CLINGAN'S CHRONICLES

By CLINGAN JACKSON

YOUNGSTOWN PUBLISHING CO. / YOUNGSTOWN, OHIO

Published by the
Youngstown Publishing Company Inc.
57 South Champion Street
Youngstown, Ohio 44503

Printed in
Youngstown, Ohio

ISBN 0-9631243-1-5

DEDICATION

Dedicated to the memory of my mother and father, John Calvin and Evalena Clingan Jackson; my three wives; and my brothers, Lamar, John and Jay.

Father and Mother never gave up on a very tongue-tied youngster and instilled in him hope that he might amount to something.

Only one of these dedicated individuals still lives, my third wife, who stood by me and helped as this book was being prepared when my sight was so far gone that I could not read a line of type.

CONTENTS

PREFACE

I did not start writing this book until I was in my eighties and was no longer able to read what I wrote. Consequently and fortunately, I received a lot of help.

Praise should first go to my wife, Loretta, for her forbearance as this project progressed.

Secondly, completing the task would not have been possible without the assistance of Andrea Wood, president of the Youngstown Publishing Company and publisher of the *Youngstown/Warren Business Journal*. Andrea served as my editor and friend, jogging my memory, when necessary, to include some historical footnote or elaborate on a subject.

Staff members of the Youngstown Publishing Company similarly worked diligently to produce and distribute this book. Artists Janice Hudach and David E. Davis designed the cover, the pages and oversaw production of the book; Eileen Webster set the type; Danny O'Brien assisted in research; Dorothy Kaglic, Monnie Ryan and George Nelson proofread the final manuscript; and Sandra Bellay handled various administrative duties. In addition, photographer Lloyd S. Jones, who began his career with *The Telegram* in 1934 then came to *The Vindicator* following the merger and is now a contributor to the *Business Journal*, provided a number of outstanding photographs from his files.

My appreciation also goes to Ann Przelomski, retired managing editor of *The Vindicator*, with whom I worked for nearly half a century and who proofread the manuscript in its early stages.

Gloria Modarelli also deserves credit for helping to organize the chapters and take down my dictation, as does Betty Yuhasz, who helped give me a start.

Others whose services were enlisted include: Richard P. McLaughlin, James Mathews, William M. Kane Jr., Mary Frech, George Lencyk, Pattie Alessi, Allison Davis, librarians at the main branch of the Public Library of Youngstown and Mahoning County and the Mahoning Valley Historical Society, and employees of Home Savings & Loan, Metropolitan Savings Bank and the Mahoning County Elections Board.

To all of these people, as well as those I have neglected to mention yet aided and encouraged me throughout the last two years as we attempted to record my journey, I owe my deepest gratitude.

INTRODUCTION

Clingan Jackson, born March 28, 1907, served *The Vindicator*, Youngstown, Ohio's daily newspaper, for fifty-four years, and spent more than forty years as its political editor.

During those years and since his retirement in 1983, he has been active in other enterprises, being a participant in as well as an observer of political affairs. Jackson has written an account of his life's journey. It may be of interest to many because of his somewhat unique vantage point as a working reporter and, at times, a public official.

The descendant of several of Mahoning County's pioneer families, clans that were deeply involved in the social and political development of this section of eastern Ohio, Jackson's higher education was largely in the discipline of a historian. As a teenager, he and his friends gathered along the railroad tracks in Lowellville, Ohio, where they placed coins on the tracks to be pressed into a memorial by the passing funeral train and sat through the night, waiting for the cars draped in black that bore the body of President Warren G. Harding to his home at Marion, Ohio.

Graduating from the University of Colorado in 1929, he returned home and went to work in Youngstown in the midst of the city's smoking steel mills. One of his first newspaper assignments was to carry stock quotations from local brokerage houses for publication, and he saw firsthand, in the statistics he was carrying, the October

1929 stock market crash.

The following year, 1930, would not be a bad year for the economy but by the fall of 1932, Jackson would see the Great Depression reach its depth as President Hoover stood on the rear of a train passing through Youngstown, which already had a "Hoovertown" located on the city dump.

With the New Deal and the National Recovery Administration's "blue eagle," Jackson would see an enlivening occur as politics reached down to the people, and the people stirred. Thousands attended political meetings, and many more marched on city halls and the Ohio Capitol, where Jackson would stand in 1934, newly elected to the General Assembly, and watch as hundreds of "food marchers" climbed the Capitol steps.

Later, in 1937, Jackson would cover the Little Steel Strike called at Youngstown, an epic event in the New Deal era that would signal the establishment of the industrial union movement which continues to affect the course of the nation. Prior to the strike, events such as the Bethlehem Steel/Youngstown Sheet & Tube merger trial at the Mahoning County Courthouse in the early 1930s had already tended to focus the nation's attention on this steel center. Few would know Gus Hall, who would rise to become head of the American Communist Party, or Philip Murray, who would become the first president of the United Steelworkers Union, as intimately as Jackson, who covered them both during the Little Steel Strike's organizational effort, which, at times, turned violent.

From 1936 through 1980, Jackson would cover every presidential campaign, attending nearly all of the party nominating conventions, and would be an eyewitness to other significant political events.

Following the assassination of John F. Kennedy, he was dispatched to Washington, D.C., where the late Youngstown Congressman Michael J. Kirwan provided him lodging. When Kennedy's body was being carried up the Capitol steps to the rotunda, Jackson's vantage point was from the oval glass above the doorway. Later, as the slain president was borne to his final resting place at Arlington National Cemetery, Jackson stood on the sidewalk as Charles DeGaulle, president of France, and a riderless black horse helped lead the solemn procession to the death-march beat of the drummers.

Marking the passage of decades, Jackson remembers Halley's Comet of 1910; keeping tab with earphones on Lindbergh's 1927 crossing of the Atlantic during the first transoceanic flight; hearing Warren G. Harding in the first presidential radio speech in 1921; participating in an early television broadcast from Cleveland; and many other historical events that would span the first decade of the twentieth century to the last decade.

Jackson served as a Lowellville councilman, a state representative from Mahoning County and a state senator from what was then the Mahoning-Trumbull district. Upon leaving the Senate, he served on four important state boards: the Ohio Program Commission, the Ohio Highway Construction Council, the Ohio Pardon and Parole Commission and the Ohio Civil Rights Commission. He has been cited as the most "commissioned" man in state history.

As a legislator, he was the author of the law that created the Ohio Department of Natural Resources, which has done much to raise Ohio's ranking among the states in natural resource conservation. Pages of the Ohio Revised Code also came under his hand including the state's first law regulating strip mining and mandating restoration of the land.

Jackson served on three Youngstown Charter Commissions and was especially responsible for the changes in the 1943 charter amendment, which provided for two-party municipal government.

As a close friend of the late Congressman Kirwan, Jackson frequently was in Washington during Kirwan's thirty-four years in Congress and came to know many of the national leaders during that period. He has sat and talked with every president from Herbert Hoover through Ronald Reagan.

Now read about this interesting fellow who comes from a background of American pioneers and began his life hearing members of his family talk about William McKinley, William Jennings Bryan and Mark Hanna.

SECTION I

DESCENDANT
OF
PIONEERS

*"*T *he first permanent settlement of white men in the Connecticut Western Reserve was here on the Mahoning River. The party arrived June 25, 1797, under the leadership of John Young of Whitestown, New York, whose feet were presumably drawn westward by the sight of Ohio-bound travelers on the Mohawk River. Mr. and Mrs. Young stayed for several years, brought children into the world, and gave their family name to the city.*

Other settlers came over the Allegheny Mountains to this foothill region to bargain for homesteads. They came the southern route through Pennsylvania to Beaver Town and followed the Beaver-Mahoning river-path into Ohio.

These pioneers were a rugged lot, worthy forerunners of a stream of immigrants into Youngstown which has continued to our day. Many were Connnecticut people who didn't like Federalist domination in their native state and Scotch-Irish from the Whiskey Rebellion counties of western Pennsylvania."*

Excerpts from a narrative written by Clingan Jackson in 1953, published by the Ohio State Historical Society to commemorate the Ohio Sesquicentennial, appear at the beginning of each chapter in Section I.

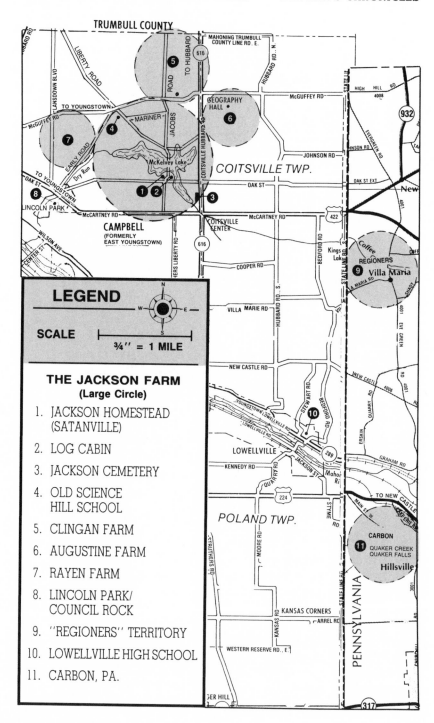

LEGEND

N W E S

SCALE ¾" = 1 MILE

THE JACKSON FARM
(Large Circle)

1. JACKSON HOMESTEAD (SATANVILLE)

2. LOG CABIN

3. JACKSON CEMETERY

4. OLD SCIENCE HILL SCHOOL

5. CLINGAN FARM

6. AUGUSTINE FARM

7. RAYEN FARM

8. LINCOLN PARK/ COUNCIL ROCK

9. "REGIONERS" TERRITORY

10. LOWELLVILLE HIGH SCHOOL

11. CARBON, PA.

"The early people were farmers, but by 1803 the first iron furnace was erected on Yellow Creek east of Youngstown. A generation later English ironmakers came, and the old charcoal method gave way to new processes. David Himrod in 1837 made iron from coal, limestone and iron ore. In 1845 the first furnace to make iron in this manner was erected below Youngstown, and was affectionately known as Old Mary. Limestone was found in abundance; Brier Hill coal and Mineral Ridge black-band ore were the other raw materials for industry."

CHAPTER 1

WHERE THE JOURNEY BEGAN

his is an account of my journey. Upper years have come and before facing my pilot, it is proper to recollect on what report to make. It is an exercise that should be taken before dotage has set in, although the possession of this malignancy often isn't noted by its recipient.

When anyone decides to inflict another book on society, he needs to find justification for his action. Without this justification, he is certain to get tired of the job and stop, if he is still eating. Moreover, when greed doesn't provide incentive to keep at the task, there must develop a belief in an obligation. For this obligation of mine, I am a depository for a long line of two families, some of whom have been worthy citizens living on land among the best for human habitation on earth.

1

Jackson

FAMILY ORIGIN AND COAT OF ARMS

Motto: *"Innocentiae securus"*
(With innocence secure)

Arms: *Gules, a fess between three shovellers tufted head and breast argent, each charged with a trefoil slipped vert.*

Crest: *A shoveller as in the arms.*

JACKSON

No doubt this family name was derived from the nickname for John and means "son of Jack." It is an old and distinguished family established in Scotland as well as other parts of the British Empire, particularly Yorkshire, England.

One of the earliest settlers on our shores was John Jackson of Tipperary, Ireland who established a home in Pennsylvania. His ancestry traces back to Sir John Jackson during the time of King Charles the Second in 1660.

American history records reveal countless persons bearing this name who contributed greatly to the development of our country. Their descendants in our country today are prominent in the political, social and economic worlds.

Many Americans are of mongrel blood. Since the humans that came to occupy this area arrived from many directions, there were more than the ordinary mixture of nationality lines. Anyone familiar with dogs knows that some mongrels do quite well.

Actually the mixture in my case includes what came to be known as Connecticut-Yankees, Pennsylvania-Dutch, Scotch-Irish and another line in there somewhere which has long been debated in the family whether it be Indian or French. (It might have been both.)

It is natural to take pride in one's ancestry. If investigation reveals some discredited elements, the proper course is to know and quickly forget. There will be little of such discoveries recorded here.

The Jackson name goes directly back to one Isaac Jackson, who landed with his four sons in Baltimore in 1713. Isaac came from a family of professional soldiers who had been recruited by Oliver Cromwell when he was the Lord Protector of the Commonwealth of England, Scotland and Ireland. After Cromwell crushed the Scottish rebels who had proclaimed Charles II king, he seized control of the English government including Parliament, and disbanded it twice over a several-year period because it opposed his declaration that the protectorate was hereditary.

Most of the inhabitants along the border of England and Scotland had been fighting with one another back to Roman times. Cromwell compensated these mercenary soldiers with 75-year land leases in Northern Ireland, but the leases ran out after the restoration of the English monarchy, and during the reign of Queen Anne.

According to some accounts at Londonderry, it was rather difficult for dissenters to get their leases renewed. Indeed, half a million of these Northern Ireland intruders immigrated to North America during the eighteenth century, the largest migration of that century. They landed in large numbers in Baltimore, Philadelphia and Charleston, South Carolina.

The inhabitants of the eastern United States didn't take kindly to the intrusion of largely illiterate immigrants. And in Pennsylvania, the Quakers, though opposed to war and arms, kindly ushered many of these immigrants to the Appalachian frontier, on occasion furnishing them with guns and ammunition to fight the Indians.

In the middle of the eighteenth century, Isaac Jackson's son, Thomas, turned up in Washington County, Pennsylvania. He, too, was illiterate; his will and that of his son Phillip are both signed with an "X." Nonetheless, they seemed to be citizens of some consequence for they had large acreages of land to dispose of in their wills.

Washington County was the site of the famous Whiskey Rebellion, an uprising against taxes that President George Washington moved personally to quash. There is no record there of the Jacksons ever fighting Indians. The Poe brothers, famous Indian fighters of Western Pennsylvania, did, however, rescue one of the Jackson boys from Blockhouse Island on the Ohio River when a band of Indians was about to practice the interesting Christian tradition of not shedding blood by burning offenders at the stake.

Isaac Jackson's clan has some relationship to President Andrew Jackson as well as to the famous Confederate General Stonewall Jackson. Stonewall's family ancestor reached this country in 1748. Andrew's family arrived in 1767, and our ancestors came here in 1713. We have some distant relationship, though closer to Stonewall than to Andrew, both of whom also go back in ancestry to the same area in Northern Ireland from where Isaac had come.

Gideon Jackson, brigadier general in the Confederate Army, was a second cousin of my grandfather, who was a captain in the Union army.

Senator Henry "Scoop" Jackson of Washington state, who served from 1953 to 1983 and had ancestors who came in the late nineteenth century from Norway, always called me "cousin." He claimed the Jacksons of Scandinavia settled in the northern section of England, where there were extensive Scandinavian inroads during the first millennium of the Christian era.

One of the only other Jacksons I have a connection with was burned at the stake for his religious beliefs in the reign of "Bloody" Queen Mary during the 1600s. Presumably, he was a Calvinist when the queen, in her short reign, proceeded to persecute the Protestants. Mary was succeeded by the great Queen Elizabeth who forever ended the persecution of anyone in England for their religious beliefs.

Early in the twentieth century, Mary Jackson, a distant cousin long deceased who lived in Sharon, Pennsylvania, searched out the history of this Jackson clan by going to England and Northern Ireland, where she was able to trace the line back to the War of the Roses. The Jacksons apparently were on the losing side in this conflict. There is a Jackson coat of arms and Mary created a rather ingenious family tree, venturing to further trace the Jackson name to the Scandinavian invasion of England, which occurred in early medieval times before A.D. 1000.

My first name is Clingan and the Clingan line goes back to a Huguenot settlement near Belfast, Northern Ireland, where quite a few Clingans are now living. The Connecticut-Yankee mixture came from the Roberts and Tylee branches of the family. The Clingans who came into Pennsylvania must have been of a more educated vein than the Jacksons. In any case, one William Clingan was one of the signers of the Articles of Confederation, which, after being substantially amended, resulted in the Constitution of the United States.

The first Clingan with any local record was a squatter on land owned by George Washington in Washington County, Pennsylvania. After Washington had the squatters kicked out, my direct ancestor appeared at West Middlesex, Pennsylvania, with his wife, a number of children, a horse and a tarpaulin.

This is the beginning of the band of Clingans who came to live in Western Pennsylvania, Hubbard, Niles, Youngstown, Struthers, and more recently in other parts of Ohio including Mansfield. Some have been rich, some poor. But looking at the traditional Clingan, you wouldn't know if he was rich or poor.

Today the Clingan family name appears on street signs in Hubbard, Youngstown, and Poland Township, Ohio. And across the ocean, Clingans show up in the Dublin telephone directory and quite frequently in Ulster, Northern Ireland.

My mother was a Clingan. In this section of Ohio, the nineteenth century practice in naming children was to give them both family names. For instance, quite often the same neighborhood would have two persons with similar names — one of them named, perhaps, Dickson McBride and the other McBride Dickson.

Both mother and father had at least two of the same ancestors — Samuel Tylee and Captain Roberts — who were the original settlers of Hubbard Township, Ohio. They came here as the surveyor and the land agent, respectively, for Hubbard, and bought the land from the Connecticut Land Company, which sold townships in what was then the Connecticut Western Reserve. Both of these gentlemen are my great-great-grandfathers twice. One of them is also my great-grandfather.

The relationship of my father and mother being second, third and fourth cousins caused the local doctor to caution my father when they were wed. He told him their children might be a little short in the cranium or possibly "unusual." Father sometimes reminded me that he hadn't made up his mind which way that went in my case.

One of my grandmothers was a McFall. The first McFall here did not own land; when he came, it was claimed by Connecticut and had not been parceled out to any settlers. He was a trapper and had a cabin along Dry Run Creek where McKelvey Lake has since been built on land that is now considered the East Side of Youngstown. His family Bible shows the birth of several children at that location a number of years before John Young led the party of trappers that stopped along the banks of the Mahoning River on June 25, 1797, and established the settlement that bears his name.

Still, the McFalls were not listed much in local history, although

The old Jackson Gulch along Dry Run Creek where McKelvey Lake now occupies the valley.

histories of Mahoning County confirm cabins existed in the valley of Dry Run Creek before the first landowners came. Scores of McFalls are still living in this section and some have also relocated to many parts of the United States.

There also was one ancestor, Daniel Augustine, with a family relationship to Augustine Washington, who was related to George. The Augustine line was Pennsylvania-Dutch.

A memory of childhood was the friendly comments my father and mother made about their respective families. Grandmother Clingan, who was a McFall, had six brothers in the Civil War. Grandmother Jackson, who was a Roberts, also had six brothers in the Civil War. During my childhood, many of my great-uncles were receiving army pensions and often visited our home on Sundays, a day when Mother was in charge. The normal Sunday found a couple of these veterans sitting on the front porch and discussing their war exploits. The gist of Mother and Father's jawing was that from Mother's angle, the Roberts, despite their patriotic service, didn't amount to much and partly lived off the government. Father's remarks were about the no-account McFalls. It was a loving family and the visitors were always treated with dignity and fed well. Mother also wasn't above complaining about all the work she had to do in the kitchen, but Dad always was an aide in carrying potatoes and such.

The Civil War was a very big affair to me as a small boy, and chasing Johnny Rebels, as some of my uncles would refer to Confederate soldiers, was entrancing talk. They also told of chasing foxes along Dry Run Valley and about many other experiences in their lives.

Not far from the Jackson family homestead, on the eastern side of Coffee Run, lived so-called "regioners," who were committed to the cause of the South and were much maligned during the Civil War as Southern symphathizers. A small town developed near the state line on the Pennsylvania side, and regioners and others came there to get blacksmith services for their horses and buy groceries and other goods that nineteenth-century farmers required.

All was not friendly, especially after the war when some of the soldiers returned to perpetrate their lives as veterans from the ranks of the Blue and the Gray. Union veterans received government pensions, which made them the envy of their Confederate counterparts, and old-timers living in the area often cited complaints about the relaxing life of Union veterans who spent their days hunting fox or playing cards at the blacksmith shop while the Confederate veterans had to dig in the western Pennsylvania foothills of the Alleghenies to "root out grub."

A cousin of mine, Monroe Johnson, had quite a military career in

*John Clingan, my maternal grandfather, poised for
a hunting expedition in the woodlots of Coitsville.*

the Civil War and we heard lots of stories about him. He had been wounded at Antietam and was discharged from the service. Monroe recovered from his injuries, rejoined the army and was at Gettysburg for the great battle. Later he was prosecuting attorney of the county and was the master of ceremonies when former President U.S. Grant came to Warren to bolster James A. Garfield's campaign for president. Grant was joined by President Rutherford B. Hayes in the campaign effort. This event, perhaps more than any other, marked the high point in what might be told of an era when Ohio held sway in the history of the United States. On that speaking platform in Warren were three men who served as president, all with Ohio backgrounds.

My grandfather, John Clingan, joined the Union Army when he was a young man. On my great-grandmother's insistence, my great-grandfather bought him out, and paid another soldier to go in his place.

Years later, the Clingan family moved west, first into Kansas and then Oklahoma, and a whole batch of Great-grandmother Clingan's children settled there. Many of that branch of the Clingans continue to reside in the area from Dodge City, Kansas, into Oklahoma. Through intermarriage, their names are difficult to trace.

In my college years, my great-aunt "Tee," Grandfather's sister, then ninety-six years old, came to Denver to visit her younger sister, Aunt Nellie. Nellie had married a Frenchman, Charles Laurent, who worked for the Denver Rio Grande Railroad. The two old aunts wanted to see their grand-nephew from the eastern home of their ancestors, and I was summoned for the occasion. Both of them had visited with my parents in Youngstown in years past.

Grandfather Clingan told me that he played cards many times with Frank James, Jesse's brother, and he also knew Jesse well. He spoke of Frank as a perfect gentleman and was a defender of Jesse, expounding on some of the contentions about the famous outlaw's way of life that have since been reported in various biographies. The railroads rode very roughshod in some of their business dealings regarding right-of-ways in Western areas, and Jesse was avenging those who had been wronged, we were told. Moreover, Jesse had a Robin Hood reputation for helping poor and suffering widows, paying off mortgages and so forth.

Besides the book that told the life of Captain Kidd and his pirating, one of the books I treasured as a youth was *The Life of Jesse James* by Jesse James Jr. As this book was circulated, many families destroyed it, fearing their children would read such accounts. It did not seem to bother my parents, yet we were still encouraged to look more to the heroic performance of Admiral Dewey in his conquest of the Philippines.

Great-grandmother Susan Hearst Clingan outside her home in Dodge City, Oklahoma, off the Chisholm Trail. Standing are uncles Cash, Frank and Cal and Aunt Nellie.

For a time, Grandfather Clingan was pretty much a man of the frontier. When I was a boy, he gave me his pearl-handled revolver, which later came up missing — somehow Mother was suspect. He taught me card games and throughout life was not a worker, as my father envisioned, but rather one who traded horses and entered into enterprises of various kinds. At one point, he was also a constable; he could ride a horse sitting erect and seemingly at perfect ease, and throughout his life he made frequent visits to western Kansas and Oklahoma where his brothers and sisters lived. As a younger man, he had herded cattle from Texas to Dodge City, Kansas, along the Chisholm Trail.

In 1889, when Oklahoma was opened for settlement, Grandfather Clingan rode into the former Indian Territory and took a land claim. Apparently, Grandfather Clingan later got into trouble out west; some surmised he was wanted in connection with a gang shooting. In any case, when he arrived in Youngstown, the family assumed he was just ahead of the sheriff. My uncle, Sidney D. Lamar Jackson, county prosecuting attorney about that time, reportedly told people that if they saw John Clingan, "Tell him to keep out of Mahoning County," because the authorities had a warrant for his arrest. Grandfather Clingan was put up in a barn in Newton Falls but the quest for him quietly ended and he lived out his life peacefully in Mahoning County on the Clingan family farm on McGuffey Road.

An Englishwoman by the name of Thompson was the mother of Joseph Jackson, my paternal grandfather. By family story, when my grandfather was a baby, she kicked him off a stone along Dry Run Creek and into the rushing waters, jumped in to rescue him, and explained that when she told him not to crawl dangerously on to a stone over the water, she meant it.

My great-grandfather was John Calvin Jackson; he was everything that a Calvinist was supposed to be, carrying his Bible to the fields. In family portraits, the curled lips of he and his wife, Marietta, revealed the hard life they had endured in the woods of Washington County, Pennsylvania, before they crossed the panhandle of Virginia (now West Virginia) into Columbiana County and northward into the Western Reserve to seek land from the Connecticut Land Company, which already had sales offices at Youngstown, a blooming town of fifteen log cabins in 1804.

Grandfather Jackson was born in 1828, and grew up in a cabin next to the creek in Dry Run Valley — a site below where the Jacobs Road Bridge now crosses McKelvey Lake. At the age of fourteen, he became a schoolteacher in Trumbull County — Mahoning County had not yet been created. For a time, he also operated a grocery store in

The Jackson family homestead on Jacobs Road, built by my paternal grandfather about the time he was elected Mahoning County commissioner on the courthouse Removal Ticket.

Hubbard that featured a barrel of whiskey sold for a nickel a tin cup. During the 1850s, he acquired a considerable portion of land in and along Dry Run Valley.

My grandfather served in the Union Army at Johnson Island on Lake Erie. It was a prison for Confederate officers, one of whom was Henry Kyd Douglas of Maryland, the youngest member of Stonewall Jackson's staff and the central figure of a historical novel, *I Rode with Stonewall*, a best-seller in the 1940s.

Serving in the 171st Ohio Volunteer Infantry, Joseph Jackson was elected captain. His discharge from the army, signed by Abraham Lincoln, lists him accordingly, and he was known throughout his civilian life as "Captain Jackson."

The 171st hurried to the defense of Cincinnati by train, as the Confederate Army thrust north and threatened the Queen City. After minor skirmishes, this inexperienced military detachment was quick to believe they had halted the Confederate threat. Their accomplishment, however, wasn't quite what they thought. A veteran Union Army cavalry unit had threatened the Confederate unit from the South; fearing capture, the rebels retreated.

This was a period when "Morgan the Raider" terrorized Ohio and volunteer attachments for the Union Army arose in many places. John H. Morgan was captured at Salineville in Columbiana County. And although short-term units had been formed to resist Morgan, it took the Michigan Cavalry to apprehend him. Morgan had reportedly boasted that upon crossing the Ohio River, he would not stop until he had destroyed Governor Tod's industrial facilities at Youngstown and watered his horses in Lake Erie.

My grandfather brought home a deck of playing cards from the Civil War. He played with them even though my grandmother — Rebecca L. Roberts, a descendant of both of the original settlers of Hubbard Township — fussed about it.

In the 1860s, Captain Jackson was a candidate for state senate, nominated by the Democratic Party during a convention at Warren. He lost that election but would eventually achieve prominence in Mahoning County government as Youngstown bested Canfield in a long-standing, sometimes bitter struggle.

Youngstown's effort to become a county seat started in the first decade of the nineteenth century, when voters began sending representatives to the legislature at Columbus who urged a separate county be carved from Trumbull County, which once had formed the entire Connecticut Western Reserve. By 1846, the effort paid off with the Ohio Legislature voicing approval by a one-vote margin. Whittling

On Aug. 12, 1876, thirty teams of horses moved Mahoning County's official records from the courthouse in Canfield to the new Youngstown courthouse located at the corner of Wick and Wood streets (pictured above). Built at a cost of $112,000, money raised by public subscription at the height of the bitter battle over the county seat, the structure served as the county courthouse until 1908. Photo courtesy of the Mahoning Valley Historical Society, Youngstown, Ohio.

off the two lower tiers of townships in Trumbull County, and joining them with the upper tier of Columbiana County townships to form the new county, Mahoning became the eighty-fourth county in Ohio.

Despite the successful efforts of Youngstown interests to create the county, Canfield was able to work out an understanding which resulted in that village becoming the Mahoning County seat. The deal was regarded as a "steal" by Youngstown politicians. At the time, Youngstown had a thriving iron industry and, with a population of about 10,000, it outdistanced Canfield as the largest community in the area.

My grandfather operated a farm, a sawmill and a cider mill in Coitsville Township along Dry Run Valley. Captain Jackson was well known in the area and, in 1874, he was elected Mahoning County commissioner, not as a Democrat but this time on the Removal Ticket, a political alignment formed to move the county seat from Canfield to Youngstown, which required a vote of the Ohio Legislature.

It was finally accomplished in 1876, when the speaker of the house cast the tie-breaker vote. Canfield residents appealed the legislature's decision to the Ohio Supreme Court which upheld the action. The matter was further appealed to the U.S. Supreme Court which, in 1879, also upheld the decision to have Youngstown as the county seat. The bitterness of that fight continued for at least another generation when no one who had anything to do with moving the county seat to Youngstown could get a vote from anyone living in Canfield. Interestingly, Canfield's attorney was James A. Garfield, who would become president of the United States in 1881.

Meanwhile, in 1874, Youngstown citizens started raising money by public subscription to build a new courthouse next to the First Presbyterian Church on Wick Avenue. Once the issue was finally settled, the public records were removed from Canfield and the building was turned over to the county with Commissioner Jackson furnishing a $10 bill as token payment.

And when the court records were brought to Youngstown, so was the only man who was ever publicly hanged in Mahoning County, an unfortunate named Charles Sterling whose trial was a sensational affair with newspaper accounts rallying public sentiment against the accused. Sterling had been convicted of the slaying of Lizzie Grombacher. He was hanged in back of the new courthouse and in later years, on moonlit nights, imaginative people claimed they saw his ghost as they crossed the path that spanned the railroad tracks at that location.

Joseph and Rebecca Jackson had four children in the 1850s and '60s. Marietta, the oldest, was a schoolteacher and married James McBride, becoming part of the McBride family of Mahoning Township in

Lawrence County, Pennsylvania. Sidney D. Lamar became a prominent lawyer and married Lelia G. McBurney, a noted teacher at Youngstown's Rayen School, one of Ohio's early high schools which rose to considerable fame for educational excellence. Jane married John A. Cooper, a Coitsville Township farmer. My father, John Calvin Jackson, married Evalena Clingan; he carried on his father's farm and operated sawmills.

Marietta can be especially remembered for her deep religious convictions. In fact, she often discussed religious questions with an Irishman who came to work for my grandfather. He tormented her by posting a sign at the old Oak Road which directed people to my grandfather's farm and sawmill and other appurtenances; it read. "Half a mile to Satanville." He also put up similar signs at a number of nearby crossroads. My grandfather, with all his businesses, had quite an accumulation of acquaintances. And, as county commissioner, he entered the name of this location as Satanville, a fact confirmed by old maps still housed in the Mahoning County Courthouse.

It was in Grandfather's corn crib on a Sunday that the legend of Council Rock was originally written by a couple of men who had visited an old Indian in Illinois. They related, or perhaps concocted, the story of Council Rock, which in Indian terms was known as the Rock of Nea-To-Ka, a large boulder that still stands on the hill above Dry Run Creek in what is now Lincoln Park on the East Side of Youngstown. Indians gathered at the rock to hold feasts and seasonal celebrations. During such a feast in 1755, the year when the Indians defeated British forces camped near Pittsburgh under General Braddock's command, this legend suggests a violent storm erupted, knocking down trees, killing squaws, children and some of the chiefs, and splitting the great rock. Fearing the Great Spirit was angered by their activities, it was purportedly the last gathering ever held at Council Rock.

This story aroused so much interest a painting that depicts the Council Rock legend hangs in the Mahoning County Courthouse, and the rock itself has long been set off as a park landmark. Indeed, Ohio history now records that during the French-Indian War, the Indians, while advancing on General Braddock, had some assembly at that rock.

As a boy, my father looked over the shoulders of these two men as they wrote this tale for publication in *The Vindicator* and signed their names. It captured the imagination of the newspaper's readers who were then interested in all sorts of Indian lore. How much truth is in it may be questionable. Nevertheless, the rock is located in the vicinity of some seventy Indian graves. It is, however, historically accurate that General Hand and a troop from the Carlisle Barracks in

Pennsylvania came through the area during Revolutionary War times, in what has come to be referred to as the "Straw Campaign" since only some "straws" were found living along Dry Run Valley.

Captain Jackson died in 1895; previously, he had suffered a stroke that incapacitated him for some time before his death. He was buried in the family cemetery, a non-profit operation today called Jackson Cemetery where hundreds have since been buried and where I will be laid to rest with those who have gone before me.

The cemetery, located on Youngstown-Hubbard Road across from the Coitsville Presbyterian Church, recalls a great deal of history. Stones there mark those who fell in the Civil War, and one stone remembers a Jackson who was buried at sea while he was on his way to the Sandwich Islands — now known as the Hawaiian Islands. He had gone to the California gold fields in the 1849 rush, and became quite wealthy before contracting tuberculosis; his estate was valued at almost $1 million and was amassed not from discovering gold, but by hiring out burros to goldminers.

EXTRA

River Played Key Role in City's Founding

John Young, Other Settlers Used It as Guide

By Clingan Jackson
The Vindicator, 1953

When Youngstown's town plat had been laid out in 1803, the year Ohio became a state, provision had been made for a town with a river flowing by.

The Mahoning River then and since has been an important avenue of commerce for this community. The first white men, John Young and his party and Col. James Hillman, reached Youngstown via the river.

First structures were built near the river bank in the vicinity of the center of the township at what is now Spring Common. In those days the river swung further to the north so that, it is believed, the site chosen for the Young landing marker by the Sesquicentennial Committee is near the actual landing place.

Arrived by River

The memorial marker is to be in the cloverleaf at the north end of Spring Common Bridge with, perhaps, steps down from the bridge level—a place for historical-minded Youngstowners to visit.

All the early settlers arrived by river or along a path cut near the river. The river was an outlet to Beaver Town in Pennsylvania, the Ohio River, Mississippi and the civilized world.

Indeed, most of the first settlers into the Connecticut Western Reserve arrived along the river. After crossing the Alleghenies on the roads opened to free the western part of that state from the French and the Indians, the settlers followed the Beaver and then the Mahoning.

Got Bad Welcome

While the pioneers fought their way in with wagons in order to bring the articles of civilized comfort required by their families, their travel afterward was much by canoe. The first census-takers came that way.

So did the tax collector from Steubenville in that brief period in territorial days when Youngstown was a part of Jefferson County, with the county seat at Steubenville. The collector was given a bad welcome here by all accounts. The settlers didn't want to pay taxes and they had a good excuse in the Connecticut claim for this land.

Roads soon stretched out from Young's Town plat. One of the first was the Mercer Road. It stretched from the location of the First Presbyterian Church out over a route very close to what is now East High Avenue and then down through Dry Run Valley, coming out near what later was known as Geography Hall on the Coitsville Hubbard Road.

Section Was Abandoned

The section from the Early Road east to Geography Hall was abandoned about 1837, but the Mariner House at the end of Jacobs Road bridge over McKelvey Lake, part of which still stands, was built in 1802 and it was built to face that Mercer Road.

Along that road young William Holmes McGuffey, of later school book fame, made his way to Youngstown for the first rudiments of his education.

But most of the communication in summer and virtually all of it in winter was via the river. Skates were used to reach Warren and Beaver Town when the water froze over. Before the coming of winter, peddler boats put in at Youngstown for settlers to buy the few articles they needed — spices, tea, coffee, sugar and some cloth. Rude utensils and powder and bullets also came that way.

Valley More Important

The river valley became even more important with the opening of the canal to Youngstown in 1839. Farm and forest products moved in boats along it. James A. Garfield, elected congressman from this district while a soldier in the Civil War, and later to be president, was one of the boys who drove tow horses.

The "black band" ores of Mineral Ridge and Brier Hill coal moved over the canal, and the first foreign ores brought into the valley from the Lake Champlain district of New York came by boat.

Young attorney David Tod, appointed postmaster at Warren in the 1830s by President Andrew Jackson, built quite an industry at Brier Hill. In 1848, when appointed minister to the court of Dom Pedro II of Brazil, Tod took leave of his Youngstown neighbors on a canal boat.

Performed Double Service

The canal gave way to railroads in the 1850s and carried its last commercial loads of limestone to furnaces in 1872. But the railroads followed the river, and made use of the towpath for right-of-way.

The river also performed the double service of bringing the water and carrying away the refuse of Youngstown for more than a century.

First municipal water systems took water directly from the river, and not until 1904 were steps taken to purify it before running it into the city mains. Now in our decade, steps are being taken to end the pollution of the river itself.

With the coming of the great factories, the river provided industrial water, and the great reservoirs, which now serve the industries, use the river as a means of transporting the water to the place it is used. All the battle for water can be summed up as effort to keep up the flow of the Mahoning. ∎

Grandfather Clingan sits with us for a family portrait, circa 1911, on the porch of the farm mansion Captain Jackson built. From left front are my brothers Jay and John; Lamar is seated behind.

*"The Ohio Canal came to Youngstown in 1839; the
railroads in the 1850s. Business boomed. In 1848
Youngstown was incorporated as a village; in 1867,
as a city. The Irish came with the digging of the canal
and the building of the railroads; the Welsh and
Scotch with the opening of Brier Hill coal fields after
1846. Many Germans came after the 1848 uprisings
in Europe. After the Civil War, southern and central
European countries contributed a share."*

CHAPTER **2**

THE JOURNEY BEGINS

his is where life began. Now that more than four-
score years have passed, it appears that the place
of the twilight is the place of the dawn. Look-
ing out from the patio made possible by good fortune — an addition
to the old house — one can envision the environment of the dawn and
childhood.

As one looks now, there is the presence of sparrows, squirrels, and
even a deer occasionally stopping at a block of salt located at the back
of the lot. This is a change from the dawn.

In recollection, on the hilltop stood a tall barn where Topsy and
Nelson lived to provide transportation to and from the farm. The barn
has long since been replaced by a garage that houses two cars,
sometimes seemingly not much more reliable than Topsy or Nelson;
either of whom hitched to a buggy would carry you well on the old
dirt roads that provided the avenues of communication in years gone by.

This picture was taken in 1900 when Lamar was still an only child and a new barn had replaced one destroyed in a fire. Mother holds Nelson, who would later come to the rescue of my pony when he was trapped in barbed wire.

I was born on March 28, 1907, at "Satanville"; here I still reside as the last years of my life impend. Doctor Stevenson, who had been a surgeon in the Civil War, delivered me at home. At the dawn, my weight was five pounds; the arrival time was about 5 p.m. Chloroform was used at that time for childbirth and I came into the world with scarlatina. The doctor's opinion was, if I survived, I would be immune to scarlet fever, a disease which afflicted many in those days.

This arriving human being had not much majesty compared to the house in which he was born, which was considered a countryside mansion. The house, which is still standing on Jacobs Road in what is now the East Side of Youngstown, was built by Captain Joseph Jackson shortly after he, as Mahoning County commissioner, received the new courthouse that had been constructed when the county seat was removed from Canfield to Youngstown in 1876.

The house, which bears the completion date of 1879, is a ten-room affair built in the Italian Farm architectural style. Most of its doors are solid black walnut; the principal rooms have black walnut paneling and the floors throughout are white oak. The lumber used in the house was harvested along Dry Run in the bleak recession days of the 1870s from the great trees that once spread along the Valley. Sawed and air-dried, the boards and planks were hand-turned to dry for several years.

The making of the V-siding was done by hand. The exterior walls of the house were built with V-siding running up and down. Within the V-siding is yellow poplar, completely covering and running the other way, making a total of two and one-half inches of solid wood walls, placed against three-by-six-inch studs of white oak, as contrasted with what generally is used now, two-by-fours.

The Jackson family homestead stood without a blemish when in the early 1950s a tornado took out twenty-five trees, uprooting some giant ones and making cavities five or six feet deep in the ground. The two driveways around the house were completely covered with fallen trees. We had to chop our way out.

As a boy, crawling on the oak floors was a prelude to the adventure of sliding down from the upstairs on the stairway's walnut banister. Young eyes would often become excited upon finding an owl or a squirrel pictured on the ledge of the back-stair casing, pictures that had been carved by the builder.

The master bedroom of the old house, the room where I was born, was the pride of the upstairs; it boasted a fireplace with a walnut mantel and was trimmed throughout including a bay window with polished walnut which was planed on the farm. There were no electric lights or indoor bathroom facilities, but the home of my childhood had books

The landmark log cabin on Jacobs Road as it looked in the 1920s. Built by my father shortly after he married my mother, the exterior's historic appearance has been preserved.

by the hundreds, if not thousands, as well as many game boards to keep us entertained.

The upstairs offered a wide range for exploration, and the attic presented foreign territory. It contained all of the equipment for making clothes — a spinning wheel and other instruments. There also hung the old Civil War uniform worn by my grandfather, and amongst his papers was the document releasing him from the service, signed by Abraham Lincoln.

The attic floor was partially covered by heaps of walnuts and butternuts that were laid out to dry. Lining the walls were trophies won from state fairs in Illinois, New Jersey and other states when the 500-acre homestead, known as the Ferndale Farm, exhibited its Red Poll cattle.

Still standing across from the house my grandfather built on Jacobs Road is the log cabin my father built in the early 1890s; it, too, is something of an area landmark. Father operated a steam-powered sawmill in the valley behind the cabin and constructed the cabin for a household when he married my mother. It was built according to standards for cabins in the pioneer days and was heated by two fireplaces at each end of the structure, with the lot enclosed by a half-circle of rail fence.

Soon after my parents began housekeeping, Father appeared at the door with Major John A. Logan, whom he wanted to introduce to his bride. Working hard to clean the cabin, my mother was in a state of disarray and hid beneath the stairway so she would not be seen. Father enticed her to come out of hiding for the introduction.

Major Logan was the son of General John A. Logan of Illinois, president of the Grand Army of the Republic who was regarded as the founder of Memorial Day and who ran for vice president in 1884 on the Republican Party ticket headed by James G. Blaine. Major Logan visited Youngstown with his father and stayed with Chauncey Andrews, a prime mover in the effort to remove the courthouse from Canfield and an aggressive businessman who built the B&O railroad through Youngstown by seizing the right-of-way on a Sunday.

Young Logan fell in love with Andrews' daughter, married her, located here, and became a prominent businessman. Logan Avenue is named after him and his vault at Oak Hill Cemetery is a landmark. He was killed in the Philippine Rebellion shortly after the turn of the century and his funeral was a big military display. Father attended the funeral, and while waiting for the ceremonies to end, Mother drove the rig over the then-new Market Street Bridge. Frightened by the imposing structure, the horse upset the buggy. My mother was taken to a home on Front Street, where she regained her composure.

My brother Jay and I dressed in our Buster Brown suits. The portrait would bring tears to my mother's eyes a half-century after Jay died.

After Mother and Father moved to the big house following the death of my grandfather, the log cabin was used as a country place. For a time, Grace Stambaugh stayed there during summer weeks; so did Harry Williams of the Commercial National Bank and his family. Currently the log cabin is the home of George Hahn and his family. They have converted the interior to a modern home while preserving the historic exterior appearance.

Behind the log cabin for many years stood a tall brick chimney which was utilized for the operation of the sawmill. Further back was a cider mill, and on the hill across the creek was housing for men who worked in the mills. Another place near the log cabin in the old days was a shoeing facility for oxen used in the timbering along Dry Run Valley. And opposite the cabin stood two giant elm trees, one of which furnished a hollow place where children could gather and play.

My brother, Jay Milton Jackson, was a year younger than I. We played about the farm yard and often the game was "war" — usually fighting the redcoats, a leftover from discussion among adults as the family celebrated the Fourth of July with firecrackers.

One of my remembrances of Jay was the two of us running around the yard, pretending to chase Pancho Villa, the Mexican who had raided into the United States. That was in the summer of 1912; Jay died in November, a day or two after Thanksgiving, and it was the first great tragedy of my life. I can recall to this day Father leading me through the pasture and explaining death to me, then my watching with deep childhood emotion the funeral cabins, drawn by horses, proceed to the cemetery and the stricken faces of my parents.

My mother's children were her jewels, and from our earliest years we knew that. Her prized possession was a picture of Jay and me dressed in Buster Brown suits, the style of that day. Fifty years later, I came upon my mother examining a box in the cupboard along the hall. It contained the Buster Brown suit that Jay, her lost child, had worn; there were tears in her eyes.

My oldest brother was Thomas Lamar Jackson; my father always called him Thomas — everyone else called him Lamar. The Lamar name came into the family when my father's brother was born in 1853 and was named after a Lamar from Mississippi who sat on the U.S. Supreme Court.

As a youngster, Lamar followed my father in political thinking. The William Jennings Bryan campaign had been a bitter one, and with the election of William McKinley, there was a lot of dissatisfaction among Democrats. When McKinley was assassinated, Lamar was a small boy, and had learned the news before my father had come home. When

My cousin, Sidney D. Lamar Jackson Jr., rides Dewey as my brother, John, mans the garden tiller.

Father drove in, Lamar ran out to tell him the news, all excited that McKinley had been assassinated. Many years later, Lamar told me he would never forget how father had taken him on his knee and explained that McKinley was every American's president and his assassination was a tragedy. As an adult, Lamar became an attorney and a Republican. At one time he served as president of the McKinley Republican Club and the Youngstown Chamber of Commerce.

Like most people, I had a share of handicaps, among them a goiter, and a tongue that wouldn't reach an arched palate to make words of any distinct sound. My parents learned to know what I was saying and my school teachers were also good at interpreting what I meant. I went through high school never able, for example, to pronounce my first name so that anyone could tell what it was. Consequently, I had a series of nicknames, "Squeak" among them. At the Stambaugh Boy Scout Camp, which I attended as a tenderfoot scout, the boys could not understand my pronunciation of Clingan, so instead they chose to call me Mascot.

My brother, John, who gave me my nickname "Squeak," always had engineering as his ambition in life. We jointly built dams to make pools on Dry Run Creek for swimming. We also put dams on the road over the ditch that fronted the family property, basically to frustrate those the township had hired to keep the ditch open. We watched in fun the frustration of the county workers as the scraper ran into these dams, heavily laced with rocks.

Other boys of the neighborhood joined us in spending summer days along Dry Run by building dams for swimming pools. Between the Haselton area, on the East Side of Youngstown, and Coitsville Center, there were at least a dozen dams over Dry Run to provide water holes deep enough for muddy swimming in the nude. In practice, one hole was reserved by a group of girls for their naked swimming; it was well surrounded by brush and trees. Needless to say, the young women were particular where they went to swim.

Once my brother had a serious catastrophe. Usually our clothing was a set of overalls we pulled on in the morning and just dropped at the side of the stream. One day a malicious cow came along and devoured John's overalls, or at least disappeared with my brother's total covering. It became necessary for him to reach home dressed as he was when he came into the world. This forced him to follow the dense hedgerows until he could make his way into the house, and it was a shock to his modesty.

There were only boys in our family and there wasn't much use for the old sidesaddles piled in the barn. Besides the driving and team

Mother (second row, third from left) and her classmates at Baldwin College, 1889.

horses, there were two ponies. My brother John's was named Jack; mine was Dewey, born on the night that Admiral Dewey captured Manila. In my mind, the admiral and my pony both had a prominent place in American history.

Dewey was a stubborn Shetland who lived in the woods all winter eating through the snow. Come spring, he was very robust and healthy, and when you rode him he looked for a tree with a low branch to knock you off. He was the most stubborn animal who ever lived and he taught his riders the value of persistence and patience.

Going to school required that we cross Dry Run Bridge, a structure that Dewey always resisted. One day, Dewey's rider was dumped five times before the bridge was finally crossed. Actually it was easier to walk to school but the other boys liked to ride the pony at recess.

One of these boys kidnapped Dewey and it was several days before we were able to locate him hiding in a shed on the East Side of Youngstown. The boy's mother appeared late one night at our home and apologized for her son's actions, and then told an old wives' tale about what had happened to her before the birth of her wayward son.

Dewey had many ugly habits such as taking a rider under an iron rod that leaned on the open barn door, thereby clipping his passenger. Nevertheless, this writer became greatly attached to Dewey. He broke his leg and had to be destroyed but he remained in my nightly prayers for years.

After all, this pony was a means of introduction to young women. The YWCA had a facility on Dry Run named Happy Hollow Camp. With the pony, the young ladies at the camp could be enticed because many wanted a ride. These girls were between the ages of twelve and fifteen and I was nine years old. They gave me the nickname "Hickey" because of my habit of saying it when I could not think of an appropriate word.

My mother was a small woman, weighing less than 100 pounds much of her life, yet she could cook for the threshing hands, milk cows, work in a garden, paint pictures and dishes, and play the piano that adorned the parlor, which was usually opened only when the preacher visited. Few women in her day managed a higher education but she had taken classes at Baldwin College and taught music, traveling with a horse and buggy from farmhouse to farmhouse to earn extra money. At one time, she had forty pupils and one student, I remember, became quite accomplished. He had no piano at home but he made a semblance of the keys to practice, and for his lesson came into a home that did have a piano. Mother also led the church choir and played the piano for the services. Her given name was Sarah Evalena but everyone called her Lena.

The fourth grade class at the old Science Hill School, 1917. The author stands third from the left in the middle row.

Mother seemed determined to instill some sense of courage and responsibility in her children. Once, coming up the brick hill of Himrod Avenue when it was a glaze of ice, she told me to get out of the buggy and lead the horse to keep him from slipping on the ice. When I was in the second or third grade and wanted to go to the schoolhouse to see a basketball game, I remember my brother had skipped away without me. I was afraid of the dark but Mother advised me to take a lantern and go to the school, which was about a mile-and-a-half away, and so I did. Returning home with the lantern, I saw quite a few hobgoblins but still made it home.

One of my earliest recollections was what she did with me when I got to tearing around the house too much. She'd hand me a hammer and nails, and suggest I hammer them into the oak rail that rimmed the porch. That oak rail came to be heavily saturated with nails. It was a way to eliminate the frustration of a child, a way which might be copied today by some child psychologist.

Christianity was a practical idea with my mother. As children we were fearful of thunder and lightning, and she always reminded us such storms were "God's fireworks." Nevertheless, she saw to it that we got into a safe place and did not take cover under trees. Once lightning struck in the middle of a blossoming buckwheat field, digging a hole in the soil, zig-zagging out and killing the blossoms of the buckwheat. This, to a child's mind, was confirmation of some almighty power.

My father never belonged to a church or a sacred society, although he read the Bible very carefully and insisted on our attending church and observing the Sabbath. My mother wasn't so much on the observance but she stopped at the idea of not belonging to the church, and enrolled her children in Sunday School. We were baptized at about age 12 in the Presbyterian Church but according to my mother's faith from the Christian denomination still then referred to as "Campbellites," with baptism only coming with the age of understanding.

As the youngest child, I had the opportunity to hear the recollections of both my parents as they grew older, and some held great interest for me. For instance, Mother recalled the famous "cowgirl" Annie Oakley who appeared at the Youngstown Fair the year that Grandfather Clingan was fair marshal and he introduced his daughter to her. Mother did not tell me that story until her last months, when she was quite ill, and the story of Annie Oakley appeared on television. She looked up and said, "I met Annie when I was a little girl," and remembered in striking detail this girl out of the Wild West Show who came to see her and fuss a little over her.

The Wild West Show also brought Indians riding horses and an

My father, John Calvin Jackson. When this picture was taken, his countenance was sometimes mistaken for William Jennings Bryan.

exhibition of Sitting Bull, the Indian leader who had scourged the whites in the Dakotas, but whom Buffalo Bill had arranged to exhibit in his shows after the Indian had been captured by the Army.

Learning that animals have intelligence is an experience that every youngster should have. Of the two horses that we used for driving, Nelson and Topsy, Nelson was the more spirited one. Once, when the family was seated on the front porch, Nelson came up to the gate in the pasture and whinnied and whinnied. When we went to the gate, he ran into the valley. We came back to the porch and he whinnied again. We finally followed him more than a mile to the back of a woodlot where Dewey was tangled in barbed wire. Nelson had seen Dewey's plight and had come for help.

We had a dog, Toss, who was very friendly. We had two fruit orchards and the boys from Science Hill Village quite often invaded these orchards. You could "Sic-em, Toss" on these invaders, and over the fence and down the road would go the boys. Years later, when I came into contact with some of these "boys" while I was on *The Vindicator* staff, they would often tell me how they had been chased by Toss.

Aunt Sarah, who lived in a house nearby, had one apple tree that she treasured. Sometimes we would steal her apples and she would always chase us away. Perhaps she was careless, or perhaps it was to retaliate that she made it a practice to tie her cow to the board strip on top of our fence — right in the center so the board would break — rather than to the post. This caused considerable rancor from my father, who probably didn't know Aunt Sarah was completely justified in her actions.

In those days, the plan of relief for anyone, particularly a widow having financial troubles in the township, was to buy that person a cow. Such animals had a complete right to the pasturage along the roads. Aunt Sarah took full advantage of this roadside grazing, but she had her own cow.

Looking out from my patio windows, it is natural to recall the woodland area; back in the right corner, the land was once filled with hemlock trees. The path led down over Wintergreen Hill into the valley. It was on this path that Aunt Jane, my father's sister, achieved attention as a girl for being able to tramp on black snakes with her bare feet when they got in her path, and scare them off. The snakes liked to lurk on the limbs of the hemlock trees.

A sight which this child was astonished to observe was black snakes in a nearby oat field coming through the grain with their heads up above the kernels on the stems. Black as they were, they had a certain satanic quality which made them somewhat fearsome to people. Nevertheless, they were generally regarded as a beneficial snake. Where they were, there were no copperheads, the scourge and danger to sawmill people and, to a lesser extent, people living around woodlands. In the summer, the copperheads would be attracted by the noise of the sawmills and come to the piles of lumber. Sawmill people in many locales in eastern Ohio carried quinine as an antidote for copperhead bites, which were poisonous and sometimes fatal.

The fields bring memories of shucking and husking corn by hand, of cropping wheat and putting it in shocks. Looking to where the old barn stood next to the granary was the chicken house, corn crib and sheep shed, all spread out and beyond the apple orchard.

Even as a child I knew that once, many years ago, the great barn had been burned and nineteen horses destroyed, although one valiant horse stood guard to keep some of the other animals from going back into the burning barn. It was a story of bravery and steadfastness that was not lost on a small child's mind. Much of what happened led children on this and other farms to try at least to follow Dante's "path direct," although it is not the lot of humans to stay on that path, not only in childhood but even as adults.

Once there were thirteen cats living about the barn. By circumstance, the family was painting the fruit house with green paint. My brother and I decided that since we had a black, a calico, an orange and a surplus number of white cats, we should also have a green cat. We painted one of the white cats green and it found its way into the house. My mother had just placed white lace curtains over the tall windows and the cat took to climbing up the curtains, leaving a trail of green. She was a patient woman, not often provoked, but this tried her beyond what was reasonable. Actually, provoked is not a strong enough term to describe her reaction; I can say that at least once I saw my mother angry, which brought about a lecture on being kind to animals.

Not too long afterward, my mother was milking a cow at the edge of the orchard, when it stepped right into the middle of the milk pail. She picked up the stool and hit the cow, smashing the oak legs off the stool. Being observant children, we reminded her to be kind to dumb animals. That was the type of interplay common in our family; the children did not adhere to the admonition that they should say their prayers and speak only when spoken to.

The air above the earth came to me in a very young age as being filled with past experiences. It could not take much imagination to know about Indians and buffaloes from the fact that a buffalo robe lay in the barn, a relic from when the buffalo roamed the West and men explored westward, living on buffalo meat. This buffalo robe, to a young mind, must have been one that Buffalo Bill had brought to the barn.

My grandfather Clingan, who had ridden into the Oklahoma Indian Territory when it was opened to white man's occupancy, had many tales to tell about the West. In fact, Buffalo Bill's aunt lived on the farm that adjoined the family homestead. The famous frontiersman and showman had stopped in this neighborhood, particularly when he was appearing in his Wild West Show. It didn't take much stretching of my imagination to believe that Buffalo Bill had visited the Jackson farm and, perhaps, given my grandfather that robe from a buffalo he had shot.

There were two aunts who had become missionaries to the Indians and appeared occasionally to offer prayers that were so long the food got cold. We heard in the family the stories of these aunts, who as young girls gave little evidence of their missionary zeal. In fact, they had scandalized the neighborhood by riding horses astride instead of sidesaddle as proper young ladies should.

Father was a history buff and knew all the stories of what had happened in the community worthy of memory. He could read out loud very well and often read to me. As a very small child, I had heard the history of Russia and knew about Ivan the Terrible. He also read from a two-volume classic work on the French Revolution, which has been read and reread over the years. We similarly heard English history and around the house were all sorts of books on the Spanish-American War. Of course, at that time we were pretty excited about Spaniards. It was a measure of my father's mind that he reminded us about the great contributions made by the Spanish in history, mentioning Magellan and other Iberian achievers. We were also made aware that neighboring Meadville, Pennsylvania, was named after the Union general at Gettysburg, who was of Spanish ancestry.

For a number of years, my brother John and I did farm work. Uncle Lamar had given me a Dorset sheep we named Blunderbust; she had two lambs. My brother and I developed a flock of fifty-seven and sold the wool. It was a profitable business enterprise. Father provided all the facilities and the extra feed for the winter. Any profit we made went into our bank accounts which our mother kept in our names at the Dollar Savings Bank.

This flock developed by keeping all the lambs and purchasing sheep from the Bailey Farm on Hubbard Road. The warning my dad gave us as we went to purchase the additional sheep was, "Watch out for the wethers." What was wanted were producing ewes, but despite our vigilance, we ended up with one wether, a non-producer.

The wool was sold to W.W. Brownlee, a Mahoning County commissioner and a merchant collecting wool in this section of Ohio at his farm on Lowellville-Hubbard Road. As the wool was stacked in a wagon for delivery to Brownlee, my father came to the wagon and advised, ''Be sure to tell Bill the wool belongs to you boys. If he thinks it's my wool, he'll try to skin me, but if he knows it's yours, he'll give you a good price.''

The wool was delivered and, with a smile, Brownlee gave us the top price and even threw in some odds and ends that we thought should be thrown away. It reflected the cordial rivalry between farmers in this section of Ohio.

The joke Brownlee often boasted about was a sale of purebred sheep to Uncle Lamar. A neighbor, Bert Marner, had tried to sell some sheep to Uncle Lamar but he didn't want them because they were not purebreds. Later, Uncle Lamar acquired purebreds from Brownlee. As he drove them home, they all ran into Marner's lane. Marner had simply processed the sheep through Brownlee and Commissioner Bill often told this story himself with a big laugh.

Sometimes, of course, it worked the other way. Once a Brownlee wagonload of logs rolled onto the Jackson property when the wagon broke down. The logs were left there too long under Ohio law and the Jacksons simply put the logs through their sawmill. After so many days, you could confiscate the logs legally.

Father worked on the farm, and many of his chores involved fence building. We had sheep that were hard to keep in, and I learned about putting in posts and fences. One day my job with him was to dig out maple trees to plant in the family cemetery. Another day Father chose stock from his lumber pile to set up a hitching rail at the Coitsville Presbyterian Church, which was built in 1869 by my grandfather with lumber from the family sawmill in Dry Run Valley. Whenever he had a day of interesting occupation and needed some help, he would write an excuse to get my brother and me out of school, explaining to us that we might learn more with him than from going to school. He was on the school board so the excuse could hardly be resisted.

Perhaps supporting the idea that trust engenders trust, through many years of my school life I had excuses in my pocket for use when needed. Most kids get to playing hooky occasionally. This happened to me, but never was one of those excuses from my father used in relation to hooky. Sometimes we got by with the hooky because there were sixty students or so in a class and it was hard for the teacher to keep track of our classmates all day long.

Looking back on my childhood, it seems every child should have a creek to play along. There were days when frog-chasing was the pastime. Sometimes we located holes they went into; on an occasion or two, we tried to eat frog legs. Using a tin can as a cooking pot, we attempted to cook them over a fire. I do not remember this repast as any great taste experience. If a salad was desired, the calamus shoots that grew alongside the creek were quite tasty.

The man-made reservoir, McKelvey Lake, now occupies most of what was Dry Run Valley. Built in the 1920s by the Ohio Water Service Company, the lake was designed to supply water for industrial use. In 1912, a dirt dam was constructed in Dry Run Valley but, a year later it was destroyed in a flood. Today, what remains of the Valley from above Lincoln Park to the Pennsylvania line — the path of Dry Run Creek — seems quite unoccupied and overgrown. But seventy or eighty years ago on a summer day, the creek area had many inhabitants and considerable activity all along its length, including children out to swim or play, some from Coitsville, Science Hill, Thorn Hill, Youngstown's East Side or Haselton. They didn't always get along. Struggles, wrestling and some stone throwing, often occurred. And when the little green apples appeared in nearby orchards, they were used in the slingshots. Sometimes battles broke out but no one was ever seriously hurt.

My father carried on the operations at the family sawmill, and he would be away from the farm months at a time. During one of these periods, he was operating a sawmill in Wise County, Virginia, at a location along the Big Sandy River, which could be reached only by horseback early in the century. He stayed at the Wise County seat in a boarding house where Sid Hatfield presided. My father recalled that Hatfield always had his pistol where he slept; the famous Hatfield-McCoy feud was not over. He also recalled that people in the little community were very religious and took care on the Sabbath to stack their guns outside the church as they entered for their weekly religious devotions. It was moonshine territory, and Father always defended the residents selling the local brews, pointing out they had no other means of turning their cornfields into money.

Another story my father told me was about Youngstown Judge William Rayen driving into the family homestead one day when Grandfather Jackson was township squire. At the time, a neighbor was talking to him, and the judge told my grandfather, "You tell him whenever he wants a sheep to step over in my pasture and take one, but leave his damn dead sheep to himself."

The neighbor man had evidently taken his dead sheep to exchange for Rayen's live one. This notoriety notwithstanding, one of the main roads in the Coitsville-Hubbard area came to be named for the man

The second dam constructed at Dry Run Valley; the reservoir it created is McKelvey Lake.

who had removed some of the judge's sheep.

Judge Rayen operated a farm next to Grandfather Jackson's property where he raised sheep. He carried the title of judge from "sitting" with a judge, as was sometimes the fashion in judicial procedures in early Mahoning County history when a judge would often have two citizens sitting beside him as he heard cases. Rayen, however, was a leading citizen in his own right, as evidenced by his generosity in his will, probated in 1857. Among other grants, he bequeathed money for what would become the Rayen School of Youngstown, a bequest made possible from profits partly generated from the sheep that grazed in the fields of Coitsville Township.

The judge wrote his will with help from attorney David Tod, who would later become Ohio's Civil War governor. The chief benefactor was a child, William Rayen Parmelee, who inherited the farm, some 900 acres on Youngstown's East Side. Although the property has been sold and resold many times over, the old boundaries of this land are still evidenced by stones marked with the initials WRP.

As Sarah Jane Peterson, a famous teacher at Rayen School and later a member of the Youngstown Board of Education, once related, Judge Rayen won his wife from a Dutchman who lived near where the Spring Common Bridge now spans the Mahoning River. Miss Peterson vowed it to be authentic that Judge Rayen stopped to see the Dutchman, took a liking to the man's wife and obtained her in a swap for his team of horses.

This has been a brief recitation of memories that give happiness to a man in his later years. Out of the dawn, this youngster had stepped into a considerable maze of childhood activity. From here, it is on to the opposite side of the Ohio-Pennsylvania border, and other events of life.

EXTRA

Ravines Played Part in Early Youngstown

Exploration Led to Discovery of Ore and Coal Seams

By Clingan Jackson
The Vindicator, 1953

With the downtown plat laid out and with the river flowing as an assurance for Young's Town, the early settlers turned to exploring the hollows and ravines that led from the river.

Indeed, some of the first settlers chose sites on these streams which offered power for grist mills and advantageous spots for the location of sawmills.

But as events were to prove, Youngstowners found more than grist mill sites in the hollows. They found the native kidney ores, coal seams, and in the very year Ohio became a state the first charcoal furnace went into operation in Yellow Creek Valley at Struthers.

Furnace Named Hopewell

Called the Hopewell, the furnace was constructed by James and Daniel Heaton. It made two or three tons of iron a week which were cast into kettles and skillet pan molds and stove plates. The Hopewell was followed by others in the creek cuts from the Mahoning and Shenango valleys.

One of the most famous was located in Mill Creek Valley at the site of Pioneer Pavilion. It had a capacity somewhat larger than the Hopewell.

Lanterman's Mill, still standing as the Mill Creek Park museum, and scores of grist, woolen and sawmills were located along Mill Creek, Yellow Creek, Dry Run, Crab Creek, Pine Hollow and other Mahoning tributaries in the early days.

Important as they were to the pioneers, the valleys proved even more important a generation later as an infant iron industry began a development here which was to lead it to a forefront place in the nation.

In the '30s, David Himrod at Mercer made iron from coal, limestone and ore. The days of the charcoal furnace were numbered. By 1845 the Mary Furnace had been constructed at Lowellville against the south buff of the river valley. It had a capacity of about 20 tons. Rebuilt and rebuilt the old Mary still operates, but its capacity has been increased at least 25-fold.

Mineral Ridge "black band" ore was discovered, the Brier Hill coal fields were developed in the '40s and by the middle of the next decade the railroad reached to Girard. It was another 10 years before rail went both directions in the valley.

In this period Crab Creek Valley prospered. The Himrod

furnaces were erected in 1859, 1860 and 1868. The first Youngstown furnace was the Eagle of 1846. Brier Hill No. 1 in 1847, Phoenix 1854, Falcon 1856 and Grace Nos. 1 and 2 in 1859 and 1860 were other early furnaces.

These furnaces along with others in the Mahoning and Shenango valleys had a combined production that made this district one of the leading iron-producing sections of the world. The Civil War boosted iron prices. Bar iron sold for $67 a ton in 1855 but by the close of the Civil War it brought $168 a ton. Many Youngstowners' fortunes date from that period.

Crab Creek has remained industrial. The W.B. Pollock Co., which dates to 1863, is one of the large industries located there. This tributary of the Mahoning also has the giant plants of General Fireproofing Co. and Truscon Steel Co. and others, including Republic Rubber division of Lee Tire and Rubber Co.

Commercial Stride Grows

With the coming of the 20th Century, gristmills and woolen mills disappeared from the industrial scene, but the commercial importance of the valleys continued. Aside from Crab Creek, many of them are the location for reservoirs which help maintain the water resources so vital to industrial production. A few like Mill Creek have been used for park purposes.

Mill Creek Park with its more than 2,000 acres and three scenic lakes has become one of the showplaces of the eastern United States. Dry Run Valley with Lincoln Park and Lake McKelvey combine both the commercial and the scenic.

In summing up Youngstown's history, from the viewpoint of these gulches which lead to the Mahoning, it is necessary to recall that stone for building has been taken from them. The first sidewalks in Youngstown were of the flat stone taken in Dry Run Valley.

In the earliest days these hollows were the most fruitful source for game. Even today the wild berries, game and small fish in the streams are relishes attractive to boys who frequent these ravines.

But Youngstown in its 150 years has not been confined to the plat, the river or the ravines and hollows. The city has taken to the hills and the great residential districts spread out over the plateaus that stretch from the river valley.   ■

*The view from the top of the Home Savings & Loan
Building on West Federal Street, circa 1920.*

"The first Italians and Slovaks came in the 1870s, but immigration was primarily from the British Isles and northern Europe until 1890. Beginning with the construction of the first steel mill in 1891 and extending to World War I, Hungarians, Italians, Slovaks, Croatians, Ukrainians, Austrians, Russians, Romanians, and almost every European people except the French and Spanish came in numbers. In all more than seventy nationalities, including the Scandinavians, came to replace the Senecas, Shawnees, Mingoes and Delawares, who once peopled the valley."

C H A P T E R 3

RELOCATION TO CARBON

he first break from what was home, to a boy who was thick in his familiarity with every barn and shed and field, was an impact on his journey. It not only meant leaving familiar scenes and animals but also somewhat the memories of Dewey and other childhood associations including the boys with whom I had always played. Years later, although memory seemingly had lapsed, meeting some of my first associations brought their names readily to mind.

In 1919, Father, who was then working at the Carbon Limestone Company near Hillsville, Pennsylvania, decided the family had better move there to be with him. Two years earlier, in order to supervise lumbering of the timber along the Mahoning River, my father had been employed to operate sawmills for the limestone company.

The company's general manager was my father's brother, Sidney

Carbon, Pennsylvania, in the 1920s, a town of company houses and company stores habitated by employees of the Carbon Limestone Company.

D. Lamar Jackson. He had been instrumental in the construction of the Market Street Bridge at the beginning of the twentieth century, a span that linked downtown Youngstown with the South Side of the city, which was then largely farm territory. With the perspective of subsequent city and suburban development, it seems ironic to recall one reason Sidney failed to be re-elected Mahoning County prosecutor was because voters complained the bridge wasted taxpayers money — it reached a scantily inhabited area.

For its mining operations, the limestone company needed ties and other timber, which were hard to come by in the World War I economy. The sawmills were located along the hillside of the Mahoning River and also in the wood lots of eastern Poland Township, Ohio.

The company built a house for us in Carbon, largely on the site of old Quakertown, an early settlement in Mahoning Township, Pennsylvania, established decades before Youngstown had been settled in Ohio.

Carbon itself had its range of company houses and the customary company store. Many of the workers had been recruited from Eastern Europe, and its boarding houses were filled with single men, mostly Croatians. As the years passed, they brought their girlfriends from the old country and made them their wives. Some of the leading citizens of this area of Northeast Ohio are among the descendants of these immigrants.

Coming into that community at age twelve, it was new and exciting open space for me, even though I had been considerably affected by moving away from my old friends at Science Hill School in Coitsville Township. I entered school at Hillsville, about a mile from Carbon, and joined the 7th and 8th grade class in an old frame building. The room was heated by a potbellied stove which stood in the center. Many of the boys chewed tobacco and as the teacher turned to put writing on the blackboard, you often could hear the sizzle of spit on the red-hot stove. Chewing tobacco was enticing to a youth exploring the way in this mad world.

Wandering about in the Carbon community resulted in many encounters with friendly people. Old Mrs. Stoner, who lived along the creek, often came up with a cookie. She was the last prominent Quakertown lady of the area, and she told me the history of the old village. I investigated the cemetery, where the headstones were testimony to the active community there that dated to the Revolutionary War period.

Quaker Creek was also something for a boy to investigate. It flowed out in clear water from the rich farmlands of eastern Poland Township into Pennsylvania, down into the Mahoning River and passed over three waterfalls, one of which was twenty-five feet high. There were places there for gristmills and, over the years, many gristmills had been built.

The main road of that early time, now obliterated, ran down the hill along Quaker Creek to the Mahoning River where there was not a bridge but a ford. At the ford, there were the remains of eighteenth century activity. A substantial stone building stood across the river; it was a factory where the workers made combs out of cow horns.

In the nineteenth century, the big falls at Quakertown became quite a gathering place for swimming, with people coming from miles around, mostly young people. The stone walls around the falls bear the initials of some who would become prominent officials in Youngstown. This community meeting place was destroyed by the coming of the stone quarries, but evidence of its existence is present today.

Limestone was first quarried immediately adjacent to Lowellville, Ohio, which reaches to the Pennsylvania line. The first limestone was transported to the iron mills of Youngstown on the old canal that moved very close along the river past the Mary Furnace at Lowellville, which had been built in 1845 by a Pittsburgh company. It was the first furnace ever to make iron from a combination of limestone, iron ore and, initially, Sharon vein coal, then later coke. From its opening in 1839, the canal continued in usage until late in the 1870s.

As limestone was taken from the hills above Lowellville and the farmlands, the mining radius reached into the Hillsville region, necessitating rail transportation, which made canal delivery of limestone a thing of the past. A Pennsylvania & Lake Erie railroad track switched up from the Mahoning River valley to serve the Hillsville quarries. During the World War I period and through the decades afterward, car after car of limestone was transported daily on this track. In fact, with the high tonnage of limestone, it was one of the most lucrative sections of railroad track in the nation.

Life in Carbon was like that in many other towns of America in the developing years of the twentieth century, with a certain roughness and toughness to the community. There was one man who always referred to himself, and he urged others to call him, "S.O.B." There was also "Crazy George," who had served a couple terms in prison, and Sam, who was badly cut in a cutting match in the barber chair. The lawman of this community in Mahoning Township was "Butcher" Bill Edwards. He maintained the law in the Hillsville area for many years and was highly regarded by all who believed in law and order.

A powder plant located in the area often had a fatality when a corning mill part exploded. The plant was built so that a blowup simply took the roof off and the base could be reconstructed. As a boy walking on the road in front of the plant, I saw parts from a man I knew from the pool hall land on the road following a blast that destroyed one of the outer plant facilities. This left a small hole in my life; on the day before, I had seen that man come into the pool room late at night after making inspections.

My first job came at Carbon, working at the store that sold everything — meat, groceries, shoes and garb. The two Croatians who operated it didn't know too much about the English language. I became a voluntary go-between for them, helping in correspondence and tabulation of the books since much of the merchandise was bought on credit.

Next to the store was a poolroom, bowling alley and barbershop combination which had an abundance of cuspidors. My morning job was to clean all the spitoons, which meant hauling them outside and hosing them out. The pay at the poolroom job was one dollar a day.

The proprietor permitted me to play pool with anyone who came in looking for a competitor. The rule was that if the houseboy won, the game had to be paid for and if not, the player had the fun of the game without cost. This had a tendency to send good pool shooters after the boy and, as a result, his skill constantly improved. Making the rainbow shot was the challenge for pool players in the 1920s. Once this was accomplished, the news went around for it is more difficult than it looks. All the pool balls are carefully put in a half circle around the table. You hit the first ball, knocking each one consecutively into the next ball, and eventually knocking the last ball into the pocket. This experience paid off in college, with my selection to stage an exhibition with the national pool champion, who paid a visit to the University of Colorado campus. We played three games; he let me win one and was a good sport.

A dollar a day wasn't much pay and, by the summer of 1921, my cousin, Sidney Jackson, who knew surveying and would later become a senior partner in a prominent Cleveland law firm, induced me to be his rod carrier. Sidney had been employed to survey a cross section of the limestone area, a task that involved thousands of acres. Much of the land had not yet been quarried, and his assignment also involved surveying the face of the quarry, which was something for young eyes to behold. The quarry face typically included about twenty-five or thirty feet of dirt and shale, a ledge of four or five feet of coal, perhaps fifteen or twenty feet of gray limestone and, at the bottom, ten or fifteen feet of blue limestone.

In the mining industry's beginning, the Mahoning Valley not only furnished limestone, coal and ore but also Black Band ore from Mineral

*Sidney and I take a break from our surveying duties,
a summer job that revealed to me the intricacies of
what minerals were buried in this part of the earth.*

Ridge, Ohio. Even before the discovery of the Black Band ore, the yellow ore of Dry Run Valley was used in early charcoal furnaces. The Mahoning Valley was soon on its way to rival Pittsburgh as the pig iron capital of the nation. The area might have fared even better in the steel industry had it not been somewhat late in going to steel, reluctant to leave the ascendency of iron. The first steel mill in the Mahoning Valley wasn't built until 1891, and by then Pittsburgh had taken a substantial lead in the beginning of the steel-making industry.

Having graduated from being a rodman in surveying, the following summer I landed a job painting for the Carbon Limestone Company. It was a job where ability to splash paint fast, rather than carefully, was needed. I carried red paint by the gallons in buckets and slopped it on the sheet metal buildings that made up the collection of structures owned by the limestone company.

The company fostered side uses of limestone other than that for the furnaces: making agricultural lime, providing crushed limestone for road construction purposes, and for the manufacturing of cement block and brick.

Some of the manufacturing facilities rose many stories high. Early adventures included climbing up to paint them — as well as some early escapes — loading agricultural lime for customers, and operating a gasoline conveyor to load trucks with granular limestone also used for agricultural purposes.

Another task I performed was relatively dangerous. I had to walk out on a catwalk above the stored agricultural limestone, and then plow and stir the flow of the final grade to a giant auger, which carried it to packaging from the vast storage building where hundreds of thousands of tons sometimes peaked up and failed to flow. A worker would have to poke the limestone with a mammoth hoe to get it flowing again; this was a perilous job. If one fell off the catwalk, he not only was drowned with almost certainty, but also was carried out in the auger. I didn't think much about the danger until one evening, when the night man fell into the bin and was killed. Then I realized the catwalk had little protection, no handholds or guardrails.

Having taken chemistry in high school, another summer job came in the chemistry lab operated by the electric plant at Lowellville, and it was quite an experience. I was taught how to do a daily analysis of the coal used to fuel the power plant, and one day I was ready to proceed when a call came from the central office, announcing a special sample of coal was arriving and the company wanted an analysis quickly. The chief chemist and his assistant were both absent. Testing the special coal samples sent from Youngstown, I was not able

Lowellville High School's class of 1925 pictured as juniors. Standing: Arthur Dickson, the author, Lyle Mencer, John Martin, John Varley, Charles Thullen. Seated: Gladys Lenhardt, Elsie Theil, Ellen Martin, Mable Krall, Rose Metillo, Lorena Beller, Edith List, Emma Davidson. Absent: Thomas Grist.

to arrive at a measurement of one element in the coal because of the breakdown of an apparatus I did not know how to fix. Taking a list of the measurements of this element from various other coals that had been analyzed, I took an average and threw it in, using the correct analysis of all the other elements in the coal, and quickly returned the results to the central office as requested.

Informed the following morning of what had transpired, the chief chemist exclaimed, "The company is buying thousands of tons of coal on that analysis!" He began to run the analysis again, and worked feverishly all day. Just about quitting time, he came to me perspiring, and said, "Your analysis was right."

For the next summer's employment, I obtained a job in the line department with the Pennsylvania Power Company. This involved walking to Kennedy's Crossing every morning, where I would get on the streetcar bound for New Castle, Pennsylvania. It was a different type of work; we dug pole holes, located poles and put up poles.

We installed electric poles from Wampum, Pennsylvania, to Ellwood City along the Beaver River, digging sometimes in sandy ground with the hole spreading out almost wide enough to look like a cellar in order to get it deep enough to erect the pole. I remember the foreman, a man named Murphy, saying, "Jackson, what do you think you're digging, a cellar?"

Some diggers are more adroit than others, some could handle pikes better than others, but part of learning is taking a flop. A pike that has been mishandled in the swinging of a pole between live electric wires could be very dangerous. Fortunately, when the task involved a tall pole rising, several pike men were on the job.

During my years in Carbon, I was once afflicted by the "Hungarian Itch" and it was necessary to remain home for fear of spreading the infection among companions. School was missed for a month, and I was ordered to bathe in a mixture the doctor prescribed to soothe my discomfort. Upon recovering, instead of returning to Hillsville School, I went to Lowellville School in Ohio. This course was taken because Mahoning Township had no high school and the district paid my tuition. Moreover, I had been born in Ohio and had more natural affinity to it than to Pennsylvania.

Entering Lowellville School in January 1920, a boy coming from "the hill" was immediately challenged by his counterparts in fist-fighting, a crude sport. But being of a stout build, I could usually do well for myself by corrupting the boxing procedure into a wrestling match. Once engaged in my early community endeavors with other boys, I was delighted when a car or two from Carbon stopped at the edge of the sidewalk in Lowellville to see that the fight was fair. Sometimes there was more than one boy on a side at a time. Nevertheless, it was not a case of knives, guns or stones; indeed, a black eye was a badge of honor.

Lowellville High School was one of the oldest in Ohio and although small, it had an unusual faculty. The superintendent, A.W. Ricksectucker, was a former Wooster Academy educator. He had some academy notions and a high standard of academic performance was required. Even so, there was always an underlying battle between the students and faculty. As my class prepared to graduate, the paint marks were put high on the chimney of the high school despite the fact seniors had been warned not to indulge in such practices.

Altogether there were only seven boys and eight girls in my graduating class, and it was the beginning of my political experience. The initial task was to elect a boy class president, and I managed to achieve this honor throughout high school. The women were usually given the opportunity to serve as secretary and do the class record-keeping.

Some of the boys came to dislike the basketball coach and a club was organized in my junior year called the Good Policy Club. Its purpose was to reorient the activity of the boy students from athletic to academic accomplishments. Two literary societies were also formed and held debates on national questions. Some of the faculty rather encouraged such activities. At one time, these societies held a program in the gym that attracted most of the town residents. Nonetheless, the club was threatened by some of the school people, yet it persisted through, at least, my high school years.

Significantly, one of the Good Policy members subsequently wrote the accepted work on Samuel Pepys, the great English diarist. Another member became one of the world's greatest mathematicians and was based at the University of Chicago.

One reflection that should be noted is that some of the professors who were not very popular really shoved knowledge into our heads. This was revealed to me upon entering the University of Colorado, and being subjected to placement tests. My scores were good; the professors had provided the proper training.

Another thing that can be remembered about my high school years was the student reaction to the Ku Klux Klan. The kids put up a flaming cross on one side of town and a flaming circle, the symbol for the opposition, on the other side. The KKK was opposed to the Catholic religion but the students were both Catholic and Protestant. They were sometimes more interested in keeping the fighting going than in profound ideas, and it wasn't unusual for them to set up the insignias to enflame the agitation.

The Klan, so far as Lowellville was concerned, disappeared because it became a joke. Years later, thanks to the performance of Lewis Meyer, a graduate of Princeton who was the Presbyterian minister assigned to Lowellville, the movement to get away from any Klan identification contributed to the peace of the community. Meyer and Father Kirby of Holy Rosary Catholic Church became very good friends, and the town rose to an outlook of tolerance that remains to this day.

A footnote about another Lowellville preacher and the inspiration he drew from the town also comes to mind. On a hilltop above Lowellville stood an old red brick house where Harold Bell Wright, a young minister from Hiram College, stayed for a time. He subsequently traveled down the Mahoning River on a raft, and eventually to the Ozark region where he would achieve fame penning stories about the Ozarks. One of his novels, *Helen of the Old House*, was partly inspired by Helen Cowden and her domicile in Lowellville while Wright served as the preacher in his sojourn there at the Christian Church.

There was a unique spirit that existed within the community of Lowellville and the community of Carbon which persists to this day. My years of residing in Carbon ended in 1932, when I married Virginia Fenton, a schoolmate who had come to Lowellville school from the other side of the river, and we made a mutual decision to reside in Lowellville.

The years at Carbon earned me friendships that continued throughout my life, particularly Michael Vanich and Joseph Yallech, Croatians who came to Carbon seeking work. Joe always claimed that he came from a high order in Croatia; he lived down by the riverbed, and Mike lived high up in the hills. Joe joked that when Mike's family planted corn, they had to come down to his area to get dirt to cover it.

These two men became prominent citizens of Mahoning County and established businesses which imparted a high regard for the Croatian immigration which came into the Mahoning Valley.

Joe Yallech arrived at Carbon in his bare feet; the Austrian-Hungarian Council at New York had given him $10 to get there. He developed a lumber company and ended life as a director of a bank, a high place from an economic and civic viewpoint.

Mike Vanich operated a store at Carbon which sold not only groceries but other goods including household fixtures such as refrigerators and radios. Located as it was, this store became one of the most popular merchandising outlets in the entire Youngstown-New Castle area. After retiring from the store, he joined with some Youngstown businessmen to build extensive grapefruit orchards at McAllen, Texas.

Virginia Fenton, my high school sweet-
heart whom I would marry in 1932.

Most of my memories of Carbon are images that can be seen today only in my mind. These images are of rows of company houses, two stores, a bowling alley, a pool hall, a barber shop, boarding houses and immigrants reaching out their hands to grasp the promise of a free America.

In the memory of a boy who walked along Quaker Creek with its water flowing down from Poland Township over the falls and into the Mahoning River, the present-day use of the old quarry spaces for garbage disposal, sending a repulsive scent into the air, symbolizes something of a better day now gone.

It should be remembered that eastern Poland Township and the Hillsville area had some of the richest farmland in this part of the country. The Henry Miller farm, for example, once had fish ponds about the big old farmhouse; from the porch you could cast your line. This farm has disappeared, first into quarry land and today adjacent to mountains of garbage. It is a development that has a bad smell for an old man who remembers pleasant, useful days in an area that once was so fit for human habitation.

EXTRA

Bridges Brought Population Shift Here

Opened Outlying Plateau Areas for Homes

By Clingan Jackson
The Vindicator, 1953

In the second half of the 19th Century, Youngstown began to reach out from the Mahoning River and the valleys cut by its tributaries. Residences and some businesses began to locate on the plateau levels of the township.

New and higher bridges were the first evidence of this. A steel bridge was erected at Spring Common in 1870 and by 1898 the Market Street span reaching from downtown Youngstown and the river bank opened the land above the south bluff of the river for development.

More than half of Youngstown's population is now located south of the river. The residential streets were laid out on high ground away from the ravines which held many homes of the early settlers.

Smokey Hollow Closed

The South Avenue Bridge was built in 1902, the first McGuffey Bridge over Crab Creek in 1901, and Mahoning Avenue Bridge in 1903.

These bridges and others which replaced older structures nearer the level of the river symbolized the rising of Youngstown to higher ground. The Oak Street Bridge and the East End Bridge which date to 1922 and 1918, respectively, tell this story very effectively.

Old Smokey Hollow was closed along Crab Creek and the East Side residential district reached down to the river. The bridge structures have tended to push the residential communities further out on the plateau.

Brought Healthier Living

At the turn of the century, homes were built along inter-urban streetcar lines to Sharon, Lowellville, New Castle, etc. These lines tended to follow the valleys.

But with the coming of the automobile and the cutting of streets in allotments across high ground, the population came to live mostly at higher elevations. Because of the smoke and fog of the valleys, this brought healthier living conditions.

This story is revealed in yet another way. At first the swimming and skating areas and other pastime places for fishing and boating were on the river. As the river became more contaminated, the swimming pools were located along the creeks. The first public pools were along the creeks, Lincoln Park being an example.

Recreation Moves Out

With the development of a source of domestic water divorced from the river and with expansion of residential streets over the plateau, the new pools have been located on high ground.

Central Square is still used for occasional large public gatherings, Wendell Willkie's speech in 1940, Adlai Stevenson's speech in 1952 for examples, but general mass gatherings for entertainment have been further and further from the downtown and upon higher land. Circuses pitch their tents out; sports areas are out from the heart of the city.

Even the parks have taken to higher ground. Mill Creek Park with its thousands of acres stretches out to have a 36-hole golf course located on relatively level land.

Annexed Additional Land

Old Lincoln Park has a baseball field and tennis courts down in the valley, but Oakland Field and other newer ball parks of the city are on the uplands.

This upward trend is associated with expansion of the city. The population increased rapidly and constantly from the Civil War period to 1930. Frequently between censuses additional land was annexed. The 1890 census showing over 1880 was partly from the inclusion of upper Crab

Creek, Brier Hill, Haselton and Lansingville. These were close to the river level.

Later annexations have been out over the plateau to take large parts of Coitsville and Boardman townships. Resistance to annexation has developed as the residential area stretched out further from Central Square.

Turns to Air

This resistance has in part been responsible for the halt in the population growth of the city. The metropolitan population has continued to grow, but the city itself has fewer residents than in 1930 when the population was 170,002.

The Market Street Bridge shows the historical trend to high land very well, but it is necessary to turn to the air for an indication of the Youngstown of tomorrow.

Since Aviation Day, Oct. 12, 1910 — the time that funds were raised for St. Elizabeth Hospital — the city has turned more and more to the air. In recent years the air above the city has also become an avenue of commerce.

Youngstown Airport tells the story. The jets from the Air Force Base streaking through the skies above are not only a security for people and things on the ground, but an indication of tomorrow.

From the river, up the ravines over the plateau and into the air is a part of the Youngstown story which in part parallels the movement of life inland from the sea. ■

A graduating senior anticipates college in Colorado.

"To add an ingredient to the melting pot which is the Mahoning Valley, numerous Negroes came to work in the steel mills since World War I. After World War II, Puerto Ricans also arrived. The Mahoning River has races and nationalities from almost all the earth trying to live close to one another on its banks. The older residents sometimes view this with alarm, particularly the intermingling of the young, but allegiance to one flag and worship of one God give assurance that here will be no modern Tower of Babel."

CHAPTER 4

COLLEGE YEARS

 raduating from high school in 1925, the next step was college. My father had given both of my older brothers support for college attendance and would do the same for me.

My older brother, John, had left Carnegie Tech in Pittsburgh after studying there about a year. He and his friend, Myron Goodman, had been on the basketball team in high school and hoped to have varsity records at Carnegie Tech. John was on the school's freshman basketball team but he had suffered a hernia and never made the varsity squad. Goodman, however, made the football team and was on the Carnegie Tech team that defeated the mighty "Four Horsemen" of Notre Dame; he subsequently played on the East team in the East-West all-star game at Denver.

By then, John was studying at the University of Colorado at Boulder and was able to see his friend play that game. John had left Carnegie Tech to marry his high school sweetheart, who had contracted tuberculosis. She had been staying at Mount Vernon, Ohio, where the state's TB sanatorium was located, and everything possible had been done there to effect a recovery. But she had lost so much weight — she was down to only seventy pounds — it was decided to take her to Boulder, a health center for tuberculosis due to its dry climate.

My father wanted to get John back in college. John and his wife had lived there for about a year when Father told me that if I went to Boulder and lived with them, he might be able to finance both of us in college. The decision was mine; I was entranced by the idea, and my parents put me and my trunk on a train in the fall of 1925.

My mother was concerned that I was to live with a tubercular patient. When she asked the family doctor about the danger to my health, he advised I would be healthier living in Colorado than breathing the air in this steel mill town, even if I was living with someone with tuberculosis. So away I went, and I lived with my brother and his wife until he graduated and I moved into a fraternity house.

My brother had alerted his friends that "Squeak" was coming; he and a couple of his friends met me at the railroad station. Shortly after I arrived, I got a job at a gasoline station working from 4 to 9 p.m., and made a little money to help out. Never being away from home more than a couple of days in my life, by Thanksgiving homesickness had taken over and by Christmas, Boulder seemed a pretty desolate place to live. Sticking it out became an obsession.

One of the first friends I made was a girl who wore a little black cap. This was a chance to make an acquaintance in a lonely block in Boulder; walking up the street with her, we took to each other. In the remaining years at college, we often paired up for a dance or a trip to the movies or some social affair at the Methodist Church, which seemed to absorb much of her interest.

Her name was Gladys Parsons, and she was the daughter of a dry-land wheat farmer from Burlington, Colorado. Her career led to a professorship in English at the University of Colorado. And upon her death in the late 1980s, a fund was established there in her name to promote the study of the English language. My friendship with Gladys lasted throughout our lives, although she married another man and I married another woman.

In fact, had it not been for Gladys I might not have been able to keep up with my studies while I was undergoing treatment to correct a speech defect. From childhood, I had a considerable impediment mentioned earlier in that I was unable to pronounce certain sounds.

This was especially irritating regarding my first name; in no way could I convey those two syllables, although by the time I went to college, I usually could talk to people so they understood what I had said.

While taking a speech course at the university, basically because I wanted to do something about my speaking ability, the professor immediately noticed my impediment and recommended a doctor in Boulder. I contacted him and he began working on my tongue. I had an arched palate and could not reach it with my tongue to make certain sounds. The cure was to lengthen the reach of my tongue and so he began to cut beneath it — a very sensitive location. The object was to nip beneath my tongue and have it stay cut; he would work at it until I blacked out from the pain. After I recovered, I would return about two weeks later for more surgery. In the meantime, often I could not talk and would attend classes in that condition; Gladys would help me in situations where conversation was needed. Eventually, one night I discovered that I could say "Clingan." I have always remembered the event as one of my life's most important.

At the end of my freshman year, I planned to return to Ohio with Bill Stoddard, a Connecticut student in the Beta Gamma fraternity both of us had joined. We purchased a 1919 Ford touring car for $50 — $25 apiece. Going through Iowa on the trip home gave me my first chance to drive a car in a rural section. Up until that point, most of the driving had been done by Stoddard.

The car's co-owner stayed on the trip until Erie, Pennsylvania, where he took a train for the remainder of his journey home. My task was to get home to Carbon, having had but feeble experience at the wheel.

I started driving south through Western Pennsylvania to Sharon. As I came into Sharon, I drove down a steep hill where a policeman had turned to stop traffic. I didn't know how to stop very well, and had usually accomplished this by pressing the reverse lever. The policeman waved at me, and I finally stopped about half a block from the intersection, which prompted the officer to wave his hand and warn, "Be careful."

There were no drivers' license tests to pass in those days — you drove what you had. I was able to use that car for going back to Boulder during the remaining years of my education.

For the sophomore year at Boulder, three of us went from Lowellville. There were no superhighways in those days, nor were there detailed road maps. One night in Kansas, we looked at the road signs and drove all night, looked at the crossroads in the morning and saw the same signs we had seen the night before.

Kansas was a muddy place and except for a mile going through the town of Manhattan, mud an inch or so thick flew under the car's mud guards (fenders). Three of four times while crossing Kansas on old Route 30 — the famous Lincoln Highway — the car became stuck in the mud, and we had to get out and dig the mud from under the fenders so the wheels would turn. Once when we were immobilized by the mud, the rear end completely broke in two. One of the boys, Chester Fenton — the brother of the woman I would later marry — informed us there was a spare rear end in the back. In one hour, Chester had installed the new rear end and we were on our way. It took four or five days to drive from eastern Ohio to Colorado, and we usually did not take time to stop and sleep.

During my sophomore year, driving home in a Model-T Ford, it was raining when we pulled into Gladys' hometown of Burlington, which was near the Kansas border. I walked around the town until I found where Gladys lived, looked through her bedroom window, and awoke her. Her mother made me hot cakes and syrup for breakfast. My traveling companions, who had not caught up with me in my search, later located her house. They had been outside in the rain but having had a good breakfast, I was fortified to join them for further journey.

Once at North Platte, Nebraska, we were drenched in cold rain. There was no top on the Ford, and we tried to get into a hotel. Sizing us up by our motley appearance, the clerk decided the hotel was full, and directed us to the rooming house by the railroad tracks, where we slept three in a bed and paid 25 cents apiece. Amazingly, the bed-bugs did not bite me but terrorized the others. This was the only night in all the trips that we had a bed; on every other trip, we slept in the car.

Bathing was not much resorted to either. Usually by the time we got home, my mother thought it was the return of some bum. That was nothing new in my thinking; I remember an occasion when I was walking with my father and his cousin, Arty. My father asked Arty what had happened to cause him to convert from a bum and become a decent citizen. He explained that one morning he awoke in West Virginia, and asked himself why not go home to his mother in Hubbard. Arty did return and the minute his mother saw him, she told him to wash in the cellar before she would have anything to do with him. He became a business leader and a pillar in the church.

A student from the East was not much known in a freshman class at Boulder. The national fraternities didn't take notice of me but there were two local fraternities — Beta Gamma and Sigma Rho — and Beta Gamma solicited my membership. With the fraternity in an economic squeeze, it was decided that I should move into the house and be its president.

Part of the initiation of Beta Gamma was a fire at dawn on the top of Flagstaff Mountain. After starting the ritual fire with two or three other pledges, I decided to go down the mountain away from the trail, took a short cut to the base of the mountain and slid down a good many places that impregnated me with cactus thorns. I had to have them removed, not painlessly, but I survived.

With one of the later pledge groups, this initiation rite started to develop into a forest fire, and we didn't hear from the pledges until the next day. It seems they had followed a high tension line eight miles up the canyon. Even though it was a relatively minor forest fire, the fraternity thereafter desisted from initiation rites atop Flagstaff Mountain.

In the 1928-29 school year, Sigma Rho went bankrupt. The fraternity owned its house while Beta Gamma rented its house. Determined to take over Sigma Rho's assets, I and several other brothers in Beta Gamma went to the bank to borrow enough money to give a percentage to the creditors. The transaction was worked out with the approval of university officials. Now we had two houses and by far the biggest fraternity on campus — about eighty members — and Beta Gamma became a political power in the Interfraternity Council.

We applied for a national Theta Xi charter, and in the process of building to meet the standards to become a national fraternity, scholarship of the members was emphasized. Beta Gamma came to have a majority in Tau Beta Phi, the honorary engineering fraternity, and it boasted about one third of the members of Phi Beta Kappa, the other chief honorary society. Beta Gamma also had heavy representation in the junior and sophomore honorary fraternities. As a result, one year we ranked first in scholarship among the fraternities and in another year, second, with our chief competition being Acacia, the Masonic fraternity that included many veterans of World War I.

Good scholarship was one of the standards required to get into a national fraternity and, in 1929, Beta Gamma succeeded in becoming the Alpha Eta chapter of Theta Xi. To receive the charter, the officers of Beta Gamma traveled to Lincoln, Nebraska, where there was a Theta Xi chapter.

A social fraternity, Theta Xi was established in the 1850s but traces ancestral fraternal organization to the beginning of the nineteenth century. As president of the newly chartered fraternity at its inception, I became Alpha Eta Number One. Pledges must know the names of all the first presidents of each chapter of Theta Xi. This was one of our traditions; consequently, all pledges to this day should know my name. The first chapter was at Renesselaer Polytechnic Institute. Many of the engineering schools throughout the country have Theta Xi chapters, including Ohio State University and Carnegie-Mellon, which used to be Carnegie Tech.

While we were at Lincoln receiving the chapter charter, an opportunity came to visit the last session of the Nebraska State Senate. Since then, Nebraska has operated on a unicameral basis with only one legislative body. At that time, the new capitol building of Nebraska had pretty well reached its completion. It is a very tall building, much different than most state capitols.

The visit to Lincoln also gave me an opportunity to see the home of General John J. Pershing who, in 1929, was still in the minds of the American people as the nation's foremost military figure from the victory in France.

Coming from a small high school where my graduating class numbered only thirteen, it was quite an adjustment stepping into the university with some 3,000 students. I majored in history and English, and did pretty well in my classes except for foreign language, and graduated in four years with a very respectable average, but short of obtaining Phi Beta Kappa honors. Some of my professors said my grades would have been better if I had spent more of my time on studying rather than fraternity business.

I became vice president of the Interfraternity Council, which was in charge of the senior graduation ball. Wearing a tuxedo and doing other things against the normal nature was a requirement, but somehow I got through. Being gracious and sharp in manners wasn't much taught or learned around boarding houses and the quarry. Once, during a banquet with four courses, I forgot the last course, stood up and had everyone leave the dining room. We had a very sophisticated housemother and without a ripple, the trays came into the parlor serving the final course as if it had always been intended that way.

Beta Gamma was a rather robust organization. We had a lady who did the cooking and so forth, an irascible woman who made breakfast for the boys before they got up. On a few occasions some of the brothers picked her up and set her in the big sink where she washed the dishes; when I came down, I had to pull her out. This was before the elegant practices initiated by Theta Xi became the custom in fraternity living.

The transition to a national fraternity also brought the introduction of a little culture. The widow of a judge was persuaded to become the fraternity housemother. Some new furnishings were purchased and all of the meals were opened with grace. In general, better conduct was inflicted on the members, all of whom did not at once accede.

As a matter of fact, the fraternity had one man who became so religious that I was convinced he was going crazy. He wanted prayers at every turn, which was not quite natural, and it could be foreseen that his fervor could end in disaster. Sure enough, many years later, the authorities arrested him after he tried to kill a member of his family with a butcher knife.

Another early experience that always impressed me in life was a prayer meeting I attended with Virginia, my first wife. The meeting was led by an emotional person who proclaimed he talked with God while plowing. My first love thought he was certainly a dedicated Christian. He, too, took a butcher knife after his father, and had to be confined.

These events led me to take excessive religious performances with a grain of salt.

Most universities do not like bad publicity, and one year at the University of Colorado, the bad publicity came as a result of almost bloody egg battles. Nearby were a large number of hatcheries, and the students took to throwing eggs that didn't hatch or were rotten. The only way to get around the campus safely was to walk through irrigation ditches, which gave some measure of trench protection.

In the egg battles, the coeds were as bad as any of the boys. They would load up their rumble seats with ammunition and drive around the streets, using the eggs as ''weapons.'' The situation reached its climax when someone got into the Kappa Gamma sorority and smeared eggs all over the walls, and out onto the street. One could smell rotten eggs all over campus.

The president of the university, George Norlin, who was regarded as a great Greek scholar, called a meeting of fraternity representatives and invited us to his house. Being a practical farmer-type, I suggested the way to end the situation was to confiscate the eggs, a proposal I made believing that our fraternity had not stored any of the ''ammunition.'' Shortly thereafter, the university rented some trucks and the drivers searched all the fraternity houses; they found twenty cases of eggs stashed underneath the porch of our house.

The egg battles had stemmed partly from fraternity and sorority rivalries. A verse to one of the favorite campus songs was ''I'd rather be a horse's butt than a Beta.'' Some of the houses had statues in their yards, and sometimes they would be decorated or just carted away.

We had a boy in our fraternity who was the grandson of Peck's ''Bad Boy.'' Peck had written a classic tale about a mischievous boy, and the term ''Peck's bad boy'' was often applied at the beginning of the twentieth century to a young man whose behavior was poor. My friend Peck was very much a boy after the original ''Peck's Bad Boy,'' yet he was decently a bad boy.

Traveling back in Peck's car from a football game at Colorado College, we came along a road that circled Palmer Lake and climbed about 8,000 feet, where a snowstorm suddenly arose. We were riding in an old Chandler car that was advertised as having a "Pike's Peak" motor. The glass on the front of it was slanted; the snow and ice would blow around so we couldn't see. Our saving grace was that we had plenty of food and hootch in the car. Using the hootch as a de-icer, we were able to melt the ice off the window, and we finally got home.

There was a good deal of freedom in Colorado in social relations at the time compared to Eastern practices. During the 1920s, Ben Lindsey, a Denver judge, had achieved national recognition in his talking and exposition on companionate marriage. It was a time when the relations between the sexes were being explored in churches and elsewhere. Lindsey came to Boulder and spoke in the Methodist Church. His ideas were the subject of debate across the United States, and young people flocked to hear him outline his somewhat liberal ideas, which advocated more intimacy in relationships than heretofore had been believed proper practice. Some of his ideas had long been adopted in European countries, where marriages were planned for months or even years ahead and those to be married often vacationed together in a companionate manner.

The University of Colorado maintained a lodge high in the Flat Iron Mountains near the Arapahoe Glacier. There are two active glaciers in the U.S., the Arapahoe and the Isabella, both in Colorado. On one warm April day, we rode up the mountain near the glacier and started to explore Gold Hill, where legend had it that General Grant had ridden on gold bars down to Boulder Canyon. There the question arose of how best to descend the mountain; it was decided to take the trail to Netherland, the community at the head of Boulder Canyon. The trail to Netherland still had areas covered with as much as thirty feet of snow or ice. Nevertheless, four stout youths in a Model-T could not only ride in the car but also, if need be, virtually carry it. Thus the university boys broke the trail and arrived at Netherland, a feat that was headlined in the Colorado Springs newspaper.

Another incident that happened while I was at the university is still sharp in my memory. I was sitting by myself back in the bleachers watching a poorly attended football game when a fellow walked up to me and asked for a match to light his cigar. After he lit the cigar, he sat down beside me. The two of us were much alone in this portion of the stadium. He seemed to be an ordinary Westerner, and his introduction to me was not unlike most any other cigar-smoker who had come up to me before and asked for a match.

Only after we started talking did I realize the man was Will Rogers, at the time America's most famous commentator, and he told me he was going to speak that night at Mackey Auditorium. Until this great man sat down beside me, I didn't even know he was speaking on campus, and even if I had, I probably would not have gone.

Rogers had recently dined at the White House with Calvin Coolidge and his family, and during his talk that night, he recalled how "Cal" had fed his dog under the table, yet worked with care to eat all of his soup. Then, the Coolidge children were much in the news for bringing animals into the White House; as I remember, raccoons.

Rogers enthralled a throng of some 3,000 gathered for his talk. He spoke for about an hour then told the crowd they ought to have the good sense to go home. Having said that, he seated himself, straddling his feet over the row of footlights on the front of the stage, and continued to humorously comment on current events for another hour. Such was Rogers' ability to captivate his audience.

For today's readers, it is difficult to comprehend how millions of Americans looked daily for the telling words of Will Rogers on the front page of most American newspapers. It was a few years later before I fully understood the good fortune I had in my time spent with such a notable American. This realization came to me in 1935 with the news that Will Rogers and famous aviator Wiley Post had lost their lives in a plane crash in Alaska.

Another memory is the University of Colorado's fiftieth anniversary program which took place in 1926 and brought to campus some of the most brilliant writers and thinkers of that time. Those invited included Sir James Jean, author of *The Nature of the Physical Universe*; Dean Roscoe Pound of Harvard Law School; Larado Taft, the famous sculptor; and John Drinkwater, the English dramatist renowned for his plays about Abraham Lincoln and Stonewall Jackson.

Drinkwater detailed why he had chosen Lincoln as the embodiment of what the Union stood for, and Stonewall Jackson for the Confederacy and what it stood for. As I recall, he pointedly explained that Robert E. Lee, the most famous military leader of the Confederacy and an aristocrat, did not have the same heartland embodiment of the South as Jackson, who had arisen from the common people.

All students were permitted to attend these lectures and during the ten-day period of the anniversary observance, it was a pleasure to sit through morning and afternoon presentations, an opportunity that few university students ever have.

In 1928, the Herbert Hoover-Alfred E. Smith presidential campaign was heated within the university community. There was a Republican campus organization for Hoover, which was very strong, and a lesser one for New York's Democratic governor who campaigned in Boulder. Smith's train backed in right below the university campus and was largely met by "Students for Smith." The governor stood at the rear of the train and made his appeal for votes. There, I had the opportunity to shake his hand as he leaned over the back of the train. My final gesture to Smith, as his train departed, was to doff a derby hat, only my hat was black.

I was the informal leader of that loosely organized group, and had been chosen to debate the presidential contest with the representative of the Hoover group. He was a polished law student and he put much emphasis on Hoover's training as an engineer. My comeback in the debate was that Smith was a great "social engineer," and I cited some of his accomplishments while serving the Empire State.

Four years of college leave lifelong memories, but only occasional opportunities arise to revisit the old college scenes or have other connections with the university, two of which remain fixed in my mind. When Youngstown College became Youngstown State University, it was a privilege to represent the University of Colorado at the ceremonial initiation of this new university. It was also my pleasure to return to the Alpha Eta Chapter of the Theta Xi fraternity as it renewed its program at the university in 1987.

The organization of Theta Xi at the University of Colorado provided my first real experience in finance and political endeavor, for the young fraternity was very interested in being active in university affairs. This was accomplished partly because of its size and having it so that its president spoke exactly what the entire fraternity would do.

Indeed, my college experiences had taught me to stand on my own two feet in financing and organization, and had given me a taste of politics, which I would savor for a lifetime. Growing up in a family that savored its pioneer heritage would also stimulate my appetite for history, which would provide me with a vantage point from which to observe as the Great Depression and other events of the twentieth century unfolded.

EXTRA

FIRST TO BE NATURALIZED IN COUNTY

COUNTRY OF ORIGIN	NAME OF IMMIGRANT	DATE
Germany	Jacob Hawns	April 7, 1847
Wales	Reese Herbert	July 7, 1847
Ireland	Matthew Kilpatrick	Sept. 7, 1846
Scotland	James Dodd	Sept. 7, 1846
England	William Pritchard	July 7, 1846
France	Barnabas Jule	June 3, 1852
Bavaria	John Shoenbarger	Feb. 28, 1855
Switzerland	George Heller	Sept. 7, 1852
Italy	John Gentile	Oct. 5, 1880
Hungary	Abraham Printz	Sept. 18, 1875
Turkey	Antonio Atames	Aug. 18, 1901
Austria	Antros Ariobis	Oct. 7, 1850
Norway	Oliver Johnson	Feb. 7, 1857
Canada	John Dowling	April 5, 1875
Greece	Gus Checkopoulos	Oct. 18, 1884
Sweden	Shoelton Hanson	Sept. 16, 1856
Baden	Christian Keller	June 7, 1854
Prussia	John Fogelberger	Feb. 28, 1854
Syria	George Deet	Oct. 6, 1896
Wurtemberg	John Frey	Sept. 21, 1852
Bavaria	Andrew Emanuell	Sept. 28, 1852
Russia	Michael Davis	Sept. 9, 1873
Saxony	Coonan Hake	Feb. 17, 1851
Denmark	Peter Jensen	Oct. 10, 1876
Poland	Christian Kindson	Oct. 1, 1878
Holland	George Grim	Feb. 18, 1892

From Clingan Jackson's records. Source: Mahoning County Courthouse

EYEWITNESS TO THE TWENTIETH CENTURY

Looking East from atop the Home Savings Building, circa 1925.

"From all indications the slogans for next fall's political campaign will be: Republicans, 'Let's put on the brakes'; Democrats: 'Giddyap, Napoleon.' The Republicans probably will reply with 'Whoa.' And President Roosevelt will possibly make a statement against anyone but the driver yelling 'gee' or 'haw' at his donkey. To conclude the matter, 50 percent of the American people will exercise their sovereignty and vote."
"By the Way" column by Clingan Jackson, The Vindicator, 1934

CHAPTER 5

1930s

very college graduate with his ears still ringing from the graduation music and encouragement offered by commencement speakers spends some thought on what he is going to do with his life. This is particularly true of liberal arts graduates who have not picked a particular line of work for college discipline.

Entering college, it was frustrating to learn my English wasn't very good. Nevertheless, after a rough beginning, I managed to come out near the top of the class in freshman English. There I met a professor who had been an English teacher at Oberlin College before coming to Boulder for health reasons. She encouraged me to write and two of my articles were published in the school's literary magazine.

One of them was about a rabid cow that had gone mad. The story was embellished with imaginative details explaining how members of the farm community drank milk from the cow which resulted in many of them also going mad after suffering from hydrophobia. The

Built in 1929 as events were transpiring that culminated in the in-
famous stock market crash, Central Tower would be the last high-
rise constructed in downtown Youngstown until the 1970s. It
originally was the headquarters of Central Savings & Loan, which
was subsequently named Central Bank and became a casualty of
the Great Depression. In the early 1980s, the building's historical
features were restored by its current owner, Metropolitan Bank.

only truth in the story was my experience concerning how a mad cow was once handled. That cow is buried along a creek across from where I was born and now live.

Late in college, I began to be interested in some diplomatic employment, but that was never effectuated. The University of Colorado had only a few courses dealing with newspaper work and not a full journalism department. The majors I followed were history and English.

Arriving in Youngstown after graduation in 1929, the outlook for finding a job was not good. Even so, I applied for a reporter's position at both of Youngstown's daily newspapers. For the time being, I obtained a job in the accounting department at the electric company now called Ohio Edison. Three months later, *The Vindicator* called and asked if I was still interested in newspaper work. I was.

So I took the job in September 1929, one month before the infamous stock market crash that would trigger the Great Depression. The pay was $25 a week, the same amount I was being paid at the utility company where my supervisors told me I was crazy for leaving because I had a good chance for advancement, and newspapermen usually became bums.

In Youngstown of the 1920s, *The Vindicator* stood out as one of the great newspapers of the nation. At the University of Colorado, the newspaper could be read regularly in the university library, where it was displayed with a dozen others from across the country. The newspaper had fought the Ku Klux Klan even when it meant losing a tremendous amount of circulation. For political reasons, including its stand against the KKK, my family had always regarded *The Vindicator* highly.

In the years spent with that great institution, a fuller knowledge of its history came. Preparing for its seventieth anniversary edition in 1938, I went over every page that had ever been printed, all the way back to the first *Vindicator*, published on June 25, 1869. This task involved cataloging the articles and information that appeared in those early newspapers. The anniversary edition became a handy record of happenings in the Youngstown area, and in it were reprinted excerpts from the considerable coverage given the two congressman from this district who would become president, James A. Garfield and William McKinley, both of whom would also be assassinated.

In these parts, Garfield was often referred to as the "canal tow boy," for as a youth, he was frequently seen in the basin area. The old canal paralleled the Mahoning River and was between the river and Front Street. East of Watt Street was Front Street, which was then called Canal Street, and from the point where the roadway turned north to run into East Federal Street, it was called Basin Street. The canal basin

William F. Maag Jr., publisher of The Vindicator, graduated from Harvard University magna cum laude in 1905, began his newspaper career as a reporter and became managing editor following World War I. His father, William F. Maag Sr., initially was the publisher of a German weekly, then bought the Youngstown Vindicator in 1887. A modest man honored for his many contributions to the economic and civic vitality of the region, it was not until Maag's death in 1968 that the newspaper was allowed to print a public testimonial made in 1941 by philosopher Will Durant, who described Maag as "a rare soul — a poet running a newspaper and making a success of it." Photo courtesy of the Mahoning Valley Historical Society, Youngstown, Ohio.

was just east of what was then the Presque Isle Bridge, and what is now the South Avenue Bridge.

As a congressman, Garfield looked to Youngstown as the center of his support in the congressional district that included Portage County and Hiram College, where Garfield had risen to fame after serving in the Civil War.

Niles-born McKinley was also a Civil War veteran and was present for the call to arms that took place in 1861 in the village of Poland, where he had graduated from Poland Seminary School, then Mahoning County's only institution for higher learning. He was elected president while residing in Canton, and had previously represented this district in Congress.

William F. Maag Jr., publisher of *The Vindicator* during most of my career, was a scholar and a gentleman in a day when all newspaper publishers were not of that ilk. In more than half a century of my experience, not once did it seem that anything but the truth was the objective for *Vindicator* reporters who were seeking news under Maag's direction. WFMJ-TV and the former WFMJ radio — both of which were founded by Maag and bear his initials — and the William F. Maag Library at Youngstown State University are tangible records of his life's footprints.

The staff of *The Vindicator* in 1929, in the 1930s and '40s included Ernest N. Nemenyi, father of Anastasia Nemenyi Przelomski, who years later would become managing editor of the newspaper. Nemenyi was then a leading business writer as well as a political writer. I would succeed him as political editor in 1936.

Others on the staff during the 1930s included George Madtes, managing editor; William Powers, city editor; George Kelley, assistant city editor; and an assortment of forceful reporters including Ella Kerber, who achieved a dominant place gathering news inside the Mahoning County Courthouse.

With *The Vindicator's* acquisition of *The Telegram* in 1936, reporters Esther Hamilton and Fred McCluer and editor Ed Salt became factors in getting out the day's news. Frank Ward was sports editor, followed by Lawrence Stolle. These folks and others were of the old-time newspaper stripe. Objective reporting was the rule. Young reporters often had a veteran standing behind them and telling them how to write proper newspaper language. The crime was to make an error of fact.

My father had known John H. Clarke who was president of *The Vindicator Printing Co.* when I was hired. In 1904, Clarke was an aspirant for the U.S. Senate from Ohio; his opponent was Mark Hanna, the famous political boss of the McKinley era. Both were natives of the Columbiana County seat of Lisbon. Then, senators were chosen by the Ohio General Assembly and not by popular vote. My father brought Clarke to Coitsville Township to make a speech during that campaign. All the workmen in his sawmills were Republicans, and my father paid them full-day wages to attend the Democratic rally for Clarke. During the Wilson era, Clarke was appointed to the U.S. Supreme Court; he resigned to serve as president of the League of Nations Association. American membership in the League was later rejected by the U.S. Senate; Clarke, however, served out his term and would subsequently lead a somewhat retired life.

Historically, *The Vindicator* was a Democratic newspaper. Old editions illustrate this political bent, especially the coverage following the defeat of Democrat Samuel J. Tilden by Republican Rutherford B. Hayes in the contested presidential election of 1876. The razor-close contest was decided by an appointed commission that had eight Republican members and seven Democrat members, and the newspaper never once referred to Hayes as president but rather as one who had gained the office by fraud.

As the twentieth century arrived, the newspaper consistently took a broader view and, under the ownership of the Maag family, served the general interest of the community rather than being a narrow political voice. By the 1940s, the newspaper came to take more of an independent view on politics than before, even on occasion endorsing a Republican nominee for the office of president. Today it is generally characterized as an independent Democratic newspaper.

My career began with a story about Quaker Falls, where Quaker Creek dropped twenty-five feet. As a youngster growing up in Carbon, it was a gathering place to swim and dance under the falling water. The walls of stone over which the falls cascaded were decked with initials such as RBJ and his girlfriend, telling observers they were in love. Many people who frequented the falls during the years of its ascendency as a recreational area took time to chisel out their names or initials on the stone ledge. My story resulted from an invitation to submit some writing after I applied for a job with *The Vindicator*.

The story was essentially entitled "If Only the Stones Could Talk." It speculated about whom the initials represented, among them one prominent man in Youngstown who served as Mahoning County auditor. His name was Elias M. Faust and the initials EMF could still be seen very plainly in the stone. Being a good newspaper fellow anxious to check the facts, it was necessary to interview certain old people from Faust's generation. They all said he had been there all right — they had often gone to the falls from Coitsville when they were young men and women, and had seen Faust there. The falls now, and even at the time of that story, had fallen into less splendor. My article was published in the Sunday magazine section, and from then on newspaper work attracted me.

As a cub reporter in 1929, one of the menial tasks I was assigned was to obtain from the city's brokerage houses the local stock quotations and carry them to the newspaper office. As the numbers fell, culminating in the Oct. 24 stock market collapse, I had a chance to look inside the board rooms at the brokerage houses, where the general hysteria of black days in all markets was occurring.

Many in the Mahoning Valley, as well as the nation, had been putting their savings into stocks, often on margin, which in a rising market gives opportunity for big earnings. Unable to meet margin requirements as the market level dropped, many were wiped out.

Word of prosperity just around the corner was frequently uttered by those who were trying to stem the pessimistic trend, but those reassurances did not calm the drifting of some people to withdraw their money out of the banks, although the breakdown resulting in the closing of all banks nationwide did not come until a few years later.

Nationally there were many suicides by persons drastically affected by the panic in the stock market, and quite a few in the Youngstown district were affected severely and doubtless felt like suicide. Nevertheless, when the collapse of 1929 occurred, there were plenty of business leaders with courage to meet local problems.

During the 1920s, James Campbell, president of Youngstown Sheet & Tube, was a familar face downtown, and the great Campbell Works arising at what was East Youngstown gave his name to that city. Then, the upper floors of the Stambaugh Building in downtown Youngstown housed the company's offices, and the Republic Iron & Steel had its offices right off the Market Street Bridge. Campbell and the president of Republic Steel were often seen at lunch in the Youngstown Club, which was then located in the First National Bank Building on Central Square.

J.C. Argetsinger, counsel for Sheet & Tube, was also a familar downtown figure, as was A.W. Craver, who had been mayor during the World War I period and was active as a lawyer with banking interests. Top figure in the Youngstown financial world as the Depression broke was John T. Harrington, who headed a law firm with offices then on the top floor of the Mahoning Bank Building; today the firm still bears his name.

The old Central Square was a clutter of streetcars at the busy hours

James M. McKay co-founded the Home Savings & Loan Company in 1889. An attorney who developed an interest in real estate law, McKay believed, "There is no more important work on the face of the earth than that of aiding the worthy and deserving people of our land to secure homes for themselves and their families." He died in 1950 at the age of ninety.

of the day, and Federal Street sidewalks, east and west, were cluttered with shoppers. The McKelveys and the Strousses themselves could be found in their great department stores on Federal Street and it was a privilege for shoppers to talk to one of them during a buying trip. There were also shoe stores and men's and women's apparel stores in numbers in downtown Youngstown, and the proprietors were always on hand to personally do business.

Hotels were busy places, all of which served meals with grandeur. Important people could also be found having a game of billiards in the Tod House pool parlor, sometimes at the noon hour.

On Fridays at noon, James McKay, the founder of Home Savings and Loan, could almost always be found walking down Federal Street, heading for the Downtown Kiwanis Club luncheon at the YMCA. Old Kiwanians still remember McKay's engaging account of his visit to the Hawaiian Islands. He enjoyed his work very much and his offspring have carried his loan company to a very high ranking as a financial institution, not only in Youngstown but in the state and the nation.

When 1929 was drawing to a close, notice came for me to serve only one more week at the newspaper. As was the custom, the key to the building had to be turned in, so at the end of the week, I presented it to the publisher.

"Do you have another job?" he asked.

"No," I said, "but I'll be looking for one."

"Just stay here until you locate another job," Maag replied, and I stayed for fifty-four years.

At that time, he was sure I wasn't cut out to be a newspaperman. But shortly after this encounter, Smith Crawford, owner of a feed company in Youngstown, was murdered. He resided at Lowellville, and I knew the family well. So I produced all sorts of information about the murder and the Crawford family. Walking in one Saturday night, the state editor exclaimed, "My god, he is a newspaperman."

From then on, I seemed to do enough to be accepted; fifty-four years of survival is some testimony in that regard.

Not too long after the Crawford murder, the writer of the newspaper's "Man on the Monument" column died. He had been postmaster of Youngstown, among other jobs, and he wrote this column for the Sunday edition. The basis of it was the Man on the Monument on Youngstown's Central Square and the Maid on the Fountain across the square. The legend was they got down from their perches and did the town after midnight and went back to their perches at dawn. The columns began in 1905. I wrote it for some years, making it a column with a good deal of history. In time, however, the paper discontinued the column, partly because of the financial stress of the 1930s which cut back advertising revenue, thereby reducing the size of the daily newspaper sometimes to only twelve pages.

During the 1930s, newspaper work wasn't a question of a career; it was a question of holding on to any job you could. This was a perilous undertaking; shortly after the stock market crash, some new employees had been dropped. At that time, monthly collections of the newspaper in bound volumes were covered with dust and out of order. Trying to hold on to my job, I cleaned, dusted and put them in chronological order.

The old Vindicator building at the corner of West Boardman and South Phelps Street had character. It was red brick and had a winding stairway that led up from the street level. Reaching the top of the stairs, one walked by a room to the right, which in the late 1920s and early 1930s was occupied by the society department, where Nellie Brown, a vivacious lady, presided. A step beyond in the hall was a large square room — the editorial department. In one corner, in a normal day of activity, Maag would be seated at his desk and typewriter. The reporters and editors would be scattered at little wooden desks with their typewriters. Throughout the room, at almost every desk, there was a cuspidor.

The staff was virtually all male, but already women were breaking into the newspaper business and they usually were referred to as "sob sisters." *The Vindicator's* best-known sob sister was Ella Kerber who covered the courthouse; *The Telegram's* was Esther Hamilton. Both of these "girls" graduated from New Castle High School in the mid-teens of this century and made their way into writing for the rival papers. In fact, Ella had actually introduced Esther to the Youngstown scene. Thereafter, considerable competition developed.

The men included Frederick Douglas, who was the editor of *The Vindicator*. He had his desk in the society department and wrote editorials. Douglas had a unique filing system — atop the seat of his chair. As the files increased, his seat was elevated. By the time of my arrival, he was a white-haired, distinguished-looking gentleman who walked downtown from the North Side for his workday. In his early days at the newspaper, one of his special duties was to scan the advertisements for corsets and such to ensure there was no impropriety. The assignment was not viewed as proper for younger male members of the staff.

All the other main editorial workers were seated in the room where Maag presided. On occasion, Maag settled difficulties arising between editors and reporters on what should be written and published.

In those days, Joe Lavery was the state editor, Frank Ward, the sports editor. Reporters included Bill Gray, Dave Lewis, and "Scoop" DePetit, the latter gaining his name by covering the police station and getting exclusive stories. He also sometimes got into his cups.

Drinking was a problem among reporters in those days. In the 1920s and during the Prohibition era, reporters usually found a way to tap into good brew confiscations made by city police, especially if the newsmen were having some kind of a party. Management, of course, frowned upon any liquor in the newsroom but sometimes a bottle was hidden in a desk drawer. This problem of too much drinking went back to the early years of *The Vindicator*.

When he was serving as the referee in bankruptcy court, attorney Jack Williams told me a memorable story illustrating this problem. Williams and William F. Maag Sr. had been elected to the state House early in the century. When the Ohio General Assembly was busy, it was quite a job to go home on weekends, and Williams recalled seeing Maag in the Neil House in Columbus one Saturday morning, pacing back and forth.

"Jack, I must go home," he confided.

Maag then mentioned two rather famous reporters of that time, and explained, "They're drunk and I have to get out the Saturday paper."

Williams also once told me another notable story. He was in Chicago in 1896 when William Jennings Bryan was nominated at the Democratic Party convention. Though he was a Republican, Williams thought he would just look in at the convention. Bryan, then 36 years old and called the "Boy Orator of the Platte," rose at the convention and made his famous "Cross of Gold" speech.

"Mankind must not be pressed down by a crown of thorns or crucified upon a cross of gold," Bryan bellowed. Almost by acclamation, the party convention nominated him for president.

"Everyone threw their hats in the air and so did I," Williams remembered. This is a significant tale about the infectious emotional level at national political conventions, considering that Williams was enough of a Republican to purchase a separate lot in Jackson Cemetery where he is buried so he would not have to lie next to his Democratic relatives.

The 1930s were a stirring era, and the newspaper's office was a stopping point for many. A frequent visitor was Reverend VanKirk of Youngstown who had designed the flag for the League of Nations, a flag of all colors flowing into white and the image of peace. Once the head of the Hobos of America came into the office and made me an honorary member; I carried the group's card for years. John Henry Titus, the

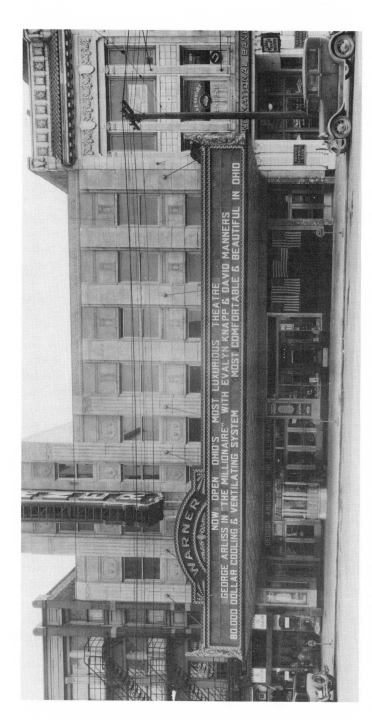

An ironic sign was the first picture the Warner Theatre showed when it opened in 1931, "The Millionaire." Built by Hollywood's Warner brothers, who hailed from Youngstown, construction followed a campaign by businessmen Fred Green Sr., Charles Owsley, Emery McKelvey and James McKay, who convinced the brothers to build in downtown's West End.

author of the "Face on the Bar Room Floor," also walked in and gave us copies of his poem. At the time, Titus was in his nineties.

Some of the reporters had real colorful backgrounds. Nemenyi, for instance, had been on an agricultural mission to Canada when World War I broke out. Because he was a lieutenant in the Austrian-Hungarian army, he was interned in Canada. As the war continued, he was transferred from an old fort near Niagara Falls to the western part of Ontario, near Windsor, to work on a sugar-beet farm as a prisoner of war. He escaped across to Detroit in August 1915, and came to Youngstown.

Here, Nemenyi was active in Hungarian societies and had worked for Republic Steel. He had also worked for the local Hungarian newspaper and then began writing for *The Vindicator*. When the U.S. declared war in 1917, and there was a problem with Hungarian nationals, it was arranged so Nemenyi could continue his employment in Youngstown. He obtained his American citizenship in 1919. I always thought he was somewhat influential in my being hired as a cub reporter.

Nemenyi continued with *The Vindicator* until his death in 1941. Much of his work was subsequently taken over by George Reiss, who is humorously noted as a "one-eyed aviator." Reiss became an authority on railroads and steel operations as well as on aviation. For many years, he was active in the promotion of air traffic at the Youngstown airport. George continued with *The Vindicator* until the mid-1980s.

Solly Adams wrote an auto industry column. Radio was growing in popularity and there was a radio writer, as well as a movie writer, Charles Leedy, who also wrote for many years a column called "Jibs and Jibes." There were others, some who worked there for a few months, some for many years.

In fact, many changes were made in the staff. In the earlier days, it was quite common for a discharged staff member to get a job at *The Telegram*, the other paper in town, quit there and come back to *The Vindicator*. An often-told story concerned a reporter who was assigned to cover a meeting but had been waylaid by some other interest. The reporter simply faked the whole story about the meeting and it was published. It was later learned that the meeting had been canceled. The reporter was discharged but management reconsidered, and a few days later he was asked to return to work. The discharged man replied he didn't want to work for a paper that wasn't any more responsible than one that would report on meetings which had never occurred.

There were telephones all over the main editorial room; ticker tapes

Built in 1931, Jones Hall is the cornerstone of the Youngstown State University campus. The building, originally known as the YMCA Educational Building, was renamed in 1966 for Dr. Howard W. Jones, the first president of the university.

giving stock quotations operated in an adjacent open room. A newcomer from the country would find it difficult to hear conversation or even talk over the telephone because of the din. Those working there simply got used to it and it didn't bother them. In my case, the noise made me nearly crazy for the first couple of weeks, and I would get a headache every day.

In my day, the Spencerian system of making letters and writing was taught in the public schools. Pupils learned to write with pencil and pen and to add without a calculator. Most reporters developed some sort of bastard shorthand system for note-taking. I used the first consonant of Youngstown and often eliminated the verb in a sentence or shortened a word with enough letters to understand what was said. Many reporters also developed tremendously good short-term memories.

One of the tricks played on cub reporters was to have the cubs pass a story from one to another for rewrite, then compare the facts in the first with facts in the last version. Often the facts didn't seem related at all. The typography men also had fun with the cub reporters. They would call the attention of a cub going through the linotype room to ''type-lice'' in the metal used to make up the pages. Then, when the cub would look, they would push the type together and water splashed up in his face. I won the reputation as being the only cub who fell prey to having his face splashed two different times.

Being a cub reporter today may not be as interesting as in the 1930s when the workdays had no limit on hours. Rather than relying on the telephone, we left the newspaper office looking for news and made stops everywhere — at bars, restaurants, the courthouse, the jails, the churches and the schools. A cub wanting to get ahead would be snooping almost night and day in order to get a story that might be a scoop over a rival news organization.

For decades *The Vindicator* and *The Telegram* waged an ongoing battle for daily newspaper circulation in the Youngstown area. This rivalry continued at high heat in the 1930s, and the thriving population on the streets in Youngstown contributed to the competition.

Each newspaper published extra editions almost daily. News hawkers moved along downtown sidewalks, shouting to sell papers, especially the extras which contained some special news account. The object was to get your extra out before the rival paper got its extra on the street, and to see how much you could beat the other's stories. This, of course, added circulation and those figures had a direct bearing on advertising rates. One incident that occurred in this circulation battle was the discovery of a large number of *Telegrams* in the Ohio River, allegedly dumped there to pad circulation figures.

Shortly before its merger with The Vindicator, members of The Telegram's editorial staff posed for a picture. Seated first from the left is Vera Etinger Friedman; Esther Hamilton is fourth from the left. Lloyd S. Jones stands to the far right in the second row. Ed Salt stands far right in the third row.

One of my first jobs was to run out into the street and get a copy of any *Telegram* extra as soon as it came out. I was always kidded about walking into the office and announcing that *The Vindicator* had defeated *The Telegram* by fifteen minutes and one hundred dead in a South American earthquake. That was the type of humorous repartee that went on.

The Telegram had been located on the edge of the North Phelps Street hill but by 1930, it was housed in a new building on West Boardman Street at Chestnut Street, which is now Vindicator Square.

At that time, *The Vindicator* could keep a closer eye than *The Telegram* on city hall, which was across the street from *The Vindicator's* office, and the county jail, which was one building away on Boardman Street. The city jail also was directly across from *The Vindicator* office. The Odd Fellows had a building next to *The Vindicator*; meetings were held there regularly and it had a cafeteria that was open to the public. The Hotel Ohio, which housed all the important guests to the city, was also close to *The Vindicator*.

The years have brought great improvements in newspapers but maybe some of the verve that existed in the old days of tangling "sheets" has been lost. Reporters ranged about the city, keeping notes on what was happening. The newspaper office was a coming-and-going place not only for reporters and other employees but also for the many citizens of Youngstown.

The practice was to type out all the known local news before closing shop for the night. This often meant working long hours. Reporters worked on weekly salaries which covered an eight-hour day, six days a week. They were also rotated to have Sunday and holiday obligations. When the day ended, if there was nighttime news to be covered, you went out to get a bite to eat, came back to the office and kept working until everything was ready for publication, sometimes long after midnight.

Morale was tremendous and the competition made it an exciting contest. Feature stories that included as many names as possible were often sought, much more than today. For a time, an effort was made to report the election of officers for as many organizations as could be found. This went to the extreme — for instance, the story detailing the election of officers for the Corn Cob Club and its activities. Finally, it was reported that the club consisted of only three members.

In those years when both daily newspapers were operating, every employee of *The Vindicator* was trained to have his eyes and ears open for any possible story. Tips came to the reporters — the telephone was already heavily used by the public — but the practice still was to make daily visits to the board of education, the library office and, of course, city hall, the county jail, the courthouse and similar places.

The union headquarters — those of the building trades and the steelworkers when they were formed — also were sources of regular news. Luncheon and service clubs almost always had reporters from both papers there; getting a free meal in the 1930s was part of the total renumerations.

In 1935, the Taxpayers League held a meeting in the old Rayen-Wood Auditorium which brought out an immense crowd to vote on the city charter; the venerable attorney J.P. Wilson was presiding. Both newspapers had reporters there, and the meeting went on and on. I decided to leave and *The Telegram* reporter stayed.

In the hallway, I encountered attorney Clyde Osborne, who had headed the Ohio Ku Klux Klan. He and the Irish leader in Youngstown were almost in a scuffle, arguing about the Klan. I took their conversation down verbatim amid threats of fisticuffs. It gave *The Vindicator* a full front-page column for the morning extra. There were two men living in Youngstown with identical Irish names, however, and in my story about the confrontation, I identified the wrong man. The one involved in the fight was good enough to call me so we could make the correction in time for the evening edition. Because *The Telegram* reporter didn't leave when I did, the newspaper picked up my first story and also printed the wrong name. The wronged Irishman sued *The Telegram*. And it was very amusing to learn that the Irishman who had been in the argument called me up with the correction because *The Vindicator* was against the KKK whereas *The Telegram* had, in earlier years, been friendly towards the Klan.

In the 1920s, *Vindicator* circulation had dropped by 18,000 almost overnight because of the Klan issue. Joe Lavery, state editor at the time, covered the KKK, and warned it would be a mistake to oppose the Klan because of the possible effect on circulation.

The only Youngstown mayor ever to run with the open support of the KKK was Charles Scheible, who was elected in 1923. Actually his administration proved to be very friendly to Catholics, some of whom played an important role in municipal government during his tenure; so much so that many Catholics came to have a high regard for this mayor.

Scheible was followed in office by Joseph Heffernan, who was a very outspoken opponent of the Klan. He was very involved as an Irish leader, and he could make a speech that listed virtually all the great men of history as being Irish. Heffernan was a very able mayor and had served as a judge. He became active in the ''Bonus Army'' of the Great Depression, which camped near the Washington Monument and demanded that World War I veterans receive a bonus that was not scheduled for payment until some years later. For awhile, the camp was accommodated but it was finally removed by a detachment of troops commanded by Douglas MacArthur. The bonus payment was subsequently effected in the 1930s and was a great help as Americans by the millions were struggling to survive.

Then, the relief list, even in Youngstown, numbered many thousands, many of whom turned to soup kitchens and such for daily food. By 1935, the state Capitol was besieged daily by hundreds and sometimes thousands of "food marchers." At the opening of the Ohio General Assembly in January of that year, the Capitol grounds and interior were teeming with people, who were usually supported by the voice of some very Communist-minded orator. The legislature looked diligently to find relatively small sums to maintain the relief programs in the stricken areas of the state.

Beginning late in 1933, the government put its hand to relief efforts, and R.A. Noble, director of relief in Mahoning County, was sent into Youngstown to employ people — sometimes a thousand or more in one day — to rake leaves, anything to get a small payment.

The Vindicator was still battling with *The Telegram*, and for a time I was able to get by telephone — sometimes at four o'clock in the morning — the decisions made at night meetings of Noble and his aides on projects for recovery. One week we scooped *The Telegram* with a morning extra telling what was coming for the day before the press conference took place at 10:30 a.m. When the reporter from *The Telegram* saw our story, she became angry and wondered how *The Vindicator* morning edition got the scoop.

Then, the battle to sustain the victims of the economic catastrophe was sharp, and citizens from all walks of life tried to put food in their hands and, at least, keep food available to the whole population. Thousands had lean eating days, but actual starvation was rare. In the Youngstown area, just one starvation death came to the newspaper's attention and it involved a man too proud to accept help.

One of the first effects from speading unemployment was the sad spectacle of men by the hundreds taking to traveling. The transient population drifting into Youngstown became a problem, and the Blaine Avenue police station at Haselton was stocked with cots where transients slept. It opened under the stress of crowding men, and some Communist spokesmen immediately took charge.

"Reds seize city flophouse," one newspaper headline read.

Later in the day, some ex-Marines decided to replace the Communist control and did so.

Central Square in the spring of 1933.

Sleeping in the flophouse to see the situation there firsthand was quite an experience for a reporter. At dawn, the fellow in the next cot leaned over, poked me and said, "Jackson, let's go home."

He was an FBI agent assigned there simply to keep an eye on developments in this hectic period.

Events subsequently settled down, but for a long period the old police station was a place for those wandering through the city to rest weary heads. Still later came flophouses that dished out food to long lines, enough to sustain those seeking a more pleasant future.

The year 1933 was a fermenting time in politics. Having won the presidency after a long drought, Democrats were following every step that Franklin Delano Roosevelt took in rallying the people from the desperate gloom into which they had fallen with the Great Depression.

Mill towns such as Lowellville were severely stricken, and warmth in homes was largely sustained by rolling coal off trains as they passed through the Mahoning Valley.

One such practice was to go down the river valley to Edenburg, Pennsylvania, where the trains slowed. Climbing to the top of the coal cars, it was no great effort to pile up a few large black chunks of the fuel and roll them off as the train speeded through Lowellville. Up the valley at Struthers, the train would slow again. The coal snappers would get off there and easily make it back to Lowellville to pick up the coal they had dropped — that is, if other members of their families were not waiting there for the dumping. Indeed, coal poaching was the sport of many citizens; afterward, they would often gather for an evening of card-playing. It was possible to play poker as if everyone still had money. Old poker chip boxes retained by some former Lowellville residents record that 13 cents or 17 cents was owed by this one or that one.

I was one of the fortunate ones who was still working, although my wife had to give up her job as a schoolteacher in Lowellville because the general rule was one breadwinner per household. In Lowellville, unemployment reached as high as fifty percent; in Youngstown, as much as twenty-five percent of the workforce was unemployed. In fact, in Youngstown some workers were paid with what was known as "city scrip," which was a promise of dollars to come, and was used in some stores for purchases. This type of currency was resorted to in many parts of the country, especially after the banks were closed in 1933.

It was a time when even surviving newspapers were anxious to get any bit of news that came cheaply. I spent part of my time hunting old photograph plates discarded in a pile which would serve in a new story if some information could be found that went with the picture.

In 1934, I began writing a daily column called "By the Way," *The Vindicator's* answer to *The Telegram's* column by Esther Hamilton. The column must have been a successful venture, as evidenced by its replacement when *The Vindicator* took over *The Telegram* and reverted to printing Esther's column. In any case, it may have earned me the title of political editor, which was given to me at that time.

Political writing was not a full-time occupation; I was also the labor reporter. News reporters did many different jobs. For instance, we had a brief account of the weather on the front page each day. There was a paragraph or two of observation about the weather. I tried my turn to write this in rhyme, but it was immediately apparent I wasn't poetic at all. I had borrowed some lines from Thomson's "Seasons," a famous English poem. When the complaining came from an editor, I pulled out the book of poetry to show him it was indeed poetry.

One of my experiences reporting the weather occurred when the temperature was ten degrees below zero and I went to the home of L.H. Copeland in Millport, Columbiana County. His family had kept daily records of the weather beginning in 1891, and I copied them for use in *The Vindicator*.

One record Copeland had collected was intriguing. It noted a seventeen-inch rainfall at Elkton in 1867, which was recorded by a scientist from the Smithsonian Institution. For a long time, this was the heaviest rainfall ever recorded in the United States. Much of Elkton had disappeared into a creek and ultimately into the Ohio River as a result of the storm.

On the way to Millport, it was an interesting trip driving through Dungannon, where the first Catholic Church was established west of the Alleghenies, and Hanoverton, a German settlement. A traveler can wander over to Navarre in Stark County, settled by the Huguenots, and also to Salem, where the Quakers settled.

Most interesting to me, however, was Copeland. His wife was a leader in the prohibition movement. But as I left, he invited me to the barn and pulled out a bottle of whiskey that was hidden in the hay.

"With the temperature what it is, young man, you should have a nip of this before you start back to Youngstown," he advised.

Copeland sent in a weekly report to *The Vindicator* for many years. Frequently this information could be made into a substantial article for the Sunday edition.

Nobody liked to write obituaries, so they put me on that job, and I did it for about thirty years. As a matter of fact, I continued to write obituaries from time to time as long as I was on the newspaper. For that reason, this writer has an abundance of information about the old dead of Youngstown, including its most promient citizens. Among the obituaries I wrote was one recalling the unusual life of John D. "Bonesetter" Reese who had been permitted by a special act of the Ohio State Medical Board to practice medicine. He was a healer who was internationally known for his manipulation of muscles and bones to relieve pain. Famous baseball players such as Ty Cobb, Babe Ruth, Honus Wagner and Walter Johnson came to Bonesetter's office on Wick Avenue in Youngstown to be treated as did Lloyd George, prime minister of England during World War I, and thousands of lesser-known people who also benefited from what he called his "knack."

There's always an attitude in the newspaper business of considerable abandonment about life, even skepticism. This was never more apparent to me than after I had been in the hospital for ninety-one days, a stay that included thirty-one days in intensive care; upon returning to work the first assignment I was given was to write my own obituary for the newspaper files. The principle followed in completing that task, as well as the one I complete now, is never to say anything bad about the dead.

Obituaries are fruitful sources of interesting news stories. After all, death sometimes comes oddly, such as one that occurred in Canfield when a dog's tail lodged in the trigger of a hunting gun, or another that occurred to an aged woman while she was playing the lead role in *Charlie's Aunt*. In the comedy, the prospective heirs are waiting for the aunt's death and are arguing over her estate in a humorous manner. In this case, at a church in Milton Township, the actress who was playing the aunt actually died on stage.

In another case, I was able to get a man who was reported dead on the telephone and he came into the office to confirm his existence at the same time as his funeral was proceeding. This story of mistaken identity was printed on the front page.

And yet, my most interesting experience was with a visitor who brought me copies of three obituaries that had been written about him which, fortunately, had appeared in other newspapers. Obituaries are a test of the quality of any newspaper, for errors in death notices are virtually always noted.

EXTRA

The MAN ON THE MONUMENT

A NATION CANNOT OUTLIVE JUSTICE WHERE LAW ENDS TYRANNY BEGINS

By **CLINGAN JACKSON**
The Vindicator, 1932

("Now there arose a new king over Egypt who knew not Joseph.")

"IT APPEARS that the Roosevelt administration doesn't altogether know the hoarders of grain of other years, but what we want to know is whether the big chisler is going to escape conviction as the big bootlegger has through the prohibition period," said the Man on the Monument.

"SCHEMING lawyers have found ways of getting around a multitude of legislative enactments, and scheming businessmen today are trying to avoid shouldering their full load of responsibility under the codes," the Veteran resumed.

"One of the tragedies of the whole matter is that many businesses have been in such condition that they have had to scheme to sidestep the code as much as possible in order to exist.

"And of course there have been businesses which have sidestepped things, believing that such is the way to display the shrewdest sense.

"We should have been out of this depression a long time ago had the people all quit hoarding when President Hoover asked them to quit and had they all fallen in line for the emergency to do the President's bidding without question.

"Bidding disorganization has gotten into people's minds. The psychology of revolution is in every wind that blows, and even the shrill summoning call of the

NRA bugle may not rally the straggling troops of humanity sufficiently to avoid a catastrophe.

People Frightened

"We know that our safety requires union, for in union there is strength, but we seem unable to resist that impulse to run for the nearest tree to a secure place from which to watch the rout."

"Now is the time that all of us ought to show a little nerve—nerve like that of the early builders of Youngstown, who didn't hesitate to stake all on the throw of the dice in human fate."

"But how many of us have lost that pioneering spirit, that spirit which declared if we lose all today we'll win tomorrow and be richer for the experience?"

"Today people seem to be frightened into the belief that society will be so stratified under the new deal that a man once down will never be able to get up again."

We Meet Uncle Sam

"I wouldn't worry about it. The corporation won't supply bonds for the park shanty you're staying in," the Veteran said jokingly.

"Well, I don't know about that. Many cities seem to think the federal government will furnish money for about every sort of improvement ever contemplated," retorted the Maid.

"The last few years of distress have brought the Washington government home to every one of us. The federal government has reached its hands down locally as it never has before. We wonder if it is a beginning of a new era when the states will be less sovereign and all government will be more centralized."

"The recent move of the administration against kidnapping illustrates the growing need for a police system that is centralized and wide-flung."

"All of these moves come right home to Youngstown. Folks here are better acquainted with Uncle Sam than ever before. Fifty years ago the Democratic party was the party of state rights, and about all national government did was that it delivered him his mail. Now the government tells him how long he must work every day and what his pay will be," said the Maid.

Age of Change

"After all we are living in an age of change. I wouldn't be surprised to see more changes take place next year than this. When the ball starts rolling, it won't stop until it finds a level spot or begins to roll uphill. But the ball is rolling in such a direction that Uncle Sam is almost certain to have more to do with you and I hereafter.

"And the vicious who Uncle Sam puts muzzles on will growl and fret about their fetters. But the lambs will rejoice, realizing how successful law and regulation have always been in protecting them from the wolves," the Veteran concluded.

"Well, I hope the wolf of Federal Street doesn't grab me as I'm on my way home," said the Maid, casting a Little Red Riding Hood smile. ∎

A view from Struthers where billowing smoke in the sky symbolized employment for thousands.

"Of course, the Communist Party and its members in the steel mills participated in the drive to organize steel and all other unorganized industries. The Communist Party joins with all democratic forces in the struggle against reactionaries, open shop, violence and fascism.

A great people's movement uniting labor, storekeepers, middle class folks, farmers, professionals and all who defend the Americanism of Washington, Jefferson and Lincoln is needed to drive out and defeat these would-be imitators of Hitler."
Mahoning County Communist Party circular, 1937.

CHAPTER 6

LITTLE STEEL STRIKE

 he Little Steel Strike of 1937, an epic event locally, involved some 32,000 area workers, and would eventually succeed in forever changing the course of labor relations in the Mahoning Valley.

It occurred twenty-one years after a bitter steel strike resulted in a rampage that caused more than $1 million in property damage. In 1916, the sight of East Youngtown in flames jarred residents in a way difficult for today's population living along the Mahoning River to understand. Then the area was largely inhabited by farmers or the sons of farmers who had come to Youngstown and helped develop the steel mills of the Mahoning Valley.

The workers for the mills and mines had primarily been imported

101

from the teeming populations of Eastern Europe looking for a future in the golden land across the sea. This tide of newcomers rose particularly in the first and second decades of the twentieth century.

As demand for steel from Mahoning Valley mills increased with the outbreak of World War I in 1914, a labor shortage developed. Thousands of single men residing in boarding houses, many just beginning to pick up the English tongue, lived somewhat of a free life that men usually lived when away from their womenfolk; saloons were the main locations for relaxation among the rank and file of steelworkers when they were not at their jobs. Wages were low and the management of industry operated in a very unrelenting manner.

When the steel strike erupted in 1916, starting at Republic Iron & Steel and then spreading to Youngstown Sheet & Tube's plant in East Youngstown, inadequate union organization enabled the walkout to take on vicious aspects. Workers broke into saloons and liquor flowed freely. On Jan. 7, 1916, a large group gathered near a bridge and a plant guard opened fire. A riot ensued — three strikers were killed and twenty were wounded — and large sections of East Youngstown were set on fire.

The fires took a huge toll. My father, for example, had supplied lumber for home construction in the strike-devastated area and had secured a lien on the properties as the only guarantee of payment. The flames of East Youngstown, which was to be rechristened Campbell in a future better day, pitched Father's business into a bankrupt condition. He managed to wiggle through, but for years afterward he continued making payments to meet the losses that were still occurring.

The riot threw a scare into the large residential district of the more settled peoples of Mahoning County, who feared the striking foreigners — then referred to as "honkies," "wops" and other derogatory, ethnic-based names. Roads and bridges were cut off to prevent groups of strikers, some of which had gatherings of actual criminals, from crossing.

After the state militia was brought in to take control and the strike finally ended, labor relations settled down. During the Great Steel Strike of 1919, when 350,000 men nationwide walked off their jobs and violence erupted elsewhere, labor and management showed restraint locally even though the steel companies crushed the strike.

In the 1920s, the trade unions developed something of a labor aristocracy for skilled workers, but the bulk of American workers still felt the repressive hand of the controllers of industrial might. What trade unions there were functioned through the United Labor Congress until the great union revivals of the Depression years.

President Roosevelt's first term resulted in the enactment of the

National Industrial Recovery Act, which brought about an industry-by-industry unionization effort that swept much of the country. Although the NRA, as it was then known, would later be declared unconstitutional based on the court's interpretation that its provisions for regulating business illegally intervened in interstate affairs, the legislation had guaranteed collective bargaining rights for labor.

Following passage of the NRA in 1933, the Amalgamated Association of Steel and Tin Workers, which had been in existence since the early part of the century as a trade union covering some of the skilled workers in the steel mills, expanded its activities in an effort to include virtually all employees of Mahoning Valley steel plants. At the same time, company-approved unions became very active. The incipient unions formed by the Amalgamated in the wake of the NRA later evaporated and, in time, the same occurred to the company-sponsored unions.

The Amalgamated, in these first efforts to include rank and file steelworkers, did not gain company recognition for its newly formed unions, which led to its decision to participate in the formation of the Congress of Industrial Organizations (CIO). The industrialization of the unions resulted in an expansion from coverage of a few specialized highly paid workers such as puddlers to include all employees across the board. The companies fought this expansion because they wanted non-union employees for the most part, if not all.

The Little Steel Strike resulted from the formation of the Steel Workers Organizing Committee (SWOC) under the CIO. This organizational effort in Youngstown created a number of very active union "lodges," as they were known then, and which would later become United Steelworkers Local 1330 at U.S. Steel's Ohio Works; Local 1331 at Republic Steel; Local 1418 representing Youngstown Sheet & Tube employees at the Brier Hill Works; and Local 1462 at the Campbell Works.

The SWOC sought recognition by attempting to sign collective bargaining agreements that regulated wages and working conditions for all workers. The steel companies always wanted a free hand in hiring and firing employees and setting their wages; they opposed the unions, fearing management would be limited in exercising its powers.

The process of achieving unions in some plants was avoided in others by the companies establishing, on their own, fairly liberal methods of dealing with employees, which usually involved adequate wages. Some companies found that providing wage rates at least as good as those prevailing in union companies would tend to keep unionization from occurring. Indeed, union successes always had some effect prevailing beyond the immediate impact.

During the 1930s, one of the arguments against unions was that they provided another set of administrative costs since the union leadership itself required operating funds. This argument claimed the men were putting a double set of exploiters above themselves rather than one set — management. Reportedly, in negotiating to get contracts, some union leaders would go so far as to claim they could get workmen cheaper for a company than it would have to pay otherwise.

The Little Steel Strike was called in Youngstown on May 26, 1937, by Philip Murray, the chairman of the SWOC who, in 1942, would become the first president of the United Steelworkers of America — successor to the Amalgamated — and was so named because it targeted companies other than the huge United States Steel Corporation — the leader of so-called "Big Steel" — which had already recognized collective bargaining rights for all workers in its steel mills and was not affected by the strike. The same was true of the Inland, Crucible and Jones & Laughlin steel companies.

Then, the CIO was headed by John L. Lewis and he poured into the SWOC experienced people from his United Mine Workers union such as John L. Mayo, who was sent to Youngstown as SWOC district director. From the start, the purpose was union recognition, and rank-and-file steelworkers not only saw this as their wish but also the wish of the president of the United States, then at the height of his popularity.

Lewis was searching for able union organizers and he turned to some Communist workers, among them Gus Hall, who would later become chairman of the Communist Party of America and run for president many times, and John Stevenson. Both reported directly to Mayo, who set up his office in the Erie Terminal Building in downtown Youngstown.

I was present when Hall and Stevenson first reported to Mayo some months before the Little Steel Strike erupted, and I immediately recognized Stevenson as a Communist who had previously been known as "Shorty" Steuben. On May 1, 1931, he had crawled under a car with me to watch as mounted police in Youngstown broke up a "May Day" Communist demonstration on East Federal Street. The Communists had a headquarters on Federal Street, and in the melee several police officers were knocked from their horses. A brick pile about where Andrews Avenue takes off from old Basin Street proved to be formidable, and some seventy police officers and demonstrators suffered minor injuries during the skirmish.

A few days later, William G. Foster, then head of the Communist Party of America, came to Youngstown and joined a parade that marched up Federal Street. Foster made a speech in front of the Stambaugh Building, which housed the headquarters of Youngstown Sheet & Tube. The demonstration seemed to petrify some old-time business leaders, who were looking out of a window. One of them lamented to me it was the harbinger of the end of society in the nation as he had come to know it.

The economic suffering that occurred in the beginning of the Great Depression began the shifts in the thinking of Youngstown's rank and file citizens, which led to considerable support for revolutionary sentiments and eventually became entwined to form tremendous backing for FDR and his New Deal. Roosevelt's administration had recognized the Union of Soviet Socialist Republics, and there was a growing warmness toward communism among the despair-afflicted people of the 1930s. In fact, there were quite a few Communists in Youngstown and in many other cities that were suffering from the economic collapse which exposed wrongdoings and excesses in American capitalism.

During the Little Steel Strike, Hall established a gathering location in Campbell, where there was a large collection of mace and other minor weapons laid side by side on benches around the room. This operation was quite separate from Mayo's and the director's office all through the strike. From the outset of the organizational effort, Mayo was always concerned about the presence of any terrorist activity. After the strike ended, Hall and Stevenson were terminated as SWOC organizers; both had been charged in connection with an explosive device that detonated near militiamen protecting the entrance to a mill in Warren.

Some 1,000 steelworkers attended a meeting at the Old Moose Hall on West Boardman Street in Youngstown, where Murray officially called the Little Steel Strike. The subsequent shutdown of the steel mills, which had previously been authorized by SWOC lodges, affected the entire country, including employees of Youngstown Sheet & Tube and Republic Iron & Steel's facilities in the Mahoning Valley as well as thousands of other steelworkers across the country.

Various national labor leaders converged on Youngstown, also bringing to the city leading reporters on union activity, among them Lewis Stark of the *New York Times*. I had become acquainted with Stark in Pittsburgh when J&L Steel had reached agreement with its steelworkers shortly before the Little Steel Strike broke out. He had shown me around Pittsburgh and introduced me to J&L executives, including William Mossman, an uncle of "Alf" Landon who had been the Republican nominee for president in 1936.

Workers line up to receive paychecks they earned before the Little Steel Strike erupted.

The Little Steel Strike was immediately effective; within hours of Murray's call, the plants were closed and prepared with security measures. At least one of the plants had a machine gun set up; I know, because I saw it. At a congressional inquiry following the strike, Frank Purnell, chairman of Youngstown Sheet & Tube, testified that one plant's arsenal contained "$10,000 worth of tear gas, 8 machine guns, 452 revolvers, 314 pistols and 190 shotguns," most of which, he explained, had been stored there since the 1916 strike.

Fearing another riot like the one that set East Youngstown in flames, Youngstown Mayor Lionel Evans ordered all liquor establishments to close, action that quickly followed in Warren. The preventative measures did not, however, succeed in averting violent picket-line confrontations.

The worst of the violence in Youngstown took place on Poland Avenue which had entrances there into Republic Steel and Youngstown Sheet & Tube. Union headquarters were established on both sides of the streets near a fire station. Strikers gathered day after day and formed threatening lines to stop anyone from going into the plants. On the most bitter night of the strike — June 19, 1937 — steelworkers by the thousands stood out on the avenue and the sidewalks as Mahoning County Sheriff Ralph Elser moved down the street with truckloads of deputies and attempted to keep order.

The situation erupted when some women, who were concerned with their husbands' picketing at the plant, arrived at Poland Avenue and joined female workers involved in the strike itself. Versions varied of what happened — police claimed they were attacked by strikers and strikers claimed they were attacked by police — but, in essence, there had been some friction between the women and security forces.

Ed Salt, a *Vindicator* photographer, and I were dispatched to Poland Avenue to cover the tense situation. It was growing dark by that time, lights were being shot out and hundreds of men were milling along the street. We parked near the fire station and started walking down the sidewalk. As we passed by a bush, we saw its leaves completely eliminated as a shotgun blast rang out. Being a brave man, I went back to the fire station; needing to take pictures, Salt pushed onward.

When I arrived at the station someone exclaimed, "Salt has been shot." Mustering my courage, I went to his rescue, and found him with his white shirt completely bloodied. I got him into the car, and we headed up Poland Avenue. Although the street was barricaded, I persuaded the pickets to let the car through by explaining I had a passenger who needed to go to the hospital.

When we finally reached the hospital, emergency room attendants laid Salt on a cot, pulled back his shirt and other clothing and discovered what appeared to be scores of shotgun pellets that had wrought some bleeding throughout his chest and legs, but nothing serious. I was able to report to the city editor that Salt had nothing to worry about except lead poisoning.

The editor ordered me to return immediately to the scene of the rioting. Traveling along Powersdale Avenue, which led to Poland Avenue, my car was surrounded by a mass of hundreds of marching union men who were carrying clubs and baseball bats; one man even had a scythe. I drove slowly in their midst, parked the car, ran across the street and ducked into a building where some union leaders were holed up. Bullets were knocking out street lights and the windows of buildings all along Poland Avenue, which by this time was free of human habitation. Although there was a lot of shooting, no one seemed to be shooting to kill.

The first man I encountered inside the makeshift union headquarters was Gus Hall, who was sitting on a bed. Throughout the night, we would stick things out the door to test if they would get shot at or not. Morning revealed that gas stations and other businesses located across from the steel mill were riddled with bullets, which had apparently been aimed from the windows of the plants. By 11 a.m., the situation had settled enough to get back to the newspaper office. In all, the riot caused the death of two strikers and injuries, mostly minor, to forty-two strikers, police officers and observers.

A few days after the violence, the strike climaxed when Governor Martin L. Davey, a Democrat, sent in the National Guard. Some 4,500 guardsmen were deployed to the plant gates and, on the evening of June 25, 1937, the back-to-work movement started. By the next day, 17,450 workers had entered the plant gates, and the strike was effectively broken.

In time, the companies reached agreements with the unions; but as far as the Little Steel Strike being an immediate success, it was not. Work resumed without labor contracts or set wages. Negotiations with Youngstown Sheet & Tube and Bethlehem Steel dragged on until finally contractual relationships were established. And it was not until four years after the strike that collective bargaining contracts with the union became pervasive.

Davey's action made for a very bitter political situation in the 1938 gubernatorial Democratic primary. That year, there was a huge outpouring of voters in the Mahoning County Democratic primary, some 48,000, which was unheard of for a party primary to that date. Many

Republicans and independents, apparently agreeing with Davey's action, turned out to vote for him in the Democratic Primary. Nevertheless, Lt. Governor Charles Sawyer, having strong support from steelworkers, won the nomination yet lost the election to Republican John W. Bricker, who would serve three terms. Bricker was nominated for vice president in the 1944 presidential quest of Thomas Dewey; he later became a U.S. senator while Sawyer went on to serve as commerce secretary under President Harry Truman.

The Mahoning County Democratic Party had backed Davey for the nomination while Sawyer's effort was headed by William B. Spagnola, an attorney. In 1939, with labor backing, Spagnola was elected Youngstown mayor, the first of Italian descent elected to the city's mayoralty.

The political reverberations from the Little Steel Strike continued for many years, but with the coming of World War II, there developed a cohesion between management and labor that enabled the maximum wartime production effort. By 1941, all the steel companies had entered into contracts with the unions and, although these contracts provided increases in wages and benefits, they materially reduced the competitive position of American steel manufacturers in the world market.

As the years wore on, some believe the steel companies too readily agreed to wage increases, passing along the cost to American consumers. The process worked for some decades, with steel technology in America sufficiently superior to that elsewhere in the world and thus able to accommodate higher prices. But with the resurgence of West German and Japanese manufacturing achieved by the attitude and actions of the American government to restore the economies in the war-devastated countries, these nations were able to produce many consumer products more cheaply and ship them into the United States for an opulent purchase.

There were punctuation marks of what was happening, which would herald the death of steel in the Mahoning Valley. For instance, the wire plant at Struthers, a facility that dated to the Civil War, finally succumbed when the same product could be produced by Japanese manufacturers and shipped to Cleveland at a lower cost than the Struthers plant was able to make it.

The Mahoning Valley steel industry boomed after World War II, but making steel for the war effort required fewer workers than the number required to meet consumer needs. During the postwar years, steel consumption became somewhat specialized and required more employees for manufacturing. And yet, all during the 1940s, '50s, '60s and into the '70s, there was relatively full production. The

Shift change at U.S. Steel's Ohio Works. The plant closed in 1983 and was demolished soon thereafter, a sad event that captured the attention of network newscasts which featured footage of the blast furnaces tumbling to the ground.

American appetite for automobiles had greatly expanded, and much of the steel made in the Valley went into automobiles.

There was also tremendous production of pipe for the oil industry as well as steel for construction purposes. American steel production exceeded that of the rest of the world. Production in the Youngstown/ Warren area alone equaled the amount produced by major countries. At one time, Youngstown mills produced as much steel as all of England. But no more! Today, American steel production falls below that of the Soviet Union.

Almost from the beginning, the unions had graduated into political action, and the CIO's Political Action Committee became a potent force in politics at all levels of government. The settling of the Youngstown district into a strong union area after the Little Steel Strike was partly achieved because the district itself had always been a favorable union nesting place.

To serve industry, the area had long been a railroad center, and rail employees numbered many thousands. The railroads and trade unions had considerable history in Youngstown before the CIO organizing effort was made in the 1930s. In fact, dating to early in the twentieth century, an active United Labor Congress existed, and rank-and-file political views leaned to the left.

In 1924, there was strong support in this area for Robert LaFollette, the Progressive Party nominee for president. In that election, the city of Cleveland gave its majority to LaFollette. Even in the early 1920s, when Warren G. Harding became president, some of Harding's Youngstown friends persuaded him to get socialist Eugene Debs out of prison. While being taken to prison in Moundsville, West Virginia, from his home in Indiana, Debs was transported into one of Youngstown's rail stations, where he was greeted by a large number of marching Socialists who paraded as he was transferred to another rail station.

During the 1940s, one of my assignments was to write a weekly labor column for *The Vindicator*. My coverage of labor pretty well ceased in 1948 after I wrote an article that pointed out while some union activists here were not Communists, they sometimes employed Communist tactics.

In the midst of this controversy, the United Steelworkers headquarters at Pittsburgh hired me to do a report on union activity in Scandinavian countries. Even though I was targeted with blacklisting by local union leadership, the Pittsburgh office still wanted me to do the free-lance job. I had been pretty close to Murray and Vincent Sweeney, SWOC publicity director during the Little Steel Strike and later editor of *Steel Labor* magazine, and there were local union officials who also gave me support. Despite my blacklisting by the CIO chieftains here in the 1948 elections, I won re-election to the state Senate. That would not be the case, however, in 1950, when there were three Democratic candidates for two seats, one of whom was a labor leader.

During my newspaper career, not only did I have an opportunity to view union organization from the standpoint of a reporter but I was also personally involved in such activities. In the early 1930s, newspaper employees became very interested in organizing unions, and members of the editorial staffs for both *The Telegram* and *The Vindicator* met to discuss their options. Eventually, about 1934, representatives from Youngstown, Akron and Cleveland reporters' groups met in Cleveland. Having been a student of guilds in medieval history, I moved to form the Ohio Newspaper Guild. Someone else in the group suggested that we call it the American Newspaper Guild. That was the beginning of the American Newspaper Guild, and it became one of the core unions that formed the CIO.

The local guild voted against joining the American Federation of Labor (AFL), but nationally the action was approved. Subsequently, the local guild established relations with the United Labor Congress, the AFL's organization here; and for a time I was a delegate to the United Labor Congress of Mahoning County, which had delegates from all the AFL unions — mostly trade unions.

With the formation of the CIO under the leadership of Lewis, the unions that wanted to become industrial — taking in all employees of a particular company — left the AFL. The local newspaper guild and other guilds throughout the nation, which had been formed largely under the aegis of Heyward Broun of New York, also voted to go into the CIO. Again, the local guild voted against going into this larger federation but was swept along. In effect, it had been swept into the AFL and then into the CIO, whereas in the origin of the guild idea, the purpose of the local effort was to professionalize journalism on the standard much as it was set in Europe.

As president of the local guild, I was a delegate to the American Newspaper Guild convention at San Francisco in 1938. I rode with Broun throughout the city and was even involved in active union picketing. Nevertheless, I voted almost alone at the Guild convention against Broun's urging of a pardon for Tom Mooney, who had been convicted for a bombing that had occurred during the 1916 Preparedness Day parade and celebration in San Francisco.

Despite years as a labor reporter, and my short time in a local leadership position, my contact with union activity was more personally felt during *The Vindicator* strike of 1964-65. The newspaper guild went on strike rather precipitously, in my opinion; I did not see the majority's justification for the walkout, a sentiment shared by quite a few others who were affiliated with the local guild. The strike began in August 1964 and did not end until the spring of 1965.

The union group published its own paper, *The Steel Valley News*, and *The Vindicator* maintained publication of the newspaper under considerable restrictions even though unions representing employees other than reporters continued to work under the terms of their contracts. No guild member crossed the picket lines but a small group did not participate in the strike effort as such, other than to refrain from working. And, when the strike concluded, three guild members, including myself, resigned from the union but continued to work for *The Vindicator*.

The coming of strong unions during the 1930s was a natural and necessary result, partly because of the excessive mastering of people by corporations. And yet, like other developments in history, it has not all been a blessing. Unions, as well as investors in corporations, sometimes have a tendency toward exploitation. As with other human organizations, unions have many dedicated members and a share of scoundrels as well.

EXTRA

Members Ruled By Small Group

Seeks to Elect Its Own Sheriff and Force Communism Down Throats of Workers

By Clingan Jackson
The Vindicator, 1948

The people of Youngstown, including the membership of Youngstown labor unions, those affiliated with the CIO and those affiliated with the AFL, ought to be concerned about the Communist tactics that are being employed here to rule or ruin.

Specifically, the present leaders of the Mahoning County CIO Political Action Committee are trying to take over the Democratic Party, trying to dictate the election of a sheriff of Mahoning County, and attempting also, to make it impossible for the city's Republican administration to function efficiently.

Principal officers of the CIO-PAC are James P. Griffin, president, who also is District 26 director of the United Steelworkers; Al Shipka, vice president; Eddie Weygandt, secretary; and Dan Thomas, treasurer.

Griffin seems to be the spearhead. Others are actively working in a campaign to force Paul J. Langley, candidate for the Democratic nomination for sheriff, down the throats of Democratic leaders, including other candidates for Democratic nomination.

The CIO-PAC has endorsed only one candidate on either the Democratic or Republican county primary tickets, Langley, but is trying to make deals with other candidates who may need CIO-PAC support in the November election.

Actions of the committee in this regard and against the 2.5-mill proposed city operating levy are all part of one pattern. The tactics are new to Mahoning County politics and new to CIO-PAC conduct here.

The CIO's largest local unions here are run by the small groups which show up for meetings. Likewise, only a small number participate in the CIO-PAC Council, less than 100 being present at the meeting which took action against the 2.5-mill levy.

Use Members' Money

Many individual union members are disgusted, particularly with the action of their unions in using funds from their dues for political purposes.

Many of those who are playing in the PAC's political game don't know they are playing with fire and endangering the welfare of their community. Others who are as far away from Communism or even belief in labor unions as they possibly can be are being walked into the Communist trap because they have become addicts of the pure materialism which mothers the Communist brood.

Citizens of Youngstown are Americans. They have equal rights and responsibilities under the charter of our city, under the constitutions of Ohio and the United States, under the flag of the United States and above all, under their God.

There is only one right which they as Americans do not possess and that is to feel themselves apart from the society of which they are members. No Youngstowner may feel himself apart from Youngstown and be a good citizen of his city, state or nation.

Few on Communist Side

Yet that is exactly what the Communists seek. When they have convinced a man he is apart from his community and his country, his soul has been won to the Communist cause.

In this battle of ideologies, democracy versus communism, all but a very, very few of our citizens want to be on the side of democracy.

But those infected with Communist ideas become effective tools for Communist infiltration willingly and unwillingly. The inspirers, who sometimes are not even known to the inspired, are clever at using other men and other institutions for their purposes.

In Youngstown, the CIO-PAC's action opposing the 2.5-mill levy fits into the Communist pattern, wittingly or unwittingly. The Communists of the Wallace meeting here Thursday heartily joined in seconding the action. The CIO group favored Ralph W. O'Neill for mayor because he had proclaimed veto day on the Taft-Hartley Act. O'Neill was defeated. The CIO clique took this to heart and doesn't like Mayor Charles P. Henderson.

Fertile Ground for Reds

This was fertile ground which Communists could use to effect the confusion in government on which they thrive. By playing on personal vanities and whatnot, their purpose has been effected.

The CIO-PAC is waging a campaign here against the levy. In Columbus and Toledo it opposed an income tax. Here it talks about a graduated income tax, well knowing that such a tax on the local level would be folly.

A straight income tax would require elaborate machinery to collect; a graduated income tax on a city basis would require much larger machinery so that a very large portion of the tax collected would be paid to make the collection.

Ever since the 1937 strike in Little Steel, when Sheriff Ralph E. Elser used a large force of deputies to preserve law and order, some CIO leaders have been out to control the sheriff's office.

This situation also was favorable for Communist plantings. The CIO-PAC went gunning to have Democrats endorse its man for sheriff. The party didn't do it.

Result: the CIO-PAC, after years of endorsing candidates for legislative and other offices who have been "fair" to labor — and most Democratic incumbents have been — turned its back on all of them. It turned its back on them because it wants no party or no office holder who will not take its orders.

The Communist-minded found their opportunity in the Democratic Party here as the result of a degree of disorganization resulting from the defeat last fall of Mayor O'Neill and the illness of County Chairman John C. Vitullo.

Seeks to Control Party

Communist tactics call for infiltration quickly into any such vacuum. Insofar as the CIO-PAC has been attempting to gain control of the Democratic Party here, it has been following that pattern.

Why did the CIO-PAC decide to oppose the 2.5-mill levy, the defeat of which will cripple the operations of the city — including many operations such as parks and playgrounds which are purely in the socialist conception of governmental functions?

Part of the answer is the desire to cripple the city administration, which was placed in power partly because of the disruption in the Democratic Party caused by the action of some CIO unionists.

But also the CIO-PAC, or its little group of power-crazed leaders who claim to represent 25,000 union members, is hungry for a victory.

Some of its leaders realized there is a group of Youngstown propertied men who in the prosperity under a free government have allowed themselves to become so materially minded that they forget the obligation they have to the government which protects them and their property.

Making Government Ineffective

Not wanting to pay more taxes, these men may vote to help nurse Communism. They should realize that the CIO-PAC's action was not taken in the interest of protection of property or in the interest of their not paying more taxes.

Indeed, vaguely and creepingly, an ideal of confiscation of capital by the state is taking hold. The idea is to make local government ineffective and unable to cope with its problems, since centralization is the first step toward such a goal.

Youngstown citizens have observed that Communism in its expansionist program in Europe takes care to seize positions controlling the police. They will be disturbed at the action of a CIO-PAC Council trying to put its man in as sheriff and at the same time crippling the city by defeating the 2.5-mill operating levy.

This is not to say that failure of the 2.5-mill levy would cause a disaster.

This is not to say that nomination and election of Langley as sheriff would result in disaster or even in full union domination of the sheriff's office.

It is to say that in these two problems, Youngstown citizens are wrestling with a developing pattern which could bring disaster. The time to strike down that type of thinking and action is now.

· · · · · · · · · · · · · · · · · · · ·

CIO Response: He Doesn't Know What He's Talking About

CIO Newsletter, 1948

Last Friday Clingan Jackson, Vindicator political editor, in a two-column front page article had a lot to say about Americanism and Communism and the CIO. In his zeal to gain support for the tax levy, Mr. Jackson said some things which must be examined for truth.

Said the astute political editor: "Citizens of Youngstown are Americans. They have equal rights and responsibilities under the charter of our city, under the constitutions of Ohio and the United States, under the flag of the United States and above all, under their God.

"There is only one right which they, as Americans, do not possess and that is to feel themselves apart from the society of which they are members. No Youngstowner may feel himself apart from Youngstown and be a good citizen of his city, state or nation.

"Yet that is exactly what the Communists seek when they have convinced a man he is apart from his community and his country, his soul has been won to the Communist cause."

Read those paragraphs again and then let's see if Mr. Jackson knows what he is talking about. We take it that he means that ALL citizens of Youngstown are Americans and have equal rights and responsibilities. But do they?

Americans, he says, have no right to feel themselves apart from the society of which they are members. What's that? Negro Americans are continually made to feel themselves apart from the society of which they are members. Mr. Jackson's paper does a good job in that respect by maintaining a separate column of news concerning colored citizens, and by even keeping the news of Negro Christian churches APART from that of other churches.

How else than "apart" can Negro citizens feel when on every hand there is discrimination and segregation?

Mr. Jackson makes it plain that he either doesn't know what he is talking about or wrote the article hurriedly without giving it much thought. He says that once the Communists convince a man that he is apart from his community and his country, his soul has been won to the Communist cause.

How wrong he is! Every Negro in Youngstown knows he is apart from his community and his country. Of that they don't have to be convinced. Yet but a few of the thousands of Negroes in Youngstown have had their souls won to the Communist cause.

The thousands of Youngstown's colored citizens are fully aware of being apart from the community, but it is an insult to dub them Communists in this name-calling outburst. Youngstown's Negroes, despite their "apartness," are as loyal to their city and country as any of Youngstown's citizens, and they are continuing their fight for first-class citizenship oblivious to the name-calling that is becoming quite commonplace these days. ∎

At the height of Mike Kirwan's power, Capitol Hill was a frequent beat.

"Charles J. Carney is expected to be seated tomor-
row in the U.S. Congress, the first new representative
from the 19th district of the Mahoning Valley in 34
years and only the second turnover of the office in
56 years.
  The late Congressman Michael J. Kirwan served
from 1936 to 1970 and before him, John G. Cooper,
from 1914 to 1936. Each of these three voices of this
industrial valley have had one thing in common, a
strong following among rank-and-file workers of the
district who seem disposed to be represented by one
of their own.''
  Clingan Jackson, The Vindicator, November 1970.

CHAPTER 7

POLITICAL EDITOR

ecoming *The Vindicator's* political editor in
1936 was the most important event in my life's
career.

Ernest "Nemo" Nemenyi had been the political writer since 1925.
President Franklin Delano Roosevelt pointed to Nemenyi at
Washington, D.C., and characterized him as "Nemo." It was not the
first use of the nickname but it helped make it stick for life.

In the course of political coverage of election procedures at the
Mahoning County Board of Elections, some scandal arose during the
early 1930s regarding the integrity of its operation. The investigation
involved board members and Nemo's alleged participation in the
counting of ballots. It resulted in grand jury indictments against several
people including board members who were subsequently removed
from office. The charge against Nemo was dismissed by the court of

119

appeals. Nonetheless, he was confined to the industrial beat and I was named political editor.

In the days before radio and television, this area of Ohio and Pennsylvania learned election results from extra editions that came out during the ballot tabulations. Naturally, the political writer and other reporters attempted to get the returns as quickly as possible. Nemo was accused of having his arm deep in the ballot box.

When I became political editor, it was still necessary for the paper to do a lot of tabulating at the elections board, but after that investigation, care was always taken to keep hands off any actual ballot. Sometimes the counting was not completed until after virtually all of the employees of the elections board had left for home.

It took courage on the part of the publisher to permit this editor to actively serve in a political career while writing about politics. Maag not only resisted the general advice of others holding important jobs at *The Vindicator* but also ignored criticism from Ohio newspapers whose editors believed anyone writing about politics should not be affiliated or take an active part in politics. In some instances, political writers did not even vote in party primaries so as to not show any bias or suspicion of bias in their work. No greater confidence was ever shown in me than Maag's holding that objective news handling was a matter of the mind, which did not forbid also being active in citizenship.

When I served on the Ohio Senate Rules Committee, which met behind closed doors and operated as an institution to lead the legislative machinery, I was subjected to considerable criticism. Never in that period did a line come to *The Vindicator* concerning legislative activity that had not been received by every other newspaper in the state.

It was surprising, too, to find a representative of a great American newspaper group come to me while I was serving on the Ohio Highway Construction Council and ask for first release of the news, assuring me *The Vindicator* would also receive the ''exclusive.'' He was told that morning and evening newspapers would take turns in getting news items first.

My first real entrance and glimpse into national politics came in 1936 when I joined President Roosevelt's campaign train in Johnstown, Pennsylvania. FDR had come to the small steel town northeast of Pittsburgh to make an inspection of the Conemaugh Valley, where the infamous Johnstown Flood — one of the worst in American history — occurred in 1889, and another less-serious flood had taken place shortly before his visit.

When I got to Johnstown, the railroad station was roped off, leaving a big open space below the platform. I didn't know what to do but finally decided to lift the rope and walk through the open space and up the steps to where the presidential train had stopped.

I climbed on the train, started up the aisle, and ran into a couple of men, one of whom put his hand on my shoulder. I suddenly realized the man directly in front of me was FDR — so easy was it in those days for most any American to reach the president. The man who had restrained me — one of his aides or a Secret Service agent, to this day I don't know which — asked what I was doing there. I told him I was a newspaperman from Youngstown.

"You newspapermen are supposed to be in the next car," he advised.

When the presidential party left the train, two automobiles full of reporters followed Roosevelt's car as he was being driven to the Conemaugh Valley. Along the way, the presidential party stopped at certain points for a closer look; reporters gathered around to hear what FDR had to say about flood control and to ask questions.

The floods of 1936 had aroused the nation and FDR wanted Congress to allocate money for flood control. Leaving Johnstown later in the day, the presidential train proceeded to a spot near Alliance, Ohio, where it stopped for the night. One could look out the window during the stopover and see the Secret Service people stationed at various locations around the train.

The next morning, the train moved to Cleveland. Leaving the Cleveland station, I walked through a broad hall that led to Euclid Avenue. I thought I was all alone. To my surprise, a band struck up "Hail to the Chief," and when I looked behind me, FDR's party was beginning to make its way to the Great Lakes Exposition, which was being held on an offshore island area.

I walked across the bridge to the island for a luncheon that the Cleveland Chamber of Commerce was giving for Roosevelt. A security guard had stopped the president's secretary after he had crossed the bridge and prevented him from going to the affair. He had no credentials, but I convinced the guard that he was indeed the president's secretary. Amazingly, the guard didn't ask me for my credentials, which was fortunate; in those days newspapermen didn't have any other than a badge identifying them as members of the press.

The same businessmen who had sponsored the luncheon were among the grumblers who were most concerned about FDR's New Deal measures. Nevertheless, after the luncheon the centerpiece flowers from the president's table quickly disappeared as those attending the affair snatched a flower or two for a keepsake. By the time I got a blossom, it was about the last one available.

When FDR got back on the train after the luncheon, there was a

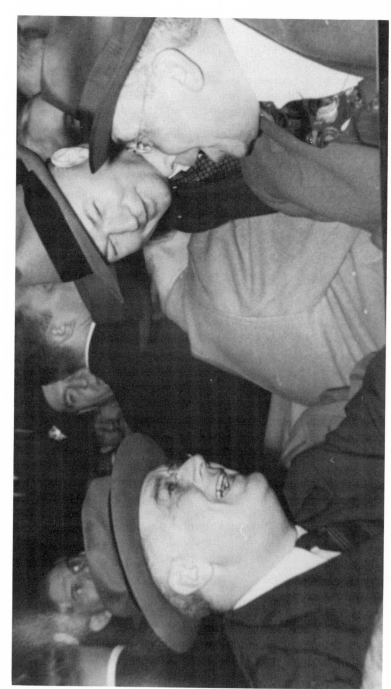

Franklin Delano Roosevelt visits Youngstown. Looking at him is Frank Purnell, chairman of Youngstown Sheet & Tube.

considerable delay in its departure and a crowd gathered. Looking from the outside into an absolutely clear window as FDR waved to the crowd, the scene was framed like a postage stamp. I was really taken by that sight — it was a case of a young American enthralled with seeing his president.

In 1936, Alfred Landon was the Republican nominee for president, and I was sent to Chicago to join his campaign train as it traveled east to West Middlesex, Pennsylvania, his birthplace, where he was to officially receive the nomination. I arrived around midnight, went inside the railroad station and inquired as to where Landon's train was parked. No one seemed to know until finally a brakeman advised, "I know where that train is — way out under a bridge."

I got a taxi and went out there. It was about one o'clock in the morning when I got to the bridge and saw the steps leading down to the tracks. There was a train parked about a quarter-mile from the bridge with a light on the end of it. I climbed on to the end car, opened the door and saw a man who was sleeping. He awoke, looked at me, and said, "Hi, Jackson."

He was from Youngstown, and I told him I was looking for the Landon train. "You're on it and I'm supposed to take over the train at the Ohio line," he explained, and fixed me up with a berth for the night.

It was a long time walking through cars jammed with people before I found Landon's car. Finally reaching it when the train was already in Ohio, and hoping to get his attention, I cast my eyes on Landon, who was seated before a desk. The car was filled with people who were also trying to get to the nominee.

The Sharon newspaper had sent a reporter who was accompanied by Senator James Davis of Pennsylvania, whose hometown was Sharon. Landon somehow registered my anxiety and beckoned me to come closer to his seat. I was able to talk to him for a few minutes, and he told me about coming to Youngstown for ice cream sodas on Federal Street in his younger days that were spent at West Middlesex.

I proceeded to write a story about Landon's recollections and when the train passed through Youngstown, the newspaper had a reporter watching for me at the Pennsylvania Station. The train slowed down, and I threw my story to him. By the time the train got to West Middlesex, where thousands were waiting for Landon on the Tam-O-Shanter Golf Course, *The Vindicator* had an extra out on the candidate's arrival.

H.L. Mencken, the famous lexicographer from the *Baltimore Sun*, was there covering the event. He liked to have someone else do the driving for him, so he rode with me. We went to several places after the speech

Theodore Roosevelt rides down Federal Street during a 1912 campaign stop. President William Howard Taft visited the city on the same day. Photo courtesy of the Mahoning Valley Historical Society, Youngstown, Ohio.

that night, and we were entertained at Lt. Governor Brown's home in New Castle. We sat on the front porch — Brown had a lot of food and drink for the reporters — and we talked with Landon until three o'clock in the morning.

This region has long spawned political leaders who won a high place in the nation's history, and it has long played an important role in determining the direction of national politics, a tradition that dates to David Tod. With the outbreak of the Civil War, he was elected Ohio governor on the Union Party ticket. The Tod House, named for his family, stood for a century as an imposing hotel on what was Youngstown's Central Square, and was the scene of many political rallies.

In 1960, John F. Kennedy spoke there and rallied area Democrats. More than six decades earlier, in 1896, William Jennings Bryan thrilled thousands as he spoke from the doorstep. Two men who served as president, Garfield and Hayes, came to the Square to dedicate the old Civil War cannons. And, on the same day in 1912, Theodore Roosevelt and William Taft passed by Central Square as they campaigned in Youngstown.

Then the Progressive Party candidate, Roosevelt came in the afternoon and rode down Federal Street; Taft, who was delayed in arriving, spoke at the old Park Theater later in the evening. The crowd was largely comprised of Roosevelt supporters who had decided to fill the seats before Taft's backers got there. My uncle, Sidney D. Lamar Jackson, was given the task of holding the crowd for Taft's arrival. He described Roosevelt as a "mighty man" and recounted the former president's great experiences touring Europe and Africa and his meetings with the czar of Russia and the kaiser of Germany. He then commented about seeing Roosevelt coming down Federal Street that afternoon with Joe West seated beside him.

"Oh, how the mighty have fallen," he humorously added.

At the time, West was an avowed Progressive and was not highly regarded by the conservative wing of the Republican Party, which felt the same way about Roosevelt, who had won the White House in 1904 for the Grand Old Party. In 1912, however, Roosevelt was considered very much on the ultra-liberal side. In his Progressive Party presidential campaign, for instance, he advocated giving Congress the right to override U.S. Supreme Court decisions.

During most of the twentieth century, Youngstown was represented in the U.S. Congress by two men who served a total of 56 years and brought respect and national attention to a region of the country then especially noted for steel production.

Republican John G. Cooper, a railroad worker, was the district's congressman from 1914 to 1936. In winning his final term, he barely survived the first waves of what would become a national political watershed; the year was 1934, and Mahoning County swung heavily into the Democratic column for the first time. With FDR's New Deal taking hold, this stampede was as pronounced in the Youngstown district in the 1930s as anywhere in the nation.

From a base which began in the Alfred Smith campaign for the presidency in 1928, the local Democratic Party organization put together a strong ticket in 1934. And to the surprise of most observers, including the party's candidates, virtually all of the Democrats won election. By that time, the local Democratic Party had become dotted with officials who had formerly been Republicans. This drift from Republican to Democrat continued after 1934 and the Youngstown area has largely remained in the Democratic camp since then with few exceptions.

Cooper was a tall, good-looking man whom I remember for his speech to the graduating class at Lowellville High School. Not a flashy person but one easily approachable and sensible, he was highly regarded within national Republican Party circles. The people and interests of the Mahoning Valley always found him concerned and helpful with their problems, and he was much-respected.

In the Democratic sweep of 1936, Cooper was defeated by Michael J. Kirwan, who was repeatedly re-elected with large majorities. Kirwan also won a high place nationally within his political party. For many years, he served as chairman of the Democratic Congressional Campaign Committee and was accorded much credit for helping the Democrats gain control of the House of Representatives during many of the years Republican Dwight D. Eisenhower served in the White House. As such, Kirwan was a national figure at his party's conventions and at some of those events, he was a major speaker.

Kirwan's entrance into politics came when he was elected to city council from Youngstown's fourth ward in the early 1930s, as the Great Depression worsened. He virtually gave his full time to serving as councilman and won the undying support of the people living on the West Side of Youngstown. It used to be told, as I remember by him, that one of Kirwan's most effective performances for his election was obtaining a key that turned the water back on in homes within his ward where service had been cut off for failure to pay water bills during the Depression.

The 1930s were a tumultuous period — unemployment compensation and Social Security had yet to be created to provide some sort of economic safety net — and Kirwan stepped into the happenings with a sure political foot. The Townsend Plan, named for a California congressman who promised a monthly government paycheck for every citizen, won Kirwan's embrace, and that helped him gain the congressional seat. It was a time when Senator Huey Long of Louisiana and Father Coughlin of Detroit expounded their views on the radio, and the whole country was listening to Long's "share the wealth" plan and Coughlin's conclusions that capitalism had victimized the working man. Long was silenced by assassination, and Coughlin was quieted by the hierarchy of the Catholic Church; but during the 1930s, their ideas were popular, albeit considered radical, even at that turbulent time.

Shortly after Kirwan was elected to Congress, he seized upon long-standing efforts to construct the Lake Erie-Ohio River Interconnecting Waterway; it was an issue that he never let go. Cooper, too, had worked on behalf of a canal to serve the steel mills of the Mahoning Valley with cheaper transportation of raw materials — coal, iron ore and limestone.

In Washington, Kirwan observed one great rule of life: He followed the leader. Sam Rayburn of Texas, in his great career as speaker of the House of Representatives, always knew that Kirwan was one of the party's troopers who could be depended upon. As American participation in World War II neared, for example, the crucial vote on the armed services draft passed the House by only one vote. Kirwan's vote was essential, and it wasn't exactly a popular vote at the time, although in retrospect it became very popular. On other wartime measures, he also demonstrated his statesmanship, and then stood with both Democratic and Republican presidents in providing means for the U.S. to maintain its posture as leader of the Free World.

An Irish-American and devout Catholic, Kirwan began his days with prayer; no one could doubt his allegiance to his country, or to his actions according to his light. He had the natural gift of seeming to be a part of any nationality group with whom he associated. Once in the 1930s, several of Kirwan's political opponents decided he wasn't an Irishman, as he represented himself, and paid for a full investigation of his background which only confirmed the congressman was in fact what he claimed to be. Born in 1886 in Wilkes-Barre, Pennsylvania, the third in a family of ten children, his first job came at age nine as a breaker boy picking slate from coal as it went over the screens. He came to Youngstown in 1907, was a railroader at U.S. Steel's Ohio Works, and served as a sergeant with the 64th artillery in France during World War I.

Kirwan's formal education was minimal — third grade was as far as he studied. He read a lot, however, had a considerable knowledge of American history, and grew in office to achieve what quite a few Americans have accomplished — graduation from the college of hard

In 1954, Kirwan proudly showed the Mosquito Reservoir to House Speaker Sam Rayburn, standing to the congressman's right. Mahoning County Democratic Chairman Jack Sulligan stands to the right of the author. In the back row (from left) are patrolman Angelo Kissos, Judge Harold S. Rickert, patrolman Ted Stiponovic, and public employees Michael Pope, James Finnessey and Carmen Fortunato.

knocks. As the result of his help in securing passage of some projects or proposals, Kirwan was awarded several honorary college degrees.

For years the congressman had a table at Young's, a famous Washington restaurant, which was set aside just for him. There he would talk to friends who came to see him, frequently to articulate their points of view about some pending political measure and, likely as not, they got the restaurant bill for the repast. That happened to me once, and it left me almost broke.

Kirwan would do almost anything for a constituent. An illustration of this is the Mahoning Valley McKinley Club, as Republican as any such group in the nation. The club had lost the scheduled speaker for its annual banquet, and Kirwan managed to get a last-minute replacement, a good friend of his and one of the GOP's best orators, who came to Niles for the affair and blasted the Democrats in mighty phrases.

He was very much a congressman's congressman, and was a ranking member of the powerful Appropriations Committee. A New Dealer who consistently supported the entire Democratic program, Kirwan became very close to Sam Rayburn. Kirwan was responsible for the $10 million appropriation that enabled construction of the National Fisheries Center and Aquarium in Washington, D.C. He was also instrumental in obtaining federal funding for construction of the Mosquito, Berlin and West Branch reservoirs, the Valley's share of more than $1 billion he had appropriated for nearly 100 dams across the nation. A strong supporter of conservation efforts in the West, he similarly backed construction of the Tombigbee Canal, which flows from the Missisippi River to the Gulf of Mexico. Part of the political deal Kirwan said he made for the Tombigbee Canal was that this area would, in turn, get the long-sought lake-to-river canal.

In 1950, Kirwan mounted his last big initiative to get funding approval for the Lake Erie-Ohio River canal, which would have utilized the Grand River Reservoir to provide water to sustain its operations. The reservoir was to have dams at both ends and overflow to Lake Erie or down the canal. As the final hearing on the proposal before the U.S. Board of Army Engineers was set, Kenneth M. Lloyd of the Mahoning Valley Industrial Council, who had generally guided the canal effort, notified Kirwan that he was unable to take part in the hearing. Republic Steel, one of the chief participants in the Council, had withdrawn its support from the canal effort, presumably because it had moved its headquarters some years before to Cleveland and its wider geographical interests had led executives to adopt a different stance. Lloyd was caught in the middle.

A few weeks before the hearing, I was engaged to take over Lloyd's

Congressman Kirwan explains hearing procedures to potential witnesses gathered at the Lee House.

job. This entailed thoroughly familiarizing myself with the proposal so I could marshal the testimony for some forty witnesses from Mahoning, Trumbull and Ashtabula counties who were supporting the effort. The witness group, myself and George Reiss, *The Vindicator's* business editor, traveled to Washington, D.C., and stayed at the Lee House.

It was a difficult assignment. The nine-member board consisted of the generals who headed one of the nine departments of the Army Corps of Engineers. We had to make our own presentation and summon witnesses to buttress our side of the question.

A favorable cost-benefit ratio had been established for building the waterway, but the government officials involved in the decision-making process worked down from the proposals that had the greatest cost benefit. Moreover, there were political overtones; some sections of the country were favorable to the canal, some were opposed. Industrial interests in Cleveland and Pittsburgh opposed the proposal because it might take commerce away from their areas. Railroad interests also opposed it, fearing lost tonnage.

The heaviest rail tonnage in the U.S. moved on rail lines going through Youngstown and down the Mahoning Valley during the first world war. One can now look at the tonnage that railroads move through the Mahoning Valley and ironically ask if the canal would have been of benefit or cost to them today.

The idea of connecting Lake Erie and the Ohio River had first been suggested by President George Washington, and throughout the nineteenth century many district congressmen diligently expressed support for the waterway in order to get elected. Since the beginning of the twentieth century, the proposal was actively worked on by Mahoning Valley interests and, in 1935, FDR had even stepped forward to authorize a stub-end canal to Lowellville. Despite more than 100 years of the best political efforts, however, it was all to no avail; the canal would never be built.

A district's congressman is the people's voice, and Kirwan never forgot that fact of political life. In his eyes, the most important people in the nation's capital were visitors from home, and he treated all of them that way. Roberta Messerly, who managed his Capitol Hill office, also jumped to attention for any visitor from the Mahoning Valley. Thousands of people in the Youngstown area still treasure some letter of congratulation from the congressman marking a wedding anniversary or a birthday. That was a way to get re-elected and, as Kirwan well knew, the first duty of any congressman has long been to get re-elected.

Kirwan's annual St. Patrick's Day Dinner at the capital city became

Vice President Johnson appears at a gathering that honored Kirwan for the bill which funded the National Fisheries Center and Aquarium, a project labeled by the press as "Kirwan's Fishbowl." Mahoning County Commissioner John Palermo stands to LBJ's left; Judge Frank J. Battisti stands to his right, beside Youngstown businessman William Cafaro.

a mecca for some leading Mahoning Valley citizens who were his friends. Men who became presidents and even the chief justice of the U.S. Supreme Court also put in appearances at the affair.

Immediately following the assassination of President Kennedy, I was dispatched to Washington, and Kirwan found me a room at the YMCA Hotel where he was staying. He also located me an observation point behind a small oval window above the steps to the rotunda of the Capitol, where I watched while Kennedy's casket was brought to lie in state for the passage of thousands of mourners.

When Lyndon Johnson became president, Kirwan was right at home in Washington. Kirwan, Johnson and Richard Nixon, who subsequently became president, had passed time playing cards together during their days in Congress.

Kirwan died in 1970, and a large congressional delegation came to Youngstown for his funeral. His death also produced a tremendous volume of testimonials about his service to the nation that were entered into the *Congressional Record.*

There have been other congressmen from the Youngstown district since Kirwan and Cooper, but only for short periods of time and not long enough to sink their teeth into the operations of the federal government. Charles Carney, who followed Kirwan, was somewhat of an exception. He came to the Capitol after a long tenure as a union official and extended service in the Ohio Senate, and consequently was able to immediately have some labor-based clout.

Others have brought mostly talk to Capitol Hill, although each has made rather conscientious efforts to serve the district.

In 1978, Trumbull County Commissioner Lyle Williams, a Republican, defeated Carney in a close election. During the months preceding the vote, Carney had been criticized heavily by the news media for distributing surplus books from the congressional library. Many of these books went to the Youngstown and Warren libraries, and also to constituents. Nevertheless, there was an investigation that involved the Federal Bureau of Investigation, and an agent even questioned me about a book I had received from Carney. If anybody from the FBI is reading this, perhaps they might want to locate the book I furnished the agent, who promised to return it to me but never did.

Another investigation involving Carney centered on his use of a gasoline credit card, furnished free of charge by a Youngstown businessman who later pleaded no contest to minor charges stemming from the incident. This, too, may have taken a toll politically.

A turn in the 1978 congressional campaign which may have also affected the election's outcome was a remark attributed to Carney about Williams being "just a barber." As a result, barber shop proprietors throughout the district tended to turn to Williams, and their establishments were places of political conversation.

In 1984, Williams was defeated by Democrat James A. Traficant Jr., who had served as sheriff of Mahoning County and continues to hold the congressional seat as of this writing. In the early days of his political career, Traficant won much support by speaking against the drug trade to women's organizations and parents' groups. Although his record as sheriff left much to be desired, he became a political folk hero when he successfully represented himself in Cleveland Federal Court against criminal charges that claimed he had been bribed by organized crime.

As a congressman, Traficant has been very adept at being Johnny-on-the-spot whenever a problem arises locally, offering to take a leading role in its resolution. He has also tried to bring back the canal issue; many observers believe this initiative was taken simply to latch on to old Kirwan supporters.

History is the setting for the political climate that has always been a large part of the people's occupation here. Political ways have much changed from the days when young Bryan was ushered up Federal Street behind teams of silver-white horses, but the game goes on; and the Valley has supplied its share of political bosses, some having powerful enough arms to impact on crucial decisions affecting the nation.

Early in this century, Edmund H. Moore was often referred to as Ohio's Democratic boss. Moore had served as mayor of Youngstown and became a nationally known lawyer. In 1920, he managed James M. Cox's campaign for the presidency, and undoubtedly had a hand in the choice of a young New Yorker who had served as a state senator and assistant secretary of the Navy, Franklin Delano Roosevelt, for the vice-presidential nomination.

In the depths of the Great Depression, local people had time for politics, and many made it their life's work. The Mahoning County Democratic Club took on new life, and a Young Democrats Club was formed. One of the early presidents of the Young Democrats was Thomas J. Barrett. With the election in 1934 when Democrats took over here, he got a job as a postal worker for the Ohio General Assembly and attended Ohio State University. Two years later, Barrett became a state representative and remained for years in that office, except for a short period during World War II. Subsequently, in a life given to political work, he served as a Mahoning County commissioner.

Operating the machinery of the two parties also gave opportunity for employment when other work was hard to come by. A young man from Himrod Avenue on the East Side of Youngstown, which furnished much of the Democratic Party's strength in its lean days of the 1920s, gave all of his time for party work which until then both parties had left largely in the hands of some lawyers and businessmen who happened to give politics only passing attention.

His name was John Vitullo; he was an Italian-American at a time when that ethnic group was just beginning to be fully accepted. Vitullo got a job as an assistant clerk at the Mahoning County Elections Board in 1936 during the clean-up process that followed the removal of the board, and there was considerable complaining about his employment. Vitullo was very disturbed about the criticism over his getting the job, which in essence made him second in command. I assured him if he did his job honestly, he would be treated fairly as far as the newspaper was concerned. He compiled a good record in his years at the board, which previously had been under much scrutiny by the Ohio secretary of state.

Vitullo went on to become clerk of the board and later a member of the elections board and chairman of the Mahoning County Democratic Party. He wove what many believed was a stout party machine. Actually, Vitullo had about 4,000 votes in the county rather solidly set under his direction. He was generally regarded as the county boss, and he made some good decisions as well as some that brought condemnation.

Vitullo earned a reputation for seeing to it that party money and party jobs went through the hands of elected party central committeemen. The central committee was built to full strength during his regime, and if a man wanted a state, county or city job during a Democratic administration, he had to have the approval of his precinct committeeman to even be considered for the job. Committeemen were paid for their work during elections from funds contributed to the party causes. Under Vitullo, candidates depended on the party for financing. Still, most elected Democratic officials would tell you that Vitullo never asked them to do anything wrong.

In my judgment, Vitullo sustained many good public officials, among them Mahoning County Sheriff Ralph Elser, Probate Judge Clifford Woodside and Mahoning County Auditor Charles Rayburn. During his time as chairman, he also kept Democratic Party politics out of elections for boards of education. Through the Depression and the ensuing years, the Youngstown school board was pretty much in the hands of leading citizens who held those offices for the benefit of the community. Some of these members were Warren P. Williamson, Charles Cushwa, and my brother, T. Lamar Jackson.

Vitullo was instrumental in getting Ralph O'Neill elected as Youngstown Mayor, and as such, he was often blamed for more than he was

Mayor Henderson inaugurates service of the Erie Railroad's Steel King. In addition to promoting rail and air service to the city, Henderson supported measures to reduce air pollution and provide for housing improvements.

guilty of. During that postwar period, the "bug" houses and the Jungle Inn were very much in the news, and the police were frequently involved in protecting these illegal gambling operations. How much of the police force was corrupt remains in question, but there is no doubt that some officers went so far as to protect locations where the betting slips were handled.

There were a few instances that came to the public's attention that suggested official corruption at some level of municipal operations, which helped in the sweep of O'Neill from City Hall in 1947, when Republican Charles P. Henderson was elected, promising to "Smash Racket Rule."

Under Governor Frank Lausche's administration, and with the urging of Mayor Henderson, the notorious Jungle Inn, a Las Vegas-style casino that openly flaunted the law, was finally closed in 1949 by state revenue agents. It was located near the intersection of Youngstown-Hubbard Road and Liberty Road in a small area that was officially incorporated as Halls Corner and was operated by gangsters aligned with the so-called "Purple Gang," who posted shotgun-carrying thugs in the balcony to keep law and order. During the peak days of the Jungle Inn, buses would line up in front of the Warner Theatre in downtown Youngstown to transport players to the casino.

Henderson's "Smash Racket Rule" campaign won national notice for the strong law-enforcement program he implemented against racketeers, which included pulling the plug on illegal, widescale operations in the city that made it the horse-race wire center for the tri-state region. Police Chief Edward J. Allen, imported from Erie, Pennsylvania, for the job, would subsequently become a nationally recognized expert on the mafia and its code of omerta — "silence or death."

Vitullo did not live to see another Democrat become the city's chief executive; he died a few years after Henderson was elected. The next man to serve a long term as Mahoning County Democratic Party chairman was Jack Sulligan, a Hungarian-American from the West Side of Youngstown who also rose to being regarded as a political boss. He, too, had worked at the elections board and had been part of Vitullo's organization. As chairman, however, he proceeded on a somewhat different basis but also managed party campaigns to victories.

Vitullo basically ran the party, often conferring with his friend, Ray Thomas, who long served as prosecuting attorney and was a Republican power inside the Mahoning County Courthouse. Thomas left the city and lived in California for quite a while, but he kept an interest in area politics, and Vitullo always kept his telephone number handy.

By contrast, Sulligan ruled through consensus. He would listen to what party people wanted and would work with them, although he was quite willing to give direction. Vitullo was more likely to have some direction already set in his mind, and so tell the party faithful.

Most unusual about Sulligan was his leadership in nurturing a Democratic Women's Presidents Club, which was often honored. Various Democratic women's organizations had previously developed in the county and they were often at odds during the primaries. Sulligan helped lead them into unity through formation of the presidents' organization.

Sulligan enjoyed wide support within the party and served as chairman until his death in 1975. He was succeeded by vice chairman Nick Bernard, with whom I served in the state Senate. Bernard did not want to keep the post; Mahoning County Auditor Steven Olenick replaced him and served until 1979, when he was defeated by attorney Don L. Hanni Jr.

In his youth, Hanni was a Republican from the East Side of Youngstown and served as president of the Young Republicans Club during the blossoming of the Democratic strength here. Hanni proceeded pretty much in the way of his life — if you can't lick them, join them — and thus became a Democrat. A successful criminal lawyer, his election as party chairman was adamantly opposed by some who held that an attorney should not be in a position to deal with judges whose elections depend partly on party operations.

The term ''party boss'' is often assigned to Hanni, and in truth his regime may be more dictatorial than party operations under either Sulligan or Vitullo. Hanni has managed more by his sense rather than by consensus with other Democrats, and consequently has not always been able to have his choices elected even in party primaries. Youngstown Mayor Patrick J. Ungaro, Mahoning County Common Pleas Court Judge Peter C. Economus and some others have remained in office even though they were not the chairman's choices. Indeed, during Hanni's tenure, his support for a candidate has frequently become something of a political liability.

His recognized ability as a lawyer and as a speaker, however, often overcomes what seems to be stiff opposition to a course he has taken. Most judges would tell you that among Mahoning County lawyers, Hanni proceeds into cases with the best preparation. Some would also tell you that Hanni, despite his party chairmanship, has never asked for any special consideration, although virtually all other lawyers do.

Youngstown has been blessed, and some would say occasionally cursed, by a series of mayors who had great influence on the development of the city. Especially to be remembered from the early decades of the twentieth century are A.W. Craver and George Oles.

A lawyer, Craver served three terms in the World War I period, when the city was much called upon to produce steel for the Allies; and he was generally credited with efficient municipal government. He went on to become a prominent banker and postmaster of Youngstown.

George Oles was an independent in the early 1920s before the operation of the city under a home rule charter, which began in 1923 with the election of Charles Scheible on the non-partisan plan provided for in the new charter. Oles won worldwide notice being portrayed as a banana vendor and merchant who rose from nowhere to lead the city. In his frequently controversial few months in office, he got wide attention before resigning to resume full-time operation of his famous downtown market and restaurant that featured buckwheat cakes made from batter which was stirred in the display windows of the establishment.

The Oles Market stretched from Phelps Street in front of City Hall to Federal Street at Central Square and to Boardman Street across from the county jail and courthouse. Oles would sit in a chair that was visible from each entrance and would talk with customers as they came through. He also wrote flamboyant advertisements for his market, and they were read as carefully as any story in the newspaper.

Scheible had been elected with support from the Ku Klux Klan, yet he proved to be a very tolerant and capable mayor in dealing with citizens of all ranks. He was succeeded by Joseph Heffernan, who was quite an orator, very capable of demonstrating that Irishmen, especially the American brand, were the light of the world.

Mark Moore, the son of Edmund H. Moore, who was Ohio Democratic Party boss in the 1920s and had also served as mayor early in the century, succeeded Heffernan. A capable lawyer, Moore passed from the political scene after serving the one term permitted by the city charter.

Lionel Evans, a Republican with the party endorsement even though it was a non-partisan election, was elected in 1935. He had won notice as Youngstown park commissioner and was well-liked and respected in the city, which was still struggling with the Great Depression.

The Youngstown of the 1930s had more than its share of brothels, and during the Evans administration, the mayor and Governor John W. Bricker were accosted by brothel ''girls'' while walking to a meeting that had been arranged especially to hear the words of the state's chief executive. The mayor's embarrassment was obvious; at that time, Boardman Street and other locations in the city had numerous brothels and gambling establishments.

During Prohibition, speak-easies abounded, and today you can still see homes that were built from such illegal gains. The Depression also forced many more women into prostitution than in prior years. A survey taken in the early 1930s by me and the late Virgil Freed, a *Vindicator* reporter, counted more than 300 places at which a man could be solicited.

Why didn't Evans completely rid the town of such establishments? No mayor has ever been able to accomplish this, even to this day; some have diligently tried while others looked the other way.

In 1939, Youngstown lawyer William B. Spagnola was elected mayor, although he received less than forty percent of the vote. This led to the city charter change providing for party nomination and partisan elections; and in 1943, O'Neill, who had been city engineer under Spagnola, won by a half-dozen votes over Republican Russell Williams.

In 1947, O'Neill was bested by Henderson, who served three two-year terms and was defeated in his bid for a fourth term by Democrat Frank X. Kryzan, who had been city council president. A war veteran, Kryzan also held the post for three terms and afterward served a long period as a municipal judge. Henderson subsequently was elected Mahoning County probate judge, succeeding Judge Clifford Woodside.

In 1959, three men struggled for the Democratic nomination for mayor: Kryzan, county engineer Samuel Gould and Frank R. Franko, who billed himself as a maverick and won a controversial two-year term. Franko was succeeded by Harry Savasten, a Republican who also served one term.

In 1963, Anthony Flask won election as mayor. Regarded as a good administrator, Flask served until he was upset by Republican Jack Hunter, a councilman from the fifth ward. Hunter's unexpected election in 1969 followed a strike-related shooting incident at Stop Five of Youngstown Sheet & Tube, where the mayor had declined to send police to keep the peace.

Hunter served four terms and was succeeded by Democrat J. Phillip Richley, who served one term; Richley was followed into office by Democrat George Vukovich.

The present mayor, Patrick J. Ungaro, has served since 1984. A Democrat, Ungaro is apparently making an unsurpassed occupation of the mayor's office. While Mayor O'Neill was instrumental in the 1940s in changing the term from four years to two years with the passage of a charter amendment, and was then unsuccessful in winning that term, Ungaro was instrumental in changing the two-year term back to four years through a charter amendment and has successfully retained the office.

Ungaro's administration has focused on economic development and jobs for Youngstown. This is a popular focus in a valley that was once one of the great steel centers of the world but today has none of the large mills still operating, forcing thousands to look for new jobs. In this respect, Ungaro has performed very capably.

Ungaro's tenure in office began after my retirement, and his election in 1983 was the first contested Youngstown mayoral race I did not poll by using the methodology I created during World War II.

Late in the 1930s, when poll-taking became fashionable among newspapers, I developed an interest in learning how to take an accurate sampling of political sentiment. At the time, poll-taking was conducted in a very dubious manner, yet the *Literary Digest* — for great reading, I suspect — had managed to conduct polls that turned out to be fairly accurate in presidential elections. Even so, in 1936, the magazine's poll completely collapsed when it showed Landon winning instead of the landslide FDR amassed.

The Vindicator's previous political writer had also conducted a poll that didn't seem to work very well. He continued to conduct the poll, but as the new political editor, I also wrote my judgments and often predicted the outcome of elections based on having my finger on what went on in politics.

I took over the poll, but I added a mechanism to make the results an actual cross section of the voters rather than relying on those who returned straw ballots. This modified poll was first used in 1943 for the Youngstown mayoral election.

My poll was hitched to registered voters; I took the names from the elections board, one in ten by random selection, and listed on the straw ballots whether they were Democrat or Republican or had not voted in the primaries. The ballots were sent to ten percent of the electorate, and voters were asked how they had voted in the previous presidential election as well as their preferences for the upcoming election.

By knowing how poll respondents had voted in the past, when the straw ballot returns came in, I printed the raw results but weighted them to show what the vote would have been had ballots been returned from a cross section of how the people had voted in the previous presidential election. Sometimes it was necessary to almost double the number of Democratic return ballots to even out the cross section. Republican voters, on the whole, returned their ballots because businessmen affiliated with the party could more easily mark the ballots and return them, whereas Democratic mill workers were not so used to marking and returning mail.

With this weighting factor applied, election predictions were normally very accurate except when some dramatic, last-minute event occurred after the straw ballots had been returned. In sending out to ten percent of the registered voters, I received about a forty percent response. Therefore, the weighting factor had to be considered to bring it to an absolute balance. I also had another way of weighting — figuring the percentage of returns by precincts. With 400 precincts in Mahoning County, theoretically each was to have 400 votes. Some precincts would return nearly all the straw ballots; some would return only a few. So, I would take the average results. By figuring the actual return percentages in each precinct and taking an average, it usually was very consistent with the percentage achieved by the other weighting method.

A third way to check was by relating the return to the party affiliation or independent affiliation indicated by the ballots. When this was weighted, it usually produced a result consistent with the other means of checking. These methods were laborious and required nights of counting ballots. Ordinarily, the weighting method on the presidential return was used. All three ways would show you how the election would turn out.

The Youngstown mayoral election was so close in 1943 that the poll predicted an on-the-nose result. I said if there were 40,000 votes cast, the Republican would be elected, but if there were 50,000 votes cast, the Democrat would be elected. I also predicted that about 45,000 voters would go to the polls, which would mean an extremely close contest. I thought the Democrat would make it; the result was that some 43,500 votes were cast and the Democrat won by only eight votes.

In 1944, it was decided the poll had been so accurate in the city's mayoral election it should be applied to the presidential contest, and the poll was extended to cover four counties — Mahoning, Trumbull, Columbiana and Ashtabula. The poll for president in each county that year came out in a percentage nearly exact in predicting how the people in Ohio would vote and, as a result, the nation.

The poll was right in 1943, in 1944 in four counties, and again in 1947, when Mayor O'Neill was opposed by Henderson. The poll predicted a 3,600 majority for Henderson; the actual count was a majority of 3,671.

In 1953, when Henderson sought an unprecedented fourth term, the poll correctly predicted that the Democratic candidate, Kryzan, would be elected by a 1,500 majority.

In the 1950 Taft-Ferguson race for U.S. Senate, the poll showed Taft a winner, even in Democratic Mahoning County, and predicted he would carry the state by more than 500,000 votes, way beyond the majorities forecast by other newspapers. Taft ended up carrying the state by about 600,000 votes. In fact, *The Vindicator* poll was so accurate that year, the *Manchester Guardian* of Manchester, England, carried a report praising the poll.

In the 1948 presidential election, my poll predicted Truman would run strong statewide; and on the Sunday report before the election, *The Vindicator* advised readers to watch the swing in results from the states along the Ohio River. The poll had proven accurate and had correctly predicted that in Mahoning County Truman would not run as strong as Roosevelt had in 1936. As a result, the poll got notice in newspapers across the nation and even one published in Shanghai, China.

The national polls were so inaccurate in the 1948 presidential election that George Gallup's poll had to undergo extensive revision to make it more accurate. When the renowned pollster called a conference to establish an effective way of polling elections, I was chosen to represent Ohio. At the time, I was a state senator.

The conference was held in Princeton, New Jersey. James M. Cox, who had served three terms as Ohio governor and who was the 1920 Democratic nominee for president, had expressed concern about whether polling unduly influenced an election. Indirectly, through my publisher, he asked me to take this up at the Princeton Conference. This I did, as well as explained my method of polling.

We met for ten days, and stayed at the Nassau Tavern. There were eight or ten of us present, including a newspaper editor from Hartford, Connecticut. We would sit around a table at the tavern talking, then go to Gallup's guest house to eat, where he would preside. I explained my method because it was the most successful one in Ohio. Later the *Columbus Dispatch* came to me seeking help in developing its poll.

One of the ways early polls attempted to balance samplings was to use a percentage of those who needed refrigerators and those who didn't. The effectiveness of my poll was that it relied on a cross section as to how people voted in the presidential election. That could only work when you had a record of how areas had voted in the past to contrast with how they could be expected to vote in the future.

Nonetheless, the more one works with polls, the more they know the results are not a certainty, especially with last-minute developments. For instance, the 1956 Suez Canal crisis rallied Americans to their president — so much so that Mahoning County voted for Republican Dwight D. Eisenhower. My poll had shown Adlai Stevenson winning in Mahoning County.

From its beginning in the 1930s, poll-taking has become much more sophisticated, and the means of taking polls have greatly expanded. The cost of poll-taking, in particular, has become a factor in the type

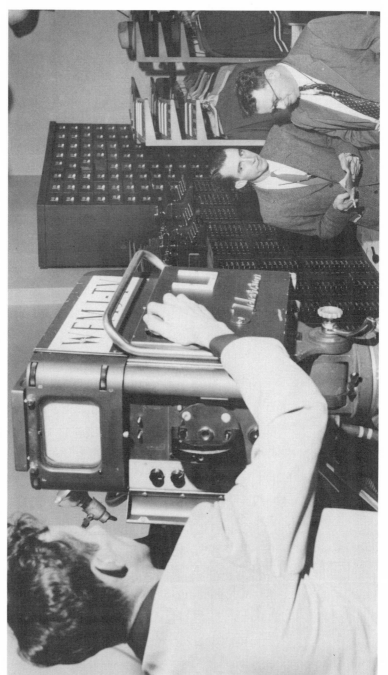

WFMJ-TV covers the 1958 primary. Ten years before, television coverage of party nominating conventions debuted.

of polls taken. At the height of my poll-taking, we covered four counties in northeastern Ohio, sending ballots to residents complete with a return stamp. When postage rates were still inexpensive, the cost of taking my poll was low; but as the years went on, postage became expensive — and thus, my type of mail poll is not much resorted to anymore. After my retirement, with the high cost in manpower and postage in mind, the newspaper contracted with Youngstown State University to provide election polls.

My years of political reporting presented many opportunities to meet famous people if they happened to visit Youngstown. One meeting I particularly remember was with U.S. Supreme Court Justice Hugo Black, who would later arouse great national debate over his former Ku Klux Klan membership. Franklin Roosevelt had appointed Black to the high court, and he became a very liberal member, winning great recognition as a jurist. He came to Youngstown and ate at the Old Oyster House on Boardman Street when he was a senator, shortly before his appointment to the Supreme Court.

Having studied at the University of Colorado, I also had an opportunity to talk to Byron "Whizzer" White, who had been my alma mater's claim to football fame — a Rhodes Scholar and a quarterback chosen for the All-American team. I met him at the Hotel Ohio, and talked to him about the quarterback I knew when I was there, a couple of years before White. The quarterback's name was Harvey Chilson, and by this time, Chilson was a federal judge in Denver. Being a good football player in college helps greatly in gaining political office.

Attorney Paul Brown of Youngstown would attest to voter preferences for recognizable names. He had been a prisoner of the Nazis during World War II but escaped into the Italian countryside. He won election to the Ohio Supreme Court possibly because of his name, as the voters did not make a distinction between him and another Paul Brown, the founder and coach of the Cleveland Browns football team and later the Cincinnati Bengals.

Brown is the most famous political name in Ohio, and Browns have long won primary elections in both the Democratic and Republican parties. For a time, Republicans seemed to have a monopoly on Browns in Ohio, but the Democrats wised up and found a Brown, put him on the ticket, and he was elected. Both Republican and Democratic Browns have served the Ohio Supreme Court at times. There have been congressmen by the name of Brown as well as candidates for governor, U.S. Senate and secretary of state. The only other name that rivals Brown in Ohio for statewide popularity is Taft; and in the 1990 election for secretary of state, a Taft unseated the incumbent, a man by the name of Brown.

Once there were three outstanding candidates for the lieutenant governor's position. One had considerable public support and one had the endorsement of the party's central committee in most Ohio counties; but there was a third candidate who had the same name as that of a famous Yankee baseball player who happened to come from Akron. Northeastern Ohio swung its support to this candidate, and he won.

In 1934 in Ellsworth Township, there were two candidates for Democratic committeeman. At the polls with his wife, one candidate met his opponent who jokingly said, "Be sure to give me your vote."

When the votes were counted, there were two votes for the other candidate and only one vote for the candidate who had brought his wife. His wife's explanation was she glanced down at the ballot and didn't see that her husband was running. At that time, there weren't many Democrats living in Ellsworth Township.

Other very peculiar things happen in elections. A Campbell precinct had twenty-four ballots in which both candidates for mayor had received a vote, canceling out each other's votes. This appeared to be a case of "short penciling" to invalidate the votes, but an inspection revealed short penciling was not involved. Instead, there had been a precinct gathering at which both candidates appeared. The twenty-four double-checked ballots occurred because citizens, in talking to both candidates, had promised to vote for each one, and they did.

Short penciling is a term applied to sticking a piece of graphite under the third finger. In the general practice of corruption, it's easy to mark an additional X when tabulating ballots. This usually amounted to filling in a vote in places the actual voter had skipped in his balloting.

With the use of paper ballots, there were many incidents of corruption. One of the means was to sneak one ballot out of the precinct polling place, mark it and buy votes by giving voters the marked ballot to take in and asking them bring out an unmarked ballot for the next voter going into the voting booth.

In one Mahoning County precinct, board members met prior to election day and decided to place a mark beside a candidate's name in a school board election if there were any vacant spaces. There were three members to elect that day, but the precinct workers knew a good many of the voters would vote for only one or two. A board member put down the marking for the second or third, tipping the election outcome very remarkably.

This stuffing of the ballot box was discovered and held up for examination because other precincts in the school district returns clearly showed that many voters did not vote for all three candidates. It could be deduced there had been tampering in any precinct that had 100 percent voting for all candidates to be elected. Simply based on the law of probability, it was possible to write a story revealing election-tampering. The ballots in question were put in a vault by the Ohio secretary of state, and the subsequent investigation revealed the suspected marking of ballots was more extensive than had been previously predicted in the story that reported precinct corruption.

Although paper ballots occasionally revealed spotty corruption during the counting, the advantage of this method of tabulation was that it enrolled a large number of citizens in the work of politics. The argument for voting machines was that they would eliminate such fraud and do the job more cheaply as fewer election employees would be needed. This was not an advantage insofar as carrying the processes of democracy more definitely into the hands of the people. Moreover, the big frauds of democracy went unnoticed by the machines.

Most elections boards now employ computerized tabulation systems, a development that came locally the year I retired. In Mahoning County, the computer system marks a return to paper ballots, only they are scanned — counted — electronically. As with any system, this one also demands scrutiny.

Generally, American democracy has worked well with two major political parties serving as the instruments for government, devoted to the election process and motivated to win a majority to the extent that often one of the parties, or both, take steps to garner voting groups that arise. Even the prohibition of liquor, although ultimately found not practical, engaged the support of both parties in its running effort.

Financing of election campaigns, however, has been the source of most major corruption in the American political process. And efforts to clean up election financing often have been misdirected and caused more corruption rather than less.

The remedy, it would seem to me, is lodging most campaign costs in the hands of the political parties, with each soliciting support from a wide range of interests. This would tend to destroy any limited special interest from having too much influence over what any officeholder does.

Additionally, the ethical usefulness in limiting the amount any candidate can spend for his own election brings big question marks. Is it better to trust one who spends his own money for campaigns or one who has collected a lot of other people's money to get elected? The answer is that the man who spends his own money is more likely to have independent judgment in what he does. After all, isn't that what the American people want in their elected officials?

EXTRA

Bombs Hang In Strings At Ravenna
Output Speeds Up
By Clingan Jackson
The Vindicator, 1943

Ravenna — Strings of "blockbuster," 2,000-pound bombs, hanging like hogs in a slaughterhouse, greeted Ohio newspapermen Thursday when they made the first official press visit permitted at the Ravenna ordnance plant since assembly lines went into full operation.

The bombs were in various stages of "dressing," not for some enticing dinner plate but for the enemy across the seas.

The Ravenna plant is loading a large number of these ton bombs and thousands and thousands of smaller ones as well, a diet which army men feel sure is too heavy for the Axis system. Ravenna alone contributes hundreds of carloads of finished ordnance for the armed forces each week—and it's finding its way into the hearts of the enemy across the Atlantic—and across the Pacific.

The bombs are hung up in different stalls. The casting of one weighs about 1,000 pounds and the inside is filled with TNT, taken from vats in which it is melted.

Workmen use rubber buckets to fill smaller bombs and a tube for larger ones. The vats are tipped to fill the buckets and bucketful after bucketful goes into each bomb. The workmen, many of them from the Mahoning Valley, must prevent a crust from forming over the TNT and leaving an air pocket.

To prevent this, the bombs are filled by stages and the crust stamped out as it forms. Inspectors take an occasional bomb out and have the chunk of TNT it contains sawed in two with a crosscut saw, then examine the texture to see whether the batch should be accepted.

Sisters and sweethearts of men in the armed services are among those who operate that TNT crosscut and do other difficult jobs. Company officials say that more than 60 percent of production personnel are women. There are more than 10,000 persons employed at the plant now.

Housewives, farm girls, erstwhile stenographers—even a grandmother —smilingly handle deadly explosives in plants spaced nearly a mile apart, and swept and dusted constantly as a safety measure.

The women roll 2,000-pound bombs around the paint room as nonchalantly as if they were beer barrels. One of these bombs, six feet long, would tear a hole 20 feet deep and kill everything within a 600-foot area if exploded.

In handling explosives, the women were given "great praise" by J.T. Power, general manager of the plant operated by the Atlas Powder Co. for the government.

"There's one woman—a grandmother—who keeps the others working right along," Power said. "She has two sons and a grandson in service, and when the line slows down, she'll say 'Come on, girls, let's keep it going.' "

The one-ton bombs are only a sample of what the Ravenna plant is equipped to turn out. It has 4,000-pounders in its storage igloos and Col. J.K. Clement of the ordnance department, commanding officer, said the arsenal could load double this size.

The plant's four miles of loading lines operate 168 hours a week.

The bombs are being painted a different color from the old "explosive yellow"—a color which will not be visible to an enemy from the air, and which blends with the scenery. ∎

EXTRA

Racketeering as Usual

Politicians Connive for Power and Spoils at Home as Nation Fights for Life

By Clingan Jackson
The Vindicator, 1943

While the boys who were expendable in the Philippines are yet unburied by the hands of home, Youngstown's potential officials are being weighed and tested in another crucible.

This is the crucible prepared by those who make money by corrupting the government which the boys in Tunisia are dying to defend. It is an old crucible, but ghastlier now because our country's blood falls drop by drop.

Each candidate for office is carefully picked and tested for each position, so there will not be any misfits. There may even be a place for an occasional honest man by the testing of this crucible—provided he is to fill an unimportant position—provided he is dumb or can wink his eye at what does not directly concern him.

Licked from the Beginning

At elections, the people play a game of chance, but these lads who fleece-line their coats from the "take" in a thousand condoned lawless practices play the game with marked cards.

What high-school basketball team would have a player on its team who is playing for the other side? Such an arrangement is common in Youngstown politics—so with cards marked and players on both sides—the election approaches.

A racket ring, a go-between and candidates with sufficient outward acceptability to commend themselves to the fine women who nursed them in childhood are the tools of corruption in city politics. This is true here—in the year 1943, the most important year to the United States since 1776.

Too High a Price

Such corruption deadens alertness, making a crystal-clear example of democracy impossible on the earth. Ultimately, war is the price paid— sons falling on the field of battle.

The candidates for office are sorted over one by one. None who are too small are picked, and none without a smile. The major places must be filled by men who are handsome and adaptable. Youngstown voters do not take to the lean and hungry.

Some incorruptible but useless morsels may be magnified and placed here and there so that the firmament won't be so bare of moral light that even the sleepy voters will recognize the shady deal.

But the slate finally completed, if viewed as a whole, will be slick and slimy. It will be extremely acceptable —and except for an occasional miscue, it is expected to have control of the city and rake in enough money not only to pay for political campaigns but also to build private fortunes for persons who have not the pluck or the guts or the ability to make their way in the world as honest men. ■

A huge crowd gathers in Sharon, Pennsylvania, in 1960 as John Kennedy campaigns for president.

CHAPTER 8

NATIONAL CONVENTIONS

he first national political convention I covered
for *The Vindicator* took place in 1940 at Chicago
for the Democratic presidential nomination. It
was an assignment in which familiarity with the city counted.

During my college years in Boulder, I became close friends with the
son of a prominent government official in Chicago. On trips back and
forth from the university, I sometimes would stop in Chicago to visit
him and he would tell me about the city. When I came to visit in 1930,
I saw the big billboard that Mayor James Thompson had erected which
depicted him as promising to punch King George of England in the
nose. Then, the city was preparing to host the Century of Progress
Exhibition, and there had been boisterous talk of arranging for British
warships to sail down Lake Michigan as part of the ceremonies.

"No!" vowed Thompson, and he rallied the citizens, particularly
the Irish-American vote, of Chicago.

Although it had been more than a century since the American

151

Revolution and the War of 1812 — often referred to as the "Second American Revolution" — Americans still viewed England as suspect in the international scene. Indeed, during World War I, most Americans sided with France, paying its Revolutionary War debt to Lafayette. Thompson's billboard is a sidelight on the silly happenings that sometimes accompany American democracy.

Another footnote from my trips to Chicago occurred while I was staying at the Palmer House, and my friend had led me to the floor where the notorious gangster Al Capone made his headquarters. Many of the delegates to the 1940 convention also stayed at the Palmer House, but Capone was long gone, having been convicted of income-tax evasion.

Highlights of my first national political convention centered around the flickering efforts of some Democrats who had not taken kindly to President Roosevelt's nomination for a third term. James Farley, who had managed FDR's earlier campaign efforts and served as postmaster general, was part of the opposition. A dramatic speech in the convention came from veteran Senator Carter Glass of Virginia, whose name stands high in history because of his part in implementing the Federal Reserve banking system during Woodrow Wilson's administration. Glass pleaded against departure from the tradition dating to George Washington's time that presidents would not serve more than two terms. Nonetheless, it was apparent from the start that the convention would easily, and almost by acclamation, nominate FDR for a third term. Already the clouds of World War II were settling close about the United States.

Roosevelt did not appear at the convention, following the custom at this time, that official notification of the nomination was made during a special event after the convention. Through 1940, at least, this tradition tended to be followed. In the case of a president being nominated for a succeeding term, however, not much was made of this tradition, and there was no precedent for third terms.

The party turned to Henry Wallace of Iowa for the vice-presidential nomination. John Nance Garner of Texas had served as vice president in FDR's first two terms, but he was a traditional Democrat and very cool to the third-term idea.

Wallace came from the progressive direction; his father had served as secretary of agriculture in President Harding's administration. The Wallace name was known nationally in conjunction with raising corn; the family's variety often received credit for producing two ears on a stalk rather than one. After he became vice president, Wallace gave me some of his family's special corn seeds. I planted them, nourished the corn along, and grew ears two-and-a-half-feet long with a few rows of white grains that had a sweet texture. Never having been much of a farmer, I did not carry on with this variety of Wallace corn.

There is not much thought about it today, but the 1940 presidential campaign very much turned on how much aid America should give to the fight against Adolf Hitler. Roosevelt had moved to give the cause of Britain considerable help. Some Americans were thinking in terms of turning their backs on Europe and looking for the future of their civilization just north and south in this hemisphere. This issue was to glimpse its resolution at the Republican National Convention in Philadelphia. Almost spontaneously, as the British troop remnants from the continent were moved back from Dunkirk to the island by all sorts of boats and Britain prepared to stand alone against Hitler's forces, there was a stir in America.

The nation was binding together to meet the full horror of World War II. In Youngstown, an Allies aid organization was formed; I served as chairman. And, to show local unity, the chairmen of both the Mahoning County Republican Party and Democratic Party served as vice chairmen of the Youngstown organization. National leaders of the effort came to a jam-packed banquet at the Hotel Ohio. There it was discovered just how many Englishmen were in the area. Because London was under siege at that time, they seemed to swarm out for the occasion. It had to be explained our organization was concerned with the defense of the U.S., not England, and steps to be supported were to be based entirely on that premise.

At the Republican Convention in Philadelphia, the chief candidates for nomination were Robert Taft of Ohio and Wendell Willkie of Indiana. It had been presumed that Taft would be nominated, but as the war and Britain's invasion threatened, more and more Americans were coming to believe this nation must inevitably come to England's defense. Taft was regarded as more of an isolationist than Willkie. At times, Taft seemed to be saying that the defense of America was on the Amazon and not the Rhine, or even the English Channel. Ohio's delegation naturally rallied to Taft. In the early ballots, Taft's strength rose to 370 votes; he needed about 500 for nomination.

I stayed at the Ben Franklin Hotel in Philadelphia, where Taft also stayed. After the second ballot, Taft gathered his supporters around him and told them Willkie would be nominated the next morning — he had gone as far as he would go.

Willkie's demand for one world campaign appealed to those who saw America's participation in the war as a certainty. After a wild performance in the hall, Willkie won the nomination. Later his official notification took place in Elkhart, Indiana, his birthplace. But in the

Republican Wendell Willkie is greeted by a large crowd during his 1940 visit to Youngstown.

interim, immediately following the convention he appeared in a room with forty reporters, he stood on a table and said, ''I can hear you and am ready to answer questions.'' And he did, with clear and concise replies. This was new for presidential candidates who often had a stand-back attitude toward the press.

Willkie was an engaging figure, and the race looked very close when he made his pilgrimage to Youngstown. Joining his campaign train at Toledo, I was standing in line behind U.S. Senator Harold Burton, who would later become a U.S. Supreme Court justice. Burton had wanted to get his wife on the train, but officials would not let her board. I could not help but notice that despite his high place in the nation, he simply told his wife to take the next train and meet him in Cleveland. Undoubtedly, if Burton had thrown his weight around, his wife would have gotten on the campaign train. Humility was characteristic of this great man.

Coming to Youngstown, Willkie rode in an open car down Federal Street where thousands were gathered, and waved to him. Everywhere he went, the local crowds treated him with courtesy, despite the fact this district was one of the heaviest pro-Roosevelt regions in the nation.

At Detroit and Toledo, however, Willkie did not enjoy such courteous treatment; tomatoes were thrown at him.

Some of the Taft people were bitter, but Taft was a loyal Republican. Earlier in the 1940 campaign, I had been with Taft in Youngstown when he was sending messages to Willkie, who had taken the nomination from him.

''He asked me to send speech information to him regularly. This I have done. So far, he hasn't used any of it,'' Taft commented.

Long afterward, when Taft was again in Youngstown, I was walking with him toward the Home Savings and Loan Building when he lamented, ''My father never wanted to be president, but he was. I have always wanted to be president, but I suppose I never will be.''

Conventions in those days didn't have the security that became extensive at the 1968 Democratic Convention in Chicago, where all hell broke loose. Nonetheless, national convention tickets were difficult to get, the auditorium being almost filled with delegates and alternates.

At the 1944 Democratic Convention in Chicago, Mahoning County Democratic Party Chairman John Vitullo managed to get all the guest tickets allocated to Ohio, so the Youngstown people attending, or wanting to attend, had pretty much of an open house. Vitullo agreed to surrender some tickets for use by other county organizations but to him, Youngstown always came first.

Early in that convention, the chairman of Jefferson County, Johnny Nolan, a powerful figure in the state's Democratic makeup, came to

Vitullo's room to negotiate for guest tickets. After leaving Vitullo, he went back to his own room, took a shower and died when a burst of steam and scalding water came from the faulty line. I heard about his death when I called the newsroom in Youngstown, even though the tragedy had occurred only a few rooms away from mine.

In another incident involving tickets, this time at the 1940 Republican Convention in Philadelphia, a group of Youngstowners wanted to get into the auditorium. One of them was John Rowland, president of Mahoning Bank, a tall man with distinguishing white hair. Rowland led the local group into the hall, and the security guards didn't bother to stop him. After all, he looked to be the ambassador to the Court of St. James.

This was the type of occurrence that historically happened at national conventions even in 1860, when Abraham Lincoln's friends had stuffed the Wigwam Convention Hall in Chicago so virtually none of his opponents could get in the hall. Lincoln, of course, did not come to the convention — as was the tradition — and instead stayed in Springfield, where he awaited official notification of his nomination.

By the 1944 conventions, America was deep in World War II and victory in the Pacific and Europe seemed to be within grasp. That year the Democratic Convention was in Chicago, furnishing Roosevelt's last trip to a convention, a visit that came only at the event's culmination as his train moved slowly into Chicago. The general consensus at the convention was that FDR wanted Harry Truman of Missouri as vice president rather than Wallace.

At that time, the Stevens Hotel was the biggest in Chicago; I stayed there, and so did Harry Truman, on the floor below my room. Upon his nomination for the vice-presidential spot, I went downstairs and knocked on his door, expecting a meeting to be held there. Truman answered and explained there would be no meeting. He quickly closed the door but almost immediately reopened it, saying the photographers would be coming soon.

We "chewed the rag" for a half-hour or so, talking about Wallace, whom he was replacing on the ballot. Wallace, who had replaced John Nance Garner as the vice-presidential candidate in 1940, had the firm support for another term, particularly from the portion of the Democratic Party regarded somewhat as to the left. While talking to me, Truman was very complimentary of Wallace and described him as a great leader. Four years later, Wallace was the Progressive Party candidate for president, but even his divergence from the Democrats was not enough to keep Truman from being elected in an edgy struggle with Thomas Dewey of New York.

After Truman and I had talked for awhile, and I had helped him turn the bed around for the family picture, Mrs. Truman and their young daughter, Margaret, came out of a side room, ready to pose for the photographers. Somehow I was not included in this portrait.

The vice-presidential nominee seized the center of attention at the convention, with Roosevelt's nomination for a fourth term taken for granted. As the nation moved forward in the war effort, the advice not to change horses in the middle of the stream seemed to be coming to acceptance in the nation.

Leaving the Chicago convention, stopping to visit my brother who lived in Springfield, Illinois, I was astounded to see the Wallace train pass by on its way back to Iowa. It still had the cornstalks on display, reflecting the will of many Iowans to uphold the Wallace name.

In 1944, the Republican Convention also came to Chicago. It was curious to see the demonstrations put on for the candidates — the demonstrators were the very same people who had paraded at the Democratic Convention.

The Republican candidate for president was Thomas Dewey, the governor of New York. In the 1930s, he had won a national following for dealing with gangsters while serving as special prosecutor for a grand jury probe of vice and racketeering in New York City.

Michigan-born Dewey was a precise man by reputation; in fact, precise as to which side of his face would be photographed. This was nothing new in politics. President William McKinley insisted on his picture being taken on only one side of his face and usually with a flower in his lapel.

One of my friends, Ohio Governor John W. Bricker, became the vice-presidential nominee with Dewey in 1944. Significantly, the Buckeye State swung to Dewey that year, probably because of Bricker's political strength. Bricker finished his campaign for the vice presidency in Youngstown's Central Square, speaking to a crowd on the Saturday night before the election.

A well-publicized remark that Dewey resembled the man on the wedding cake stuck during the entire campaign. This image of Dewey as an exuberant groom was adjudged to be very telling in the voting. In any case, both Dewey and, of course, the reigning president, were four-square in support of the American forces moving toward victory.

The principal aid coming to the Republican candidate was the question of the worsening physical condition of President Roosevelt. FDR overcame this by openly campaigning in New York in the rain so as to display his vigor. Roosevelt was elected, and started his fourth term in January.

The next event crashing in on the memory of an observer of the

In 1948, it looked like Thomas Dewey would win the presidency when his campaign stopped in New Castle, Pennsylvania.

national scene was word of FDR's death, which was felt by every American. I was riding home from the Ohio Senate with Senator Maurice Lipscher; we had reached Doylestown when news of his death came over the car radio. The eyes of the nation turned to Warm Springs, Georgia, then followed his funeral train to Washington and finally to Hyde Park, New York, where he was buried.

Attending conventions for forty years would give anyone a sense of how considerate and friendly most Americans are. This was to be proved to me again in Philadelphia, where both the Republican and Democratic conventions were held in 1948.

Dewey had made a few inroads into FDR's strength in 1944, so from the beginning of the Republican Convention, it was apparent that Dewey would be nominated a second time. The only possible alternative, it seemed, would be Senator Taft. He had received a lot of convention votes in 1940, and continued to be one of the nation's outstanding senators, winning national and international attention for his response on the Nuremberg trials. Taft came out with a statement that brought people to their senses. Simply put, he questioned the neutrality of a winning nation putting on trial war personnel of the losing countries.

What Taft would do at the convention was up in the air. One night at the Ben Franklin Hotel, I happened to see Taft with a group of men going into a room. I sensed something was going on, so I sat in the hall by the door. Hours later they came out of the room and hurried up the hallway toward the freight elevator, with me following after them. When we got to the elevator, they rushed in and the door slammed shut before I could get in, but Taft opened the elevator and beckoned me to join them. There, he gave me a statement which ended a lot of conjecture concerning his actions. I shot it to the newspaper and the Associated Press, the wire service with which *The Vindicator* was affiliated. It was something of a national scoop, reporting that Taft had taken himself out of the field of candidates.

Wandering around the Dewey headquarters, I was tired after having spent long hours at the convention. There was a bed in a room, so I dropped down to doze. It was a good place, for some of the southern delegates to the Republican National Convention were being brought there for negotiations. In 1948, decades after the Radical Republican Reconstruction period, the South was still regarded as the ''Solid South,'' solid for the Democratic Party. Whatever delegates were chosen for the Republican convention were allegedly subject to receiving financial considerations or perhaps being given an opportunity for some kind of job. These people had no party mooring because the southern states didn't even have the Republican Party on the ballot. Nonetheless, the

GOP was trying to maintain a national orientation.

Bascom Timmons, a correspondent for *The Vindicator* based in Washington, had been in charge of some of the arrangements for the press at the 1948 conventions. He set me up with a seat well to the front of the press section, with nationally syndicated columnist Walter Lippmann seated to my left and David Lawrence of *U.S. News & World Report* to my right. I think Timmons did that because he thought I was a reporter from the sticks who might appreciate a good seat assignment, and I did.

Other such evidence of Americans' general kindness — and specifically within the ranks of the fourth estate, which might be frowned upon by reporters today — occurred in 1940, when Willkie came to Cleveland with a group of important Washington correspondents. The national press people picked me to ride in their car and fling my arms about in the back seat. Most of the people who gathered along Euclid Avenue and waved to Willkie that day did not know that who they had actually seen and waved to was a young reporter with long hair. For security purposes, Willkie had been taken another way, with scarcely any escort, to his meeting in Cleveland.

There had been no certainty in Dewey's expectation, once he was nominated in 1944, for he was to meet that master, FDR. But in 1948, the atmosphere in Philadelphia was one of certainty that the first Republican president since Herbert Hoover would be elected.

This was a general conclusion; the Democratic Convention, also convening at Philadelphia shortly afterwards, similarly demonstrated this belief. Coming to Philadelphia for the Democratic meeting, an astonishing sight was a huge billboard displaying pictures of Dwight D. Eisenhower, in hopes he would seek the Democratic nomination for president; no one knew then that his time would come four years later, but not as a Democrat.

Staying at the Bellevue Hotel, and snooping around a little bit, it was apparent to me that some kind of an effort was to be made on behalf of President Truman for the nomination, even though Truman's national approval rating had reached a low level and it was generally agreed only time remained until the United States had another president. The convention went on during a stretch of sultry Philadelphia weather. Eisenhower was not interested in being president, he indicated, and Truman became the nominee without too much effort.

It was well after midnight when Truman was nominated in the crowded convention hall, where the temperature was extremely high. For the first time, the heated lights of TV hung above the speakers' dais, forever changing — albeit heating up — the national political atmosphere.

Indeed, the temperature was about 120 degrees in that section of the auditorium. Men's suits were soaked with perspiration, and on several nights, I had to go back to the hotel so I could wring out my suit. I remember the sight of Dorothy Thompson, famed foreign correspondent who had won national recognition reporting from Berlin as the Nazis took over. She was completely soaked in perspiration, as was everyone else, yet the convention continued.

The operators of the convention released doves that flew perilously about, and the bald-headed convention chairman, Sam Rayburn, frequently looked up apprehensively as they flew above him. Watching all this take place was the convention secretary, Jeanne Kilpatrick. She later became a Republican and served as ambassador to the United Nations and has since been urged to run as a Republican vice-presidential or presidential candidate. Such are the topsy-turvy developments in politics. Willkie is another example of successfully switching parties; nominated on the Republican ticket in 1940, he was considered a prominent Democratic leader in 1936.

Once Truman was nominated at the 1948 convention, he came before the assembly and made his famous "Turnip Day Speech," vowing to call the Republican-dominated Congress back on Turnip Day, July 17, to pass laws to halt rising prices and to meet the housing crisis. From that speech, the national tide began to turn, coming to a climax during Truman's famous whistle-stop campaign as his train traveled from larger to relatively small towns, especially across the Midwest. The result was dramatic.

In 1948, James A. Rhodes, later four-time governor of Ohio, was mayor of Columbus and went to pay his respects to the president when the train reached Columbus, and Truman recited his famous "Give 'em hell, Harry!" speech. Throughout his later campaigns, Rhodes often referred to Truman, telling the story of David and Goliath in describing Truman's come-from-behind win over Dewey. Although a Republican, Rhodes never ceased to admire Truman.

By breathing his Missouri soul out to the public, Truman stole the hearts of old-line Americans living in much of the Midwestern part of the nation. Some states that had been for Dewey in 1944 left him and swung the nation to Truman's election, including Ohio. But it was an election so close that even the *Chicago Tribune's* first editions streamered, "Dewey Wins."

Truman was a relatively young president; nominated for vice president was an old senator from Paducah, Kentucky, Alben W. Barkley. Americans usually have not known their vice presidents very well, sometimes not even their names. This was the convention of the

"Veep," so called by Barkley's grandson, and the nickname stuck to the office as well as to the man.

Every time I had a chance to talk to Barkley, a very pleasant man, he reminded me that Ohio had more institutions of higher learning than any other state in the union, and that Ohio had become famous for Antioch College and its great educator, Thomas Mann, as well as William Holmes McGuffey, a native of Coitsville Township.

Parenthetically, it always seemed important to me that I lived by the valley to which the young McGuffey tread to and from Youngstown for his early training at the city's First Presbyterian Church. McGuffey was a professor at Miami University in Ohio, where a collection of his memorabilia is maintained. He later became president of Ohio University in Athens, and concluded his career at the University of Virginia as the Civil War swept the country. He is best remembered as the author of the *McGuffey Reader* series which spread in use across the nation during the nineteenth century. Mark Sullivan, one of the great syndicated newspaper writers from the World War I period, observed that McGuffey had more effect on what four generations of Americans believed and stood for than any other man because his *Eclectic Readers* had instilled moral principles and a love of reading.

In my possession are the original records noting the formation of Coitsville Township, including the minutes from trustees' meetings for more than ten years after the township's formation: Some of these have a small note at the end, signed William Holmes McGuffey, who was then a youth writing the records. Alexander McGuffey, William's father, was an officer of the township when it was founded in 1807. While serving on the Ohio Highway Construction Council, it was my privilege to see that a marker was placed on state Route 422 honoring McGuffey and Coitsville, his boyhood home. The importance Barkley ascribed to this great educator was not lost on me and, hopefully, will not be on generations to come.

Four years after the convention that nominated Barkley for vice president, the city of Chicago was offering fine inducements to both parties seeking a site for their 1952 gatherings. Parties always have had trouble financing national conventions and presidential campaigns, and sometimes the eventual selection of a city or a candidate hinges on money. A little-known case in point happened in 1920. The Democratic Party was strapped in its funds for the convention at San Francisco, where FDR was nominated for vice president, perhaps because the party planned to use Roosevelt's home at Hyde Park for its national headquarters during the campaign. Former Ohio Governor George White, who was national Democratic Party Chairman in 1920, told me that story when he wandered into my room in the Neil House in Columbus years later. He sat down to talk a little about old times and explained he was looking for his hat, which prompted him to recall that when he was governor, the hotel looked after his hat much better.

Given the incentives offered by the "Windy City" in 1952, both conventions were set for Chicago. Rumor had it that since the party meetings had been in Philadelphia in 1948, it made good economic sense to have the conventions in the same city again. Some paraphernalia from the first convention could be used for the second, and many of the same people engaged in the demonstrations and such put on for candidates could be hired more cheaply for both conventions — two for the price of one.

The Republican Convention promised a bitter struggle in 1952. Taft was the odds-on favorite for the nomination, but before the convention opened his opposition had turned to the great American general, Dwight D. Eisenhower. "Ike" was not an orator, stumbling a little in his talks with reporters. Nevertheless, I was very proud when he came into a hotel room where reporters were assembled and walked directly across to shake my hand.

The Ohio delegation was for Taft and he swung considerable support, but a military hero such as Ike was hard to overcome given that professional politicians were seeking a sure-fire way into the minds and hearts of American voters. After all, being a successful military leader has helped many others to become president: George Washington, Andrew Jackson, William Henry Harrison, Zachary Taylor and Ulysses S. Grant.

Ike really swung the nomination when the deal was made to get the support of the California delegation, an arrangement shepherded by Earl Warren, who had been governor of California. At Warren's direction, a senator by the name of Richard Nixon met the California delegation's train somewhere in Oklahoma, and the rest is history.

The 1952 Democratic National Convention brought the same team of demonstrators. President Truman and others had turned to Adlai Stevenson, governor of Illinois, as the party's hope. Stevenson's father had been vice president under Grover Cleveland, and Adlai, a lawyer, was extremely articulate. With his nomination, members of the press stood up and joined in the standing ovation; I had never seen that type of reaction within the press section.

Stevenson accused the Republican Party of having a schizophrenic personality, and convention delegates went wild. During the ensuing campaign, Stevenson came to Youngstown and spoke to a large crowd gathered at Central Square. He was not, however, able to win much

Eleanor Roosevelt and Adlai Stevenson greet the political editor at the 1956 Democratic National Convention.

national strength for the election, mainly because rank-and-file Americans seemed to regard him as an egghead. Stevenson would sit at his typewriter and write his own speeches, some of which will live through the ages. Perhaps most remembered is his veto, while governor of Illinois, of the cat-licensing bill, when he humorously pointed out the feline habit and disposition are not subject to legal control or regulation.

The 1952 election put the Republicans in control at Washington for the first time since 1932, marking a change of direction in American politics. As president, however, Eisenhower did not prove to be a Republican ideologue; his administration encompassed and continued much of what had been New Dealism in American politics.

In 1956, it seemed logical for it to be another race of Eisenhower versus Stevenson, although the elder statesman Truman, who had retired, was not so hot for Stevenson again. Moreover, there was a movement within the Democratic Party to support Governor Averell Harriman of New York for the nomination. Harriman's name was associated with great wealth and corporations such as the Union Pacific Railroad, which was built by his father. It was quite an unusual scene to see Communists marching with what appeared to be executives from the Union Pacific or other Harriman enterprises in a push to articulate Harriman's effort for the presidential nomination. Truthfully, quite a few American Communists thought well of Harriman because of his performance as ambassador to Moscow after recognition of the Soviet Union during FDR's first term. Stevenson, nonetheless, was nominated.

In the last week before the 1956 election, the Suez crisis developed, and the American president stood against the action of France and England to militarily hold the Suez Canal. Americans flocked to the support of the president, including many of Irish background who never seemed to have too much in common with English aspirations but who were Democratic historically. Mahoning County, which in some previous elections had furnished the highest Democratic strength north of the Mason-Dixon Line, also gave Ike a majority.

In 1956, a young man by the name of John F. Kennedy aspired to the Democratic Party's vice-presidential nomination but was defeated in a close convention vote that nominated Senator Estes Kefauver from Tennessee. Kefauver had made a name for himself during a congressional investigation of the mafia which included testimony from former Youngstown Police Chief Edward J. Allen, who detailed some aspects of underworld operations in Youngstown.

By 1960, when the party's convention was held in Los Angeles, JFK was not seeking the vice-presidential spot, but rather the presiden-

Mike Kirwan hosts John and Bobby Kennedy at the Idora Park Ballroom during JFK's 1960 campaign for the nomination.

tial nomination. Senator Lyndon Johnson of Texas was the choice of party veterans, and Eleanor Roosevelt, FDR's widow, appeared at the convention and made an appeal for Stevenson as her "kind of man." Johnson called reporters to a press conference and proceeded to recite Kennedy's legislative record, maintaining that the senator from Massachusetts did virtually nothing on Capitol Hill and was mostly absent during his term. Two days later, Johnson became Kennedy's choice for vice president.

The day after the convention ended, I was privileged to attend a rather interesting going-away gathering, where Sam Rayburn, speaker of the House of Representatives, presided. It was a breakfast meeting; Kennedy sat at Sam's left and Johnson at Sam's right.

"We have nominated the right ticket but we made one mistake," Rayburn said. "It should have been Johnson for president, and this young fellow for vice president. We started too late to nominate Johnson. Everywhere we went, 'Old Joe' Kennedy had been there first. But we are going with the ticket, and we are going do our best."

The campaign appeal of Johnson throughout the southern states has been generally credited for the success of the Democratic ticket in 1960. The Republican Convention at Chicago had nominated Vice President Richard Nixon for president, and the contest brought one of the closest outcomes in the history of American elections.

Kennedy came to Youngstown, Salem and Niles, Ohio, and Sharon, Pennsylvania. To show how touchy the campaign was, while I was sitting in a car next to Kennedy, it stopped so the candidate could pick up some apples at a farm. JFK took a few bites from an apple and then threw the core in a ditch. My recalling of this incident in a *Vindicator* column made some readers very incensed; they claimed my intent was to portray Kennedy as a man who would throw garbage in the road. Actually, the nominee's action revealed him as a very human man, possessed of boyish charm. I have always thrown apple cores into the ditches along the road and I am sure every farmer also finds the practice acceptable. But people were touchy in 1960, and watched political events carefully.

The Catholic issue, which was most pronounced when Alfred Smith was the Democratic Party's presidential candidate in 1928, bobbed up again in 1960. But Kennedy met with a lot of Protestant support, climaxing in a meeting with a Protestant group in Texas. Hopefully, Kennedy's success in 1960 put an end to the prejudicial thinking with regard to religion of the American president. After all, the nation has suffered a lot of Presbyterians and Episcopalians, but now at least it can list a Roman Catholic and a Unitarian.

After Kennedy's assassination, Lyndon Johnson took the reins of government and carried through successfully on many of the promises of JFK's campaign. By 1964, there was not much doubt about Johnson's presidential nomination for he had enjoyed remarkable success in picking up Kennedy's "New Frontier" program, enlarging it and getting it accepted by Congress. Indeed, LBJ was at the height of his popularity.

Nevertheless, the Republicans were determined to put a conservative social program into effect. Senator Barry Goldwater of Arizona had aroused much of the Republican electorate, and one of his strong supporters was a man in the movie business in California, Ronald Reagan. Like the Democrats, the Republican Party has its right and left. Governor Nelson Rockefeller of New York was the figure on the left, or as one might say, more moderate in his views on social issues.

Goldwater came to San Francisco where the GOP convention was held, and throngs of young people embraced his views. He walked on stage at one of the rallies at San Francisco, raised his arm and bellowed, "I'll be your tiger!"

Ohio Governor James Rhodes came to the 1964 convention as the state's favorite son, a political practice to enhance a state's king-maker potential. At another convention where Rhodes was the favorite-son candidate, he was the recipient of whiskey packaged in specially decorated contraptions for dispensing. Rhodes, however, was not a drinking man. One night a knock came at my hotel room door; two of his daughters appeared with the whiskey and related their father thought I might like to have them. I still have one of these gallons; the other was carried away by a scamp who married one of my daughters.

One of the most fascinating things about national conventions for reporters is the opportunity to encounter many famous people. Franklin Roosevelt Jr. and I drank beer together. Even though he was a beer-drinker, you still got the feeling you didn't quite belong to his class; and, of course, you didn't. By contrast, Harry Truman gave you the feeling he was one of the gang, and yet he always conveyed the impression that he knew exactly where he was going.

After the Republican Convention in 1964, *The Vindicator* editorial and circulation workers went on strike. As a result, I did not attend the Democratic Convention in Atlantic City that nominated Lyndon Johnson for an elected term and Minnesota Senator Hubert Humphrey for vice president.

It was apparent that Johnson would sweep the land. I voted for Goldwater and his running mate, William Miller, a congressman from Buffalo, knowing in my heart that Johnson would win. Truly, if the election was at all close, I would have voted for Johnson. I have always hoped to keep a balance between the two parties; I liked Johnson, but I knew Goldwater was going to be kicked to death.

By 1968, American involvement in Vietnam had led to Lyndon Johnson's decision not to be a candidate. The Chicago convention of that year was the most disruptive of any national convention held to nominate a president in the history of the United States. Much of the disturbance took place along Michigan Avenue in front of the hotels located across from the statue of General Grant. A long line of police guarded the front of the Stevens Hotel as young people, angered by the Vietnam involvement, conducted protest rallies. Before the police set up, the protesters literally invaded the hotel and messed up the stairway and lobby beyond any civilized conception. This activity revealed there were individuals in the mob who possessed total animal tendencies, even to the point of using the floors and stairways as a toilet.

The convention set up security as had never before been necessary. Even those with credentials had to punch in with a key to show their identity. Electronic security was in its infancy at this time. My key produced a red light instead of a green light, at which time the officers would come to examine my credentials, and repeatedly mine would still fail. I did feel rather secure at the hotel; Chicago police had asked to utilize my room on occasion because it overlooked the boulevard where much of the agitation was centered.

The Vietnam protestors were not exactly from the rank and file. Looking out of the window at the end of the hall opposite my room, I would occasionally see a woman dressed in luxurious furs come out and get into a chauffeur-driven limousine. She later appeared on the speakers' platform in the park area opposite the hotel where various agitators also appeared.

This woman was staying in the same hotel where Eisenhower had his headquarters in 1952. "Hinkey" Dink's widow also had a suite in that hotel, and from there she would routinely feed the pigeons, other birds, and squirrels that would come in the window. Hinkey was a famous political operative who had control of three or four wards in Chicago. At the peak of his power, the bums carried cards signed by Hinkey Dink which entitled them to burial and other benefits; their only obligation was to come back to vote in Chicago.

Some of the delegates to the 1968 Democratic Convention were struggling to prevent Chicago Mayor Richard Daley from being seated; the credentials committee ruled in Daley's favor. And, despite all the turmoil, the conventioneers eventually succeeded in nominating Vice President Humphrey for president and Edmund S. Muskie, a senator

In 1968, Hubert Humphrey stopped in Youngstown for a rally on the steps of Stambaugh Auditorium. At his side is Harry Meshel, who would later succeed Charles Carney as state senator.

from Maine, for vice president.

At the Republican Party National Convention in Miami, the GOP again turned to Nixon, who had failed in 1960 to win the presidential election. This time, the "New Nixon" chose as his running mate Maryland Governor Spiro Agnew, who came to Youngstown for a campaign meeting at the Holiday Inn in North Jackson. Thanks to his Greek descent, Agnew had quite a number of followers locally. I don't remember much about his speech because of being distracted by a female reporter sitting next to me who was too much in her cups.

With Alabama Governor George Wallace running as a third-party candidate, the '68 election was close, and some believe Humphrey would have defeated Nixon if the election had been held a week or so later.

In 1972, the Democratic presidential nominee was Senator George McGovern of South Dakota, with Sargent Shriver, John Kennedy's brother-in-law, as his running mate. At the convention, Senator Thomas Eagleton of Missouri received the vice-presidential nomination, but it was soon thereafter reported that Eagleton had undergone treatment for mental problems and he withdrew.

Shriver came to Youngstown, but the Democratic effort in the 1972 campaign was very weak. Nixon won a sweeping victory after being re-nominated at the convention in Miami, which attracted among other celebrities actress Jane Fonda and fellow anti-war activists.

At the Republican Convention in 1972, there was a group, which included James Rhodes, that wanted Nelson Rockefeller nominated for president. The Republicans were a little to the right of Rockefeller, who had been governor of New York. Ronald Reagan was also a name that was on the lips of many. But it was not to be this time for either of them.

One of the Youngstown delegates was Walter Paulo from Canfield, head of the Isaly Dairy Company. He told me a story that left an impression: Isaly's could put out a wheel of Swiss cheese, cut it in two, put a sign on half of it saying it was imported, and it would sell out twice as fast, at twice the price, than the half posted as American-made. This reveals the tendency of Americans to go for foreign-made products, even though it may not be in the country's best economic interests — something Chrysler Chairman Lee Iacocca has since warned must cease.

The experience I remember most from this convention, however, is being in a small group to whom Attorney General John Mitchell was speaking. One of the delegates from Illinois was raising a question about an election law violation involving some political activity

Campaigning in Warren in 1972, Richard Nixon's motorcade pauses as he receives a plaque from city officials.

in that state. The advice he was given by Mitchell was there had to be pretty liberal attitudes about what active politicians did in campaigns. It should have been adequate warning to me that the Watergate scandal was on its way. Apparently, the Republicans wanted to posture themselves so the Democrats would overlook any off-center performances in the heat of campaigning. Looking back, it often appeared to me that the Nixon administration wanted a liberal policy toward any indiscretion during active political campaigning.

As the Watergate affair got under way, Larry O'Brien, national chairman of the Democratic Party, came to Youngstown. Mahoning County Auditor Stephen Olenick and I picked him up at the Pittsburgh airport and brought him here. During the short trip, I asked O'Brien why anybody would be looking for the party records when they didn't mean anything. O'Brien muttered a few words and gave me the impression it would be pretty hard to specify what the actual damage would have been except bothering office arrangements at party headquarters.

In 1972, it was a Nixon sweep; but four years later, the Democrats bobbed back up. The Watergate scandal had taken its toll — Nixon's resignation — and for the first time, the U.S. had both a president and a vice president who had not been voted into office. Prior to Nixon's departure, Agnew had resigned under scandal and was replaced by Gerald Ford, a congressman from Michigan who had served as House minority leader. With Nixon's resignation, Ford became president, and Nelson Rockefeller was later appointed vice president.

The 1976 Republican Convention was in Kansas City, and the battle was between Ford and Reagan for the presidential nomination. It was a close one, but Gerald Ford won. A lot of people wanted Ford to turn to Reagan as vice president, but there was small chance Reagan would accept second place. Instead, Senator Robert Dole of Kansas was nominated.

The 1976 Democratic National Convention was held in New York City. Georgia Governor Jimmy Carter was nominated for president with Minnesota Senator Walter Mondale as his candidate for "Veep." Carter had traveled the primary route through the states, generally telling people nothing more than, "I'm Jimmy Carter and I'm running for president." He hadn't been heard of much until the Iowa caucuses, but he struck a cord with party rank and file.

Carter came to Youngstown twice in his campaign. I rode once with him from downtown to the airport. Some Democratic women handed me a batch of two-dollar bills and asked that I get Carter's autograph. I told him about their request, and he quietly took the bills and autographed them all.

He was a graduate of Annapolis, and while the United States has had a number of army men as presidents, including graduates of West Point, Carter was the first navy career man to win the presidency. On the side, he raised peanuts in Georgia.

Seeking re-election, Carter also came to Youngstown in 1980 and made one of the final appearances of his campaign. *The Vindicator* endorsed his bid even though relatively few Ohio daily publications supported him that year.

I did not attend the 1980 conventions because of the death of my wife shortly before I was to report to the Republican convention. Of importance to me, however, was the passage of a resolution offered by Ohio Congressman John Ashbrook, marking my long attendance at conventions and expressing condolences in my absence.

In 1980, Ronald Reagan was nominated for president, and George Bush for vice president. Iowa had selected Bush in the state's party caucus, which had awakened Reagan. From then on, Reagan took all the delegates and subsequently won the general election.

After years of watching national conventions, it seems both party affairs are dominated by professional politicians, a characteristic typical but not subject to any ideological conception. No matter what the nominated candidates may say, they are committed first to their party's winning. What the political parties are actually deciding in the direction of the conventions is how to get the most votes.

In this century, the Democratic Party, often regarded as the liberal left of the political spectrum, has nominated on at least two occasions men who were regarded as ultra-conservatives; namely John W. Davis in 1924 and the "gold" candidate in 1904, Elton Parker, a considerable shift from William Jennings Bryan's "silver" candidacy of 1900, 1896 and 1908. Bryan had advocated the free coinage of silver; but in 1904, the party decided to try the other side of the question and in support of gold maintaining its dominant place in financing.

On the other hand, the Republican Party, more recently regarded on the conservative side, has nominated some very liberal candidates.

And yet, perhaps neither the Republicans nor the Democrats have ever nominated quite so liberal a candidate as former President Theodore Roosevelt when he was the nominee of the Progressive Party and the chief threat to Democrat Woodrow Wilson's election in 1912.

I think the genesis of vote-getting behavior by political parties was best demonstrated in the first convention to nominate a presidential candidate, which was held by the Anti-Mason Party in 1831. The delegates nominated for president a 33rd-degree Mason.

As the Civil War conflict was seeming to arise in the political ferment of the 1840s and 1850s, the Whigs were very anti-slavery. Yet when that party assembled to nominate a candidate for president, the Whigs called upon Zachary Taylor, a Louisiana slaveholder and military hero.

The process seems to be that parties nominate a president, then try to figure out who is in opposition to what that candidate stands for, and pick a vice-presidential candidate who is well regarded in that opposition stance. So naturally, there is frequently a political swing when a president dies in office.

The prime example came when the Republican Lincoln, in his second term, had as his Union Party running mate Andrew Johnson, a true cross-party ticket. In Lincoln's first term, Johnson was a Democratic senator from Tennessee, the only senator from a Confederate state who remained loyal to the Union and then returned to his state as the war governor. Upon Lincoln's death, Johnson became president and faced continuous opposition, primarily over Reconstruction and from the Radical Republican leaders in Congress. Johnson survived impeachment by only one vote.

And yet, tremendous steps often have been taken by American statesmen to assure the political unity of the nation in times of crisis. As World War II threatened the nation, FDR brought Republicans into the cabinet. And when Lincoln took his oath of office as president in 1861, Stephen Douglas, his Democratic opponent for the office, stood with him and held his hat. With Washington under siege from the rebelling Confederacy, Lincoln and Douglas stood together for the Union.

In the Civil War period, David Tod of Youngstown became governor of Ohio as the Union Party's candidate. He had twice run for governor as a Democrat in the 1840s, losing by small margins, and had been ambassador to the court of Dom Pedro, the king of Brazil, under President Polk. Despite his Democratic affiliation, Tod was offered the appointment as treasurer in Lincoln's cabinet.

But times do change; and the Tod family, still prominent in Youngstown, has since become a strong Republican factor in state and local politics.

EXTRA

Choice of Candidates Hints 20-Year Trend Is Ending

By Clingan Jackson
The Vindicator, 1952

Government in the U.S. is almost certain to pull in a different direction as the result of this year's nominations by the two parties of men familiar with government but not bound to the political organization of the last 20 years.

Even the people at the Democratic Convention sensed that the end has come to the trend which has been sustained by the electors since 1932. The Republicans responded to nominate, in Dwight D. Eisenhower, a champion who has promised a crusade.

But in nominating Eisenhower, the party moved in a direction of absorption of much of the New Deal as contrasted with repudiation represented at least to an extent in U.S. Senator Robert A. Taft's candidacy.

If the Republicans recognized the staying quality of many of the steps of the last 20 years and the necessity of sustaining much of the present foreign policy, the Democrats appeared to understand that an era in American history has ended.

In nominating Adlai E. Stevenson for president, the party was choosing a man whom the records indicate may be a sympathetic student of the New Deal with a depth of understanding of its relationship to the foundations of our government. He is sure to tie closer to the historic basis of his own party.

It was notable, I believe, that he repeatedly mentioned the Republic in his addresses. It is not to be the vibrant Democracy of days of extension into new fields, but a reckoning with the forces of our time which might conceivably bring tranquillity to the American scene.

In the nomination of both Stevenson and Eisenhower, the process through which a Republic works to seek strong leadership in days of crisis appeared. The circumstances that brought about the nomination of both to some degree seemed to unfold from a higher power than the politicians and, indeed, a higher power than the people themselves.

Whether even strong leadership will succeed is problematical. In their own way, however, both Stevenson and Eisenhower seemed to sense the momentous issue of the presidency. Stevenson spoke of ferment in the world and summoned the people to patience and sacrifice.

Eisenhower presented the issue, perhaps, more simply in a soldierly way. What he has to offer is organizing ability, experience in getting along with others and adjusting to difficult situations. With it all, the campaign will offer him an opportunity to display the depth of his insight.

In Stevenson, the insight from a political viewpoint is there from the start, but one may wonder whether he has experience in organization to the extent of Eisenhower or whether the magnitude of the job, considering that he must deal with an incumbency of his own party, might be overwhelming.

Certainly the Stevenson record is a promise of the end of General Vaughans and mink coats if the Democrats are continued in power, but there are other and deeper aspects of the materialism which has engulfed much of the world and has had its day in the U.S., which may not be so easy to reckon with.

Taft greets two employees of Youngstown Sheet & Tube during a campaign visit.

With the tenseness of the two national conventions as seen at first hand in panorama, in contrast with the spotty observation which came over television, there were a few dramatic situations that stood out.

Senator Taft seemed to choke up—to those who saw him after the nomination of Eisenhower. It was a final frustration to a long and I think sincere preparation and seeking for the presidency. The choking up came to others than Taft who believed in his way. He took it like a soldier of his party.

In the Democratic Party, Vice President Barkley's bitterness showed through despite his kinship with the nominee. The Democrats answered that situation with a guarded display of emotion for the party's old warrior.

Eisenhower himself met the Taft situation by going directly to the Ohioan after the nomination in tribute to a great American instead of waiting as is the custom for the vanquished to acknowledge the victor.

The convention system has come in for much criticism since the televising of the Chicago events, but anyone who attended still feels the forces unleashed in them, bringing America to the surface, days after the actions in them have begun to take their place in history. ∎

The dedication of Pine Hollow Park in Lowellville in 1946 was a special occasion for the former village councilman, who is flanked on the dais by editor William Powers (far left) and Mayor Charles Quinn to the right.

"Youngstown, Ohio, has a famous old and beautifully named newspaper — The Vindicator — who has as its pollster a political editor who is also a state senator.

In this dual role, careful, conscientious Clingan Jackson last spring forecast his own defeat in the primary — and he was right."

Bascom N. Timmons,
Vindicator Washington Bureau Chief, October 1950.

CHAPTER 9

POLITICAL CAREER

he political bug struck me most forcefully one cold fall day in 1932, when Mayor Charlie Quinn of Lowellville asked me to serve on the village council. Shortly after my marriage to Virginia Fenton, Doctor Erskine, a veteran member of the village council, died, and it was my task to write his obituary. Quinn and a couple of councilmen later appeared at my door one night and asked me to take his place. Subsequently, I was elected to the post.

Being chosen to run in 1934 for the Ohio General Assembly, partly because I was a Lowellville councilman, was my second step in the political field. The leadership of the Mahoning County Democratic Party, then chaired by John Farrell, had become disgusted with candidates always being beaten by Republicans, and a slate was drawn up with a man from Sebring, one from North Lima, one from Struthers, one from Canfield, and one from Lowellville — a geographical sampling outside Youngstown city limits. Several candidates also came from the

179

city, which had two-thirds of the population of the county, and they, too, were chosen because of the broad sector they represented. Moreover, care was taken that no religious or ethnic group dominated the slate.

The Republicans, as was usual in those days' primary elections, drew about ten times the number of voters as the Democrats did in 1934, and no one gave Democratic candidates much chance of prevailing in November. But a new spirit was in the air with FDR's New Deal taking hold, and when the general election came, to the great surprise of even the Democratic candidates, most were swept to victory. In my case, with a majority of 20,000 votes, I led the ticket. This Democratic sweep in 1934 was all the more surprising because the Republicans who were defeated were incumbents. It was the start of a long period of Democratic Party prominence in Mahoning County politics, a condition which prevails to this day.

For a young freshman legislator interested in history, exploring the Capitol and its grounds was a fascinating experience. On a marking between the Supreme Court Annex and the Capitol, for instance, was the spot where Abraham Lincoln had appealed for support from Ohio. He was on his way to Washington to be inaugurated as president; already Confederate flags were waving in some southern states, and Lincoln made numerous stops to rally northern states for the Union.

It was more than seventy years after Lincoln's trip from Springfield when I came upon an old man standing on the winding stairway of the brick building that previously housed *The Vindicator*. The day was Feb. 12, the birthday of the American president who had come to face, with wisdom and almost superhuman insight, the worst crisis that ever confronted the nation.

The old man looked at me, then young and frisky, and exclaimed in a fervent voice, "I saw Lincoln!"

He explained that at the age of four his father had awakened him at the family farmhouse in Columbiana County, loaded him and the other members of his family into a wagon, and drove them through the rain and mud several miles to Alliance, where Lincoln's train pulled in for a stop. The tall, gaunt lawyer and president-elect spoke in the rain from the rear of the train, and appealed for continuation of the Union, just as he had in Columbus.

This old man had tears in his eyes as he recalled the Great Emancipator, and my thoughts were drawn to the fourteen or so remaining survivors of the Tod Post of the Grand Army of the Republic who maintained quarters in the basement of the Mahoning County Courthouse and still marched on occasion, recalling the honor of Union soldiers during that time of crisis.

The crisis facing the nation in the 1930s, however, was the Great Depression, and the 1934 election had sent sixty-eight Democrats and sixty-nine Republicans to the Ohio House of Representatives. One Republican joined Democrats to elect the Speaker of the House, and with the Ohio Senate fully in the hands of the Democrats, the party pretty much controlled the legislature.

In the new legislature, Mahoning County had three representatives elected at large. Winning a place on the school committee, I was named its secretary.

I first became aware of the intricacies in school funding legislation as a reporter. At the time, the U.S. Office of Education was studying the Youngstown municipal school district, and George Roudebush was the superintendent of city schools. Roudebush was regarded as one of the state's top educators; he later became superintendent of the Columbus school district.

I kept tabs on Youngstown school operations and the study on an almost daily basis. The city schools depended heavily on locally levied taxes for their support, and Roudebush armed me with ample information suggesting what should be done on the School Foundation Law, ideas that partly originated with the U.S. study. He had also worked closely with other school superintendents in the state to set forth the needs to be met in the proposed law.

With the stock market crash of 1929, Youngstowners looked to employment in the large steel mills for their future. At the beginning of 1930, the mills had orders on their books and it appeared employment would be sustained. But with the hard times, orders were canceled and the resulting unemployment was tremendous. In fact, Youngstown was one of the hardest-hit cities in Ohio; tax collections dropped, and school income was seriously affected.

In the midst of this economic chaos, the people of Ohio voted to cut from fifteen mills to ten mills the mandatory real estate levy which funded local governments. I always believed one of the reasons for this statewide vote was the political pressure that came from financial institutions, which had been saddled with a large number of homes and commercial buildings through defaulted mortgages. The argument for the millage reduction was echoed by everyone who still owned a home, and it passed overwhelmingly. This further reduced revenue, and local governments suffered along with the public schools.

Two veteran legislators had their name on the School Foundation Law in its enactment, but I was proud to have been a factor in the form it took. The remedy was a state measure providing a certain sum for each pupil based on average daily attendance for the schools. Passed during the 91st Ohio General Assembly, the impact of the law was tremendous. It had a tightening effect on school and local government financing and also resulted in the passage of the Sales Tax Act, which provided more state revenue to subsidize schools and government subdivisions.

Experience quickly showed, however, that average daily attendance was not a reliable measure upon which to base school funding. Some school districts had consistently reported perfect attendance, their superintendents not all-honest, not all-crooked, in trying to get money for their schools. As a result, the present law includes an amendment basing tax distribution simply on enrollment. School districts have to be in operation a specified number of days a year; no attendance standard is required.

The objective is for the state to provide about fifty percent of the revenue necessary to operate public schools. This has rarely been achieved, yet the state money has been a godsend. Some districts have a tremendous tax duplicate behind each pupil, but the state foundation money per-pupil goes to every district without regard to property tax valuations.

My credit is small. I was secretary of the Ohio House Education Committee when Representative Grover Traxler of Wyandot County left for a new position, and House Speaker J. Freer Bittinger designated me chairman; work on the bill had already been completed. The previous legislative session had started to prepare a school funding bill, which was sponsored by Representative R.J. Kiefer of Logan County, a retired school superintendent who was well-versed in the needs of Ohio schools. Traxler joined with Kiefer to give the measure, officially known as the Traxler-Kiefer Bill, bipartisan play for passage.

The 90th General Assembly had wrestled with measures trying to meet the problems that arose from the reduction of the mandated levy, and it passed a temporary sales tax law which ran out in 1935. But it was left to the 91st General Assembly to enact a permanent sales tax and a funding formula to sustain local governments and education.

The Ohio House finally passed the permanent Sales Tax Act well after midnight, and the chamber and the galleries were full of people. State Representative Hugh Fuller of Trumbull County, who opposed any sales tax, arose and asked for recognition; but the speaker, knowing what Fuller was up to, would not recognize him.

A man in his seventies who had hearing problems, Fuller was seated well in the front of the assembly hall. Upon being ignored, he climbed on top of his desk, raised a bony finger at the speaker, and yelled, "I was sent here to represent the people of Trumbull County, you son-of-a-bitch, and I will be heard."

Fuller was heard, which always seemed to me dramatic evidence of the voice of the people.

As with any young first-term legislator, it was natural to think about how I would stay in office through subsequent elections; but there were a couple of issues that arose in the 91st General Assembly that mitigated the possibility of my ever being re-elected.

The most politically charged issue — the first and only time in the history of Ohio that it came to a vote — was the Parochial School Bill. Due to the Depression, the parochial schools were also in terrible shape, and their superintendents came looking for a direct appropriation of money, a request obviously unconstitutional on the grounds that church and state must be separate. Even so, legislators were deluged with letters and petitions, and I was in such a position that either way I voted, I was finished politically.

Some of my friends advised me not to vote — I had both Catholic and Protestant friends. The Protestants armed up against the Parochial School Bill and the Catholics armed up for its passage. I voted "no," and the measure went down to defeat by a margin of two-to-one. Most Ohio dioceses didn't penalize their legislators who had voted against it; but as I cast my vote, I turned to a colleague and predicted, "Here ends a budding political career."

During my term in the state House, my contribution was slight, outside of the school committee. Yet, two laws bearing my name as author were passed, and both have gained some notice in state history. One involved county welfare, the other township government.

Faced with huge welfare problems which stemmed from the Great Depression, Mahoning County interests were instrumental in the authorization of county welfare departments. Previously, welfare had been primarily the responsibility of each subdivision of the county; practice had long been for townships to meet their responsibility to destitute widows by buying them each a cow and permitting that cow to graze in the grass along township roads. The act, passed in 1935, enabled welfare to be put on a more modern, county-wide basis. The bill was drawn up in Mahoning County and, in its original state was handed to me by William F. Maag Jr. It was the only legislative request my publisher ever made of me, and he did so on behalf of Mahoning County.

There was also a situation that occurred in my own bailiwick which was difficult at that time. Coitsville Township then included the city of Campbell, and according to the law, a township could not spend any money or collect heavy taxes in the city. Actually, the township tax on property in Campbell was one-tenth of one mill. The remainder of the township, however, paid about three mills or thirty times as much as city residents.

Moreover, Campbell had a large population and its majority elected township trustees. Not being able to spend money in the city under restrictions of Ohio law, Coitsville Township trustees tended to use a considerable portion of the funds available to improve roads adjacent to the city and to neglect those in more remote areas of the township. They also sought to evade the requirements that regular employment be directed to residents living in the township outside the city, and instead employed Campbell residents once they moved them to a boarding house located adjacent to city limits.

Receiving a copy of the Ohio General Code — a printing of all the laws of the state — I pieced words into the township section of the code, introduced it as a bill, and secured its passage. The state high court eventually held it to be constitutional. This measure simply permitted a majority of freeholders of property in the area of a township outside a city to petition county commissioners to exclude that city from the township. The commissioners were mandated by the majority to so act, having direction from the general code as to how to divide the assets of the township fairly with the excluded city.

Once passed by the Ohio House, the problem was to get the welfare and township measures approved in the state Senate. The legislative session was nearing an end, and I began to worry my bills might die on the vine. First, I tackled Senator Paul P. Yoder from Dayton, president pro tempore; he promised to put both bills on the Senate calendar for passage. Then I persuaded Senator Maurice Lipscher from Youngstown to move for their approval. Under the wing of the president pro tempore, they were passed with little discussion.

Sometimes a township takes action previously adopted by other townships or counties; sometimes a county takes action adopted by the state, and the states have long been testing laboratories, with successful measures frequently finding their way into all states and even federal enactment. For example, several states had prohibition laws before the 18th Amendment was enacted; child labor laws and women's suffrage were also first enacted by states, then the federal government. Similarly notable in history is the fact that not only were most of the states free states, but there were proposals in several southern state legislatures for freeing the slaves which had not been acted on when Fort Sumter was fired upon.

The law to provide for the welfare setup which Mahoning County sought was the basis for many Ohio counties establishing welfare departments. The law sought by Coitsville Township to enable free-holders in the township area outside a city to exclude the municipality was employed by other Ohio townships.

In 1935, the annual salary of legislators was just $1,000, and law-makers paid their own food and lodging expenses while working in Columbus. Since the 91st General Assembly, which lasted seventeen months, legislative sessions have been shorter in duration but legislators have been paid more — recently a great deal more. And yet, the School Foundation Law, the permanent Sales Tax Act, and other basic steps in Ohio law taken in that session remain very much as then enacted.

Notwithstanding the fact that a young fellow by the name of Robert A. Taft Sr. of Cincinnati had been defeated for state senator in the 1934 balloting, the 91st General Assembly included some outstanding individuals. Some members later served in the Congress of the United States, including William McCulloch of Miami County and L.A. Moorehead of Harrison County; others rose to become presidents or chairmen of major corporations, such as Jacob Davis, chairman of the board of the Kroger Company, a large grocery store chain.

I spent two-thirds of my time in Columbus during the 91st session — sometimes five days a week, other times four days a week. I still worked for *The Vindicator*, but I paid the salary of a replacement on the days I was away. Later in life, I saw this replacement while he was an inmate at the Ohio Penitentiary. As I was walking through the prison to speak at a gathering of inmates who were about to be parol-ed, he shouted his greetings to an old friend across the yard. I had gone my way into politics and he had gone another way.

One of the continuous battles during 1935 was to provide money for general relief to the unemployed and their families. The gover-nor's office consulted various legislators on what was needed in their districts. A check of welfare officials indicated that at least $200,000 was necessary to carry the relief load in Mahoning County. I asked for $400,000 and it was allocated, which kept local relief operations in the black.

These were the days when crowds of hungry marchers came to the Capitol, often filling the steps and the rotunda. The marchers usually had a legitimate purpose in their attempts to persuade the legislature to enact some bill or other measure to help them. Yet, all too fre-quently, their spokesmen appeared to be Communists. After all, Com-munism did not seem so hideous to these economic victims in the hungry days of the 1930s.

Another issue during the 91st Ohio General Assembly involved passage of a gasoline tax increase. The fraternal organization known as the Eagles had sent telegrams opposing the tax. According to a story legislators passed among themselves, Governor Martin L. Davey warned Eagle officials to recall those telegrams or there wouldn't be a slot machine operating in an Eagles lodge. Whether this is true or not, the telegrams were recalled and the bill was passed.

Governor Davey, a Democrat, was accused of using various means of gaining legislative support for his programs, even among members of his own party. With statewide unemployment ranging from fifteen to twenty percent, all legislators were trying to find employment for residents of their districts; and there were some indirect negotiations, I suspect, for state jobs. One legislator from Youngstown, also a Democrat, virtually accused the governor of buying votes. The allegation was reportedly made following a meeting between the legislator and the Ohio Democratic Party chairman at the Deshler Hotel in Columbus.

I had accompanied my colleague to the hotel. While he talked to the chairman, I sat some distance away and read the comics section of the newspaper.

The story of the legislator's claim was broken by the Cleveland *Plain Dealer* and it was suggested another legislator had heard the substantiation of the allegations. By the time I reached Columbus for the opening of the session on a Monday, there was a stream of reporters crowded about my desk. I simply told them I knew nothing and had heard nothing.

The Telegram, rival to *The Vindicator*, editorially commented, "Jackson has a convenient memory."

Not long after, I walked into a gathering of Democrats at the Miramar, a favorite Columbus eating place, where the governor was presiding. He arose as I walked through the door, pointed his finger at me and said, "Here comes the only gentleman in the Ohio legislature," implying I did indeed have a convenient memory.

This was about the first time Davey had recognized me, although some legislators, including myself, had often gathered around him as he played the piano and sang at the Neil House.

The upshot of this incident was that both I and my Mahoning County colleague, John Hewitt, were called before the Franklin County prosecuting attorney. The prosecutor more or less said that I knew nothing and exonerated me, but Hewitt might have some involvement. It was the last ever heard of the incident.

To the end of his service, Davey was a controversial yet most artful governor. Although he liked to come into a town with a motorcycle escort and other accompaniments, he had a very common touch in dealing with people. It was a day before terrorists; governors and even presidents walked among citizens with little, if any, concern for security.

Folks in the Youngstown-Akron area all knew Davey, who was often referred to as the "Duke of Kent" because of his flamboyant nature. His family had developed the famous Davey Tree Service, and Davey won great attention from his radio broadcast during the gubernatorial campaign when he recited Joyce Kilmer's famous poem, "Trees." The Davey family had lived in Hubbard before moving to Kent.

An interesting footnote about the 1935 legislature was that I had as many as four of my colleagues sleeping in my room on cots, for which they paid a quarter apiece. I paid $1.50 per night for the room in the Neil House, located on High Street across from the Capitol. At least one night, I remember, two or three of the legislators did not have the money for the cot and slept on the floor. There was, at least to my knowledge, one who arrived at the legislature by riding railroad boxcars; he couldn't afford to come any other way. Nobody had any money in those days.

During much of that time, some Ohio Supreme Court justices slept in their offices. Even Chief Justice Carl V. Weygandt was set up to sleep in his office in the Capitol Annex.

Many justices and officials would eat in the Mills Cafeteria as well as several trusties from the Ohio Penitentiary. One was the trigger man from the Purple Gang, who was incarcerated for much of his life. The Purple Gang had ravaged Toledo and Detroit, and purportedly moved into the Youngstown region in the 1920s when bootlegging was an extremely lucrative enterprise.

One fellow I met in a beer and sandwich shop across from the Deshler Hotel had red hair and drank beer with the fellows there. His name was Bob Evans. He was from Rio Grande, Ohio, and he was always talking about trying to start a business. From this lowly beginning in the midst of the Depression, he founded the chain of Bob Evans restaurants that engage a multitude of diners in cities throughout Ohio and other states. His restaurants feature honey and homemade biscuits along with Bob Evans sausage, which has captured the tastes of many Americans, including me.

When legislators were serving on committees, one habit was to adjourn the panel at a time when they could corner the lobbyists, who would provide a free meal. The railroad lobbyists, in particular, would serve you as much shrimp as you could eat. Other lobbyists were also generous. I would go from one such gathering to another to see what my fellow legislators were up to. Of course, I, too, would eat.

And yet, honest purpose always seemed to be the guiding rule among the members. Some were very strict about accepting any favor from any special-interest group. Most of the legislators would take a meal

STATE REPRESENTATIVE

CLINGAN JACKSON

DEMOCRAT FOR

CONGRESSMAN

In 1936, it was too late; Michael J. Kirwan
was in the right place at the right time.

or a cigar from a lobbyist, but very few would permit other payments such as hotel bills. Some lobbyists operated on a very ethical basis — some not quite so ethical.

During the 91st General Assembly, the so-called "wets" and "drys" were still battling. The wets wanted to keep the age low at which Ohioans could legally buy beer, and the drys wanted to raise the age. They wrangled on the floor of the House, voting on amendments of one kind or another. Finally a vote was taken, and the measure was overwhelmingly passed with only three votes against it. I had no set opinion on the subject, but I watched the amending process very closely and voted "no" as the measure swept through. After the vote, we moved peacefully to adjourn and then went home.

The next day, the *Plain Dealer* headlined, "General Assembly Votes Beer for Babes." The amendments had tangled up both sides so much the wets and the drys each voted for the bill, believing it contained language to their liking. In truth, neither side wanted it because it eliminated any age requirement for buying beer. I became, temporarily at least, a hero to the Women's Christian Temperance Union. On the Monday following the vote, the returning legislature aborted its action, remedying its mistake.

The memory of this legislative fiasco was refreshed many years later when I was campaigning for governor in a farming area near Beloit, and stopped at a gasoline station to put out my literature. The proprietor said, "If you have a little time, my mother lives close by. She's always wanted to meet the man who voted against Beer for Babes."

In 1936, knowing the trouble I was in politically following my "no" vote on the Parochial School Bill, I decided not to run for re-election to the state House and instead became a candidate for the Democratic nomination for Congress. It crossed my mind that I might as well be defeated for Congress rather than for a lesser office.

Youngstown was then part of the Cleveland Diocese, and Bishop Schrembs insisted on political retribution. The Sunday before the primary election, the diocesan newspaper carried my name in bold black print at the top of the front page with an arrow signifying I was to be defeated.

In 1936, the outlook was for another Democratic sweep, and in the congressional primary I ran very strong outside of Youngstown and Mahoning County; but Michael J. Kirwan won the nomination and would continue in office for thirty-four years. Kirwan's win in the general election was over Republican John G. Cooper, a Republican who had represented the district for twenty-two years and barely managed to survive a very weak opponent in the 1934 Democratic sweep in Mahoning County.

My close friends had urged me to seek the congressional nomination in 1934, but I heeded the wisdom of veteran politicians. Had I run for Congress in 1934, I don't doubt that I would have been elected. I was twenty-seven years old then, just two years older than required to serve in Congress. Many times I have pondered what trouble I might have gotten into had I listened to my friends.

Being of stubborn nature, I tried again in 1938, this time for the nomination to the state Senate. My support improved a little, but I was defeated — some were still reminding everyone of the Parochial School Bill vote.

By 1944, this "transgression" was largely forgotten or forgiven and I was nominated for state senator. The fall campaign turned out very well, and I began six years of active service in the Ohio Senate.

During my first term in the state Senate, my colleague, Maurice Lipscher, and I introduced a fair employment bill. Modeled after the Quinn-Ives statute in New York, it was vigorously opposed, and it wasn't until fourteen years later before Ohio was able to move forcefully in this civil rights effort to eliminate employment discrimination by imposing penalties for any such violation.

The arguments against our original bill were quite vigorous during committee hearings. A senator boldly pointed his finger at me and declared, "You are a Communist!"

Later we became fast friends.

As bitterness over the fair employment bill intensified, my colleagues serving from Mahoning County would appear in the committee room and take their seats in an apparent effort to show that our section of Ohio stood for the measure.

World War II ended in this session of the Senate, and postwar planning began for the expenditure of many millions of dollars that had accumulated in the Ohio treasury during the war, when restrictions were put on all domestic improvements.

One of the postwar issues was to bring more efficiency into Ohio's conservation efforts. The state parks were then supervised by various departments, forestry by another. In addition, no one had done much about erosion along the Lake Erie shoreline.

Professor Arthur E. Morgan, a consulting engineer from Antioch College in Yellow Springs, Ohio, who initially headed the Tennessee Valley Authority, had drawn up a consolidation proposal. A small group forming a committee of the Postwar Commission heard him read it at a meeting in the Deshler Hotel. This was the beginning of what became legislation establishing the Ohio Department of Natural Resources.

Morgan's proposed bill was a couple of pages long. By the time existing Ohio judicial decisions and law had been reviewed, the measure needed more than 150 pages in order to preserve court decisions involving services that were consolidated in the department with its nine divisions and, in general, put conservation efforts under one head. Final action on the bill did not take place until 1949.

In the 1947-48 session of the Ohio Senate, my chief contribution was the Strip Mine Act. Aside from that, some achievement was made in amending Ohio election laws along the lines requested by the Mahoning County Board of Elections, plus some other routine steps that included amending the general code for distribution of tax receipts to and from the local government fund, and amendments dealing with taxes on intangible property.

The Strip Mine Act had stiff opposition from mining interests, but it managed to awaken Ohioans to the need to save the soil, water and what this earth has to offer. The people residing in the areas of strip mining — other than those profiting from it — were very anxious for regulation. The problem was to alert people throughout the state so legislators coming from areas not affected by strip mining would not listen to lobbyists and others working to oppose effective regulation.

In preparing the original strip mine law, emphasis was placed on the concept of returning the soil to a gently rolling surface with quality planting. How this would be implemented varied from location to location. In some sections, trees were grown, or occasionally even orchards. Some mining companies had already proceeded with restoration efforts on their own or had provided for reclamation at the time the mining rights were obtained from the original landowners. Although some of the original owners had been exact in their requirements, the enactment, undoubtedly testified to by experience, effectively restored strip-mined areas more so than before envisioned.

In subsequent sessions, the original strip mine law was amended; and, unfortunately, Ohio still needs to generate greater effort toward conservation of the land. But in 1947, the 97th General Assembly enacted the measure very much as it had originally been written. Interestingly, passage came partly from the support of Republican Governor Thomas Herbert, whose gubernatorial campaign had been rather heavily promoted by many in the mining organizations. After he was elected, Herbert reportedly told industry lobbyists that it was "high time" for state regulation regarding strip mining.

To me, this enactment was particularly warming. When I first considered running for the state legislature, my father, who worked for the Carbon Limestone Company near Hillsville, urged me to make

Governor Thomas Herbert signs the Strip Mine Act; the measure's author stands at far right alongside the bill's co-sponsors.

it my business that firms stripping the land should be required to return that land to such a shape as to provide future usefulness to man. Regretfully, Father did not live to see me elected to any state position. He died accidentally when a side-track rail train at the limestone company backed into him while he was walking home.

When I first became a candidate, Mahoning County had such a history of Republican domination that my father warned me that seeking the Democratic nomination for state representative would be a good experience, but he doubted a Democrat could be elected. Six months after his death, however, the political tides had turned.

There were many interludes in my legislative service that were fascinating, such as the two principal finance bills in the 98th General Assembly — the Biennial Appropriations Bill and the Additions and Betterment Bill.

The latter bill was for various projects made possible by surplus money available during the postwar years. As chairman of the Ohio Senate Finance Committee, I joined forces with Senator Al Daniels, who had headed the committee in a previous session; our chief purpose, as we saw it, was to channel this money into capital improvements.

Since Ohio had a furniture industry dependent on an adequate supply of hardwood, much of it was allocated to create a state forest. A substantial amount also was allocated for the construction of dormitories and other improvements at state universities. Kent State University, for example, acquired eighty acres for its expansion. With the GI Bill, college enrollment had jumped by the thousands.

There also was a desire to preserve for public use some frontage along Lake Erie. As a result, today beach areas can be found in state parks — one near Toledo and another between Cleveland and Ashtabula. These recreational areas are accessible to all Ohioans.

The House version of the appropriations bill in the 97th General Assembly did not meet the favor of the Senate, so Senate and House versions had to be meshed together through the agency of a conference committee. The committee traditionally had three members from each house. Under the legislative rules on conference committees, both the majority and the minority were to be represented; I was the minority member of the Senate committee in 1947.

Usually final approval of the appropriations bill is put off until toward the end of the session. But practice had shown that too much delay from too much political debate would cut off funds to pay thousands of state employees and other governmental expenses.

In 1947, however, the conference committee was not wrangling over anything very important. Senate Republicans advocated appropriations for some veterans' organizations, but House Republicans wanted to cut out money for these groups. The conferees ended up in the governor's office, negotiating through much of the night. I stood up for the position taken by the House Republican conferees and kept citing how much cutting funding for veterans would help the Democratic Party. After hearing my arguments, House Republicans decided to accept the view of their counterparts in the Senate and agreed to funding for veterans organizations.

As daylight was breaking, we concluded, and I walked out of the governor's office. At some distance from me was Senator Daniels, who then chaired the Senate Finance Committee. He came up to me and remarked, "You son of a gun — you knew what you were doing, didn't you?"

"Yes," I replied.

"Well, we are marking up the Additions and Betterment Bill upstairs. We want you to have what you want, so come up and help us," he offered.

"They wouldn't get me sitting down in such a Republican meeting," I joked. He told me to figure out what I wanted for my district and give the information to him.

The next day I told Daniels I wanted funding for eighty acres at Kent State University, which officials there had been seeking. I also wanted appropriations for Beaver Creek State Park near Rogers, and the Yellow Creek Project in Jefferson County. There were a couple of other items this district had been concerned with, and dutifully the Additions and Betterment Bill provided them.

My final term as state senator brought to fruition a number of measures that interested our area. For instance, I authored the law providing for the licensing of practical nurses and setting forth the standards involved. The Bobwhite Quail Bill also came up.

At the time, I had been writing a daily column for *The Vindicator*, but on alternate days the column was written by Larry Flint, a very able poet and writer. One day Flint wrote his column and asserted that anyone shooting a bobwhite quail would shoot his aunt. Someone in the newspaper composing room forgot to change the byline on the column, and the hunters' association immediately jumped on the neck of the guy they thought wrote the piece. So, by natural request, I became the Ohio Senate's champion of bobwhite quail.

For many years the state had protected the birds from hunters; violators were prosecuted by game wardens. Contending there should be open season for hunting bobwhites, sports organizations argued the birds had become too numerous and inbred their flocks. A good many farm groups favored continuing protection. The bird was regarded as beneficial to agriculture since a few bobwhites could keep down the potato bug population and were in general regarded as an aid to gardens and other plantings. The influence of the hunters, however, prevailed. Although Governor Frank J. Lausche vetoed the act, it was overridden; since then, open season has been permitted.

Interestingly, women senators approved of shooting the bobwhites; I thought I'd have their approval at least. It was the only time I ever heard that killing something was beneficial to its health. The quail population has since radically dropped in Ohio, perhaps not due to hunting but because the rail fences along which they first came north in search of new homes have largely disappeared during the last fifty years. Not native to Ohio, bobwhite quail migrated from the South.

In the primary election of 1950, defeat came to me again — this time in a three-candidate race. The Mahoning-Trumbull senatorial district had two state senators, Nicholas Bernard and myself. One Senate seat for this district was eliminated in the 1950 election; the two of us ran against each other for re-election and the CIO put in a third candidate, Charles Carney who, with strong labor support, edged both of us out.

During my last term as a state senator I was chairman of the Ohio Program Commission; and soon after leaving the Senate, Governor Lausche named me and two others as his commission appointees to serve two-year terms. This would be the beginning of nearly thirty years of service on various Ohio boards and commissions.

EXTRA

FOR AN EFFECTIVE VOICE IN COLUMBUS
RE-ELECT State Senator
CLINGAN JACKSON
DEMOCRAT

LOCAL GOVERNMENT FUNDS—Senator Jackson evolved the "Youngstown Plan," part of which was adopted, giving local governments in Mahoning and Trumbull Counties more than $500,000 additional in funds during 1949 and 1950.

CONSERVATION—Senator Jackson was the author of the act creating the Ohio Department of Natural Resources which consolidates conservation work in Ohio for the first time.

STRIP-MINING—He was the author of strip-mine legislation passed by both the 97th and 98th General Assemblies, designed for the sloping, leveling and planting of strip-mine spoil banks. Time will show what this means to the Ohio countryside.

ECONOMY—As chairman of the Senate Finance Committee, Jackson proposed a cut which balanced the state budget and saved approximately $7,000,000 for the tax-payers of Ohio.

SCHOOLS—Jackson has fought for a square deal for Northeastern Ohio schools in the distribution of state funds. He has actively sought laws to provide more money for schools and school employees.

LABOR—No legislator has a more consistent record through four terms of supporting legislation designed to better the position of laboring men. Unemployment compensation and workmen's compensation amendments have been actively supported by him. He voted against passage of the Ferguson Act and other anti-labor legislation.

Jackson is chairman of the Senate Finance Committee and the Ohio Program Commission, positions which enable him to act effectively for this district.

Jackson will continue his effective work in the state capital if you give him support in the Democratic Primary, Tuesday, May 2nd.

JACKSON FOR SENATOR COMMITTEE

M.W. Vanich, Chairman   **Mrs. Ann Stanko, Secretary**

EXTRA

POLTICIAL ADVERTISEMENT 1950

It's the Same

Old Story

**Every flea has
Little fleas, and
They have fleas
To bite 'em;
And even these
Have parasites—
And so on—
Ad infinitum.**

And Every
Stooge Has
HIS Stooge!

We've always contended that Political Editor Clingan Jackson is a stooge of *The Youngstown Vindicator*.

* * * *

And last Sunday *The Vindicator* had an editorial explaining that State Senator Nicholas Bernard is JACKSON'S stooge.

* * * *

Of course *The Vindicator* didn't use the word "stooge."

* * * *

They were very, very, VERY clever about the matter.

* * * *

They merely said that Mr. Bernard had been "GUIDED" by Mr. Jackson in Bernard's work in the Senate.

* * * *

After looking over the voting record of Mr. Bernard we're forced to agree. Mr. Bernard was "guided" all right, and that's for sure!

* * * *

We could go further, and say that Mr. Bernard was not only "guided" but was actually SHOVED!!!

* * * *

So, if you don't relish VIN-DICATOR RULE, you certainly will not want Mr. Jackson for State Senator.

* * * *

And, if you do not relish Mr. Jackson, you most, most CERTAIN-LY couldn't stomach Mr. Bernard.

* * * *

To clean house at Columbus it is very necessary that both these "individuals" be EXTERMINATED from public office, and

* * * *

to insure a breath of fresh, clean air in the State Senate

VOTE
For a
FIGHTER
Instead of a
"PUSSY-FOOTER"
VOTE FOR

X	Charles J. Carney

DEMOCRAT FOR
STATE SENATOR
Primaries, May 2, 1950

**Carney for State Senate
Committee**

**Eddie Weygandt,
Treasurer**

Ohio Attorney General William O'Neill, second from the left, joins members of the Highway Construction Council as they inspect a project.

"Everyone has heard of the one rotten apple that spoils the barrel. But in human relations, the effect a good apple can have cannot be overestimated. Street-corner gangs need a seed from such a tree, but often because of the stratification of society, such a seed is missing.

Zoning or segregation is partly responsible. Communities should [be planned] so [children] will have the advantage of the interplay of old and young, rich and poor and the simply different. The advantages of intercourse among the elements of society are being denied at peril."

Clingan Jackson, The Vindicator, 1960

CHAPTER 10

STATE COMMISSIONS

y association with the Ohio Program Commission began with its inception, a step taken as World War II came to a close and the Ohio General Assembly believed preparation had to be made for the postwar period.

Initially, the program commission was comprised of representatives from both houses of the legislature and appointees of the governor, and was called the Ohio Postwar Commission. As the immediate postwar period passed, the name was changed to the Ohio Program Commission. Beginning in 1947, I was one of the Senate representatives. In 1949, the chairmanship became my job and, when I failed in my bid to be re-elected to the state Senate in 1950, Governor Lausche named me to the commission as one of his appointments.

199

The commission studied Ohio's needs by setting up committees of volunteers that formed study groups on problems facing the state. For example, there were studies on the highways that eventually produced the basis for the Ohio Highway Construction Council, which regulated and designated the major thoroughfare system and interstate highways of Ohio. There was also a study group on education, and one we called a little "Hoover Commission," which was designed to recommend more efficient use of state funds much in the same way as the famed Hoover Commission did for the federal government.

Important people gave the commission their time to help calculate what might be done by Ohio government for capital improvements and to make state operations more efficient. It is important to note as historical fact some of the famous Ohioans who served. One study group was headed by Dr. Andrew Fleming, president of Ohio Wesleyan University and who would later serve in President Eisenhower's cabinet. George Roudebush, then superintendent of Columbus schools, headed a study on education. Howard Jones, president of Youngstown College, headed a study on employment. Other famous Ohio names were also on this list — Harvey Firestone Jr. of the tire company and George Kettering, who invented the self-starter for automobiles and after whom the city of Kettering is named, were just two.

Many improvements in Ohio law were the direct result of the studies, among them the creation of the Ohio Department of Natural Resources, for which the final form took place in the legislature. The commission also implemented a study of highways which enabled Ohio to rank high, if not first, among the states in completing its interstate system.

Throughout Ohio history, much of state government's performance had come about in a topsy-turvy way. The important work of the commission was focusing legislators' attention on various means to put government into a position for efficient operations. At least one member of the commission was in each study group, and the commission itself had several members from both houses of the legislature, which facilitated the process of getting planned changes into law. Moreover, the commission provided a link between the floors of the legislature back to citizens from various parts of Ohio. Public meetings were frequently held, providing opportunities for citizens to voice their concerns and opinions.

During the 1940s and into the '50s, the Program Commission furnished much of the impetus for the vital legislation enacted to bring Ohio government into the last half of the twentieth century. By the 98th General Assembly — 1949-50 — the General Code of Ohio needed major changes. Some of the laws were virtually beyond understanding, and others had ceased to have any meaning. Fifty-five of these laws were repealed in one single act. Action also was taken to change the Ohio fiscal year from beginning in January to beginning in July.

With the fiscal year beginning in January, when the new General Assembly came to Columbus, the task always had been to pass a six-month appropriations bill. This was usually accomplished in a hurried manner since legislators couldn't get their pay until its enactment. At such junctures in the 1930s, the state treasurer would loan money to arriving legislators against their pay. With the new enactment, the legislature passed a two-year appropriation measure which gave the incoming legislature no need for an appropriation enactment through the first six months of their service.

During 1949 and 1950, Loren Glosser was the commission secretary, and when the Ohio Program Commission went out of existence, he came to head the agency that was set up permanently to write bills and prepare statistics to aid the operation of the general assembly. Thus, the work of the Program Commission was carried on by paid state employees with the service of volunteer citizens no longer a factor. I was subsequently asked to serve on another state board, this time overseeing state highways.

In 1947, the Automobile Safety Foundation had been hired to make a study of Ohio roads. The foundation's final report was made to the Ohio Program Commission in 1949, but implementation of those recommendations was left to be done.

A great deal of money was required to meet the needs as set forth in the highway study. Since the state of Ohio cannot go into debt except by a vote of the people, the legislature proposed to submit a $500 million bond issue to the voters. With a Democratic governor and a legislature controlled by Republicans, a provision was put in the proposed constitutional amendment whereby a Highway Construction Council would be established to control the expenditure of the bond money. The council was to be appointed by the governor subject to the confirmation of the Ohio Senate.

The idea was this council would serve as an effective watchdog over the Ohio Highway Department in implementing the construction program. It also was given the task of classifying and, in effect, determining the major thoroughfare system network within the 18,000 miles of state highways. This major thoroughfare system of approximately 6,500 miles would include some 3,000 miles of four-lane interstates.

The legislature wanted safeguards in the expenditure of funds from the bond issue, and the three-person council, which was to be a blue-ribbon panel, was their answer.

Governor Lausche made three nominations for the Highway Construction Council but the Senate refused to confirm them; he thereupon appointed three others. For his first appointment, the governor chose Jesse Van Fossan, who had once been named America's National Farmer and was a Democrat of national prominence. Then he appointed a Republican, Wilbur Cotton of the National Cash Register Company and one of the first city managers in the United States. Finally he chose me, presumably because I had served in the Senate and he thought I was a Democrat the senators would confirm.

The Senate quickly confirmed all three appointees; the other two commented that since I knew my way around Columbus, I had better be chairman.

The three of us set up operations in the state office building, and hired a secretary and a stenographer. Council members proceeded to travel the 18,000 miles of Ohio highways, inspecting and evaluating them, section by section. We recommended eliminating some miles from the system, and in some cases provided for highways at new locations to be added to the system, including thousands of miles of interstates, almost all through new right-of-ways.

The commission was put in control of a program to set priorities on highway construction and to authorize the expenditure of bond issue and other funds that came into the state treasury via enactments by the legislature for such purposes. During its existence, the council authorized the expenditure of approximately $1.1 billion.

We saw to it that there was a major thoroughfare into each county seat and to all important Ohio historical monuments. To ensure the money was going into adequate highway construction, the Federal Bureau of Highways supervised the flow of federal funds for interstate highways. The way it worked, the state designated where a highway would be built, such as Interstate 80, for example. The federal bureau was interested in statistics showing why each should be an interstate highway, and the standards for which that highway would be built. In general, the state highway department and the council were in charge, but representatives of the federal bureau retained what might be considered a strong hand.

The federal highway people never numbered more than a dozen or so. The state highway department had more than 15,000 employees, headed by a corps of engineers comprised of career people. The state highway director was also a career engineer.

The state highway department was responsible for major thoroughfares, highways, the interstate system and all state roads. The council's job was to approve or disapprove and, by classification, set up a priority system which would edge the highway operation toward as much efficiency as possible. The highway department developed the projects and the council set the priority for their construction.

In so doing, the council came up with a rather unique system to establish priorities, which seemed to work fairly well. It graded the highway projects as A, B or C, basically on the importance of the individual roadway. Then it set against the A, B or C a one, two or three for the speed of construction, recognizing that urgency was not always in direct proportion to the size or eventual importance of any particular project.

By that method, some A, some B, and some C projects were slated for rapid construction, even though the C-1 might be rather insignificant compared to an A-1 or an A-2 project that could not be undertaken in the near future due to the availability of funds and contracting facilities — materials, manpower or both. The council was also responsible for authorizing the expenditure of some $140 million to build access roads to the turnpike.

Armed with the highway department's statistics on road travel, maps of the highway system and the study proposals for major cities of the state, council members inspected the layout of the interstates and interstate plans by air. Most of the highway inspection, however, was accomplished by traveling on the ground and evaluating miles upon miles, section by section, to determine how such highways were to be classified. Working with the state highway department, the council was also instrumental in setting the standards for Ohio highways, moving to the use of concrete as the real backbone of the roadways and major thoroughfare systems.

Some of Ohio's veteran engineers have stated the best thing that ever happened to the highway department was the Highway Construction Council. The council encouraged the department to adopt some new ways of thinking and was a factor in its success. Even in the years after the council ceased to exist, Ohio rated first, or close to first, in the race to complete the country's interstate highway system. This was quite a feat considering that highway construction in Ohio is very difficult compared to many states, since the soil and the climate combine to make the task much more expensive than in many regions of the country.

The interstate highway system in Ohio was in full operation by the 1970s, quite an accomplishment when it is recalled one of Governor James M. Cox's slogans in his 1916 gubernatorial campaign was "Get Ohio out of the mud." Cox and his macadam roads were a far cry from the limited access interstate highway system that came within a half-century to the state. The governor, however, was a far-sighted man. Tourists can venture off the main highways and still see some of the old "S" bridges that opened the trail into the Northwest Territory, and at some locations they can also see the monuments characterized as the "Madonna of the Trail," which depicted a Conestoga wagon with a woman driving the team west. It was Governor Cox who preserved this part of Ohio's history.

In classifying state highways, council members encountered some unusual situations, especially when it came to eliminating highways from the state system that were deemed unnecessary. For instance, in southern Ohio near an old Civilian Conservation Camp that had been erected during the Great Depression, the council traveled down a road which was no longer important. In fact, the road was overgrown with weeds as tall as a man, yet members were shocked to find that highway markers there had just been repainted. This road was immediately removed from the state system.

In western Ohio, the council found several lanes which had been put on the state highway system because a former governor once had a camp nearby and he wanted the roads improved. There were other improprieties discovered by the council. To the credit of highway department officials and the governor, corrective steps were quickly taken.

In northern Ohio, we were somewhat astounded to find a project for widening a bridge that was already forty feet wide, with construction scheduled immediately. A quarter-mile away on the same highway, there was an eighteen-foot bridge not scheduled for widening at all. These types of mistakes were often uncovered and the situations were rectified.

One of the most interesting events that occurred involved State Highway Director Samuel Linzell, who was somewhat miffed when such problems were discovered.

"Come with me and I'll show you Ohio's not too bad," he said one day, and proceeded to drive us to West Virginia where a divided highway had been built for several miles, but with only single-lane bridges across a creek that curved in and out over the highway.

Across the Ohio River from West Virginia, however, the commission discovered an impropriety along Route 7 in Ohio that also may have miffed Linzell. The highway hooked around a business which would have been removed if the road had followed a direct line. It seems this loop in the highway had been engineered for a friend of one of Ohio's governors.

On Route 62 just east of Alliance, the council encountered another example of political influence. The roadway had a sharp left turn, where a garage and filling station was doing business. Members sought to remove the sharp turn, which would have placed the business some distance from the highway.

One night, on my way home from Columbus, I stopped at the gas station and engaged the proprietor in conversation about the project to straighten the highway. He did not know I was on the council, and during our chat he repeatedly insisted the roadway would not be straightened. The council had already appropriated $50,000 for the project, but we were told in a highway report it would take much more. An additional amount was then provided, but this, again, was found to be insufficient, whereupon we earmarked $200,000 and ordered that the job be completed. Eventually, the roadway was straightened for slightly less than the original $50,000 authorization.

Early in the council's efforts, attorneys for the highway department maintained that bond monies could only be spent for improvements to existing highways. But council members believed bond monies could be used on projected new highways they would designate, including new right-of-ways. Court decisions subsequently sustained the council's point of view.

Interestingly, although the council enjoyed good cooperation from the governor, the attorney general and officials who represented the major cities, it had considerable difficulty with Youngstown city officials. Indeed, the first projects in the Youngstown area were entered into by the highway department with considerable reluctance.

One of the basic complaints was that in making estimates for the purchase of new right-of-ways needed for some of the projects, three independent estimates had to be secured. In Youngstown, highway department officials discovered whenever they met an owner to negotiate for property, the owner already knew what the highest estimate was. The city was a participant in the financing of the projects, usually a ten percent share, and Youngstown City Hall was kept informed of all the steps involved in building the highway. The confidential information apparently leaked through to those who were selling right-of-ways. This problem arose particularly in the widening of Oak Street; in some instances, the state sent in different appraisers to work out costs.

In Ashtabula, harbor businessmen and the city's chamber of commerce were seeking money to improve the road from Kingsville on Lake Erie to Route 90. The council informed them the money could be provided if the road was extended to East Liverpool.

Sam Gould, Mahoning County engineer, and I persuaded his counterparts in Trumbull, Ashtabula and Columbiana counties to have their respective boards of commissioners provide $10,000 apiece for the engineering study, with the Highway Construction Council supplying the additional funds necessary to complete the study. As a result, Route 11 came into being and serves as a means of rapid transportation between East Liverpool and northeastern Ohio, as well as in the movement of goods north to the Buffalo area.

The Highway Construction Council completed its work with the Ohio Highway Department without any scandal involving highway projects. The blue-ribbon panel may have helped some, but the state highway department itself has had a long reputation of integrity. Moreover, many of Ohio's governors have tried to keep highway construction on a high level.

As chairman of the council, I often had breakfast with Governor Lausche at the beginning of each workweek. Anytime the council had problems, the governor would help resolve them.

When a serious legal problem arose, it was taken to the attorney general, whose job it was to represent the council. At the time, the attorney general was William O'Neill, a Republican who would later become governor and chief justice of the Ohio Supreme Court.

"Tell Governor Lausche about this. He'll eliminate the problem immediately," O'Neill always advised.

Lausche of course, was a Democrat; O'Neill's advice confirmed that honest officials perform their duties regardless of politics.

Some little-used roads lead to historical monuments, but they were intentionally kept on the state highway system. For instance, there was a recommendation to eliminate the road that leads to General George Custer's monument near his birthplace at New Rumley, but the council decided that millions of Ohio school children had seen depictions of Custer's last stand and kept it on the system.

Over the hill from Ripley on the Ohio River is the Rankin House, which is maintained by the state. This house was the main depot on the Ohio River for the underground railroad through which thousands of slaves escaped to the north and Canada. It is also the house from which Harriet Beecher Stowe, author of *Uncle Tom's Cabin*, had supposedly looked out the window and over the river to envision Eliza crossing on the ice. The council wanted the road to this historic place kept on the Ohio highway system. Traveling to the house, we crossed a small stream, looked under the bridge, and discovered only one support of the four was holding up the span. It was subsequently repaired.

Another historic place in Ohio is located on one of the state's most heavily traveled routes. In Point Pleasant, on the highway that runs east from Cincinnati along the Ohio River, stands the small cottage where General U.S. Grant was born. His father was Jesse Grant, the man who drove the coach for Trumbull County Judge George Tod, the father of David Tod, who would become Ohio governor during the Civil War and turn down Abraham Lincoln's request that he serve as secretary of the treasury.

We tried to keep the system open to all of Ohio's chief historical places — some of which include Thomas Edison's birthplace in Milan and President Rutherford B. Hayes' home in Fremont. Members also worked in connection with the highway plans of large cities so they would mesh. In most instances, this worked out very well.

Those seeking highway funds to improve Ohio Route 40 north of Dayton advocated building a new bridge rather than keeping the existing road over a dam. Appearing before the council was an army general who testified about the value of Route 40 as a defense highway, and the necessity of keeping it at a high level of construction. I was less interested in this project than in those needed for highways in northern Ohio with heavier truck traffic. At the time of his testimony, I was reading the book written by Dwight D. Eisenhower, recounting the triumph of American arms in Europe, and noted the passage where Ike explained it was easy to knock out a bridge by air bombing, but very difficult to knock out a dam.

I copied his statement on the back of a letter, got up at the hearing, read it to the general who was testifying, and asked, "Who do you suppose said that?"

"Some damn fool, I suppose," he replied.

I informed him the statement came from the army's commander in chief. The final result, however, was the bridge was built. I lost that round, but it makes for a good story.

Another incident involved the construction of Ohio Route 21 north of the Akron area, which meant taking a right-of-way through a rather beautiful part of a prominent Clevelander's country estate. This necessitated a hearing, and the owner was pretty upset. From the viewpoint of location, the highway could go a short distance the other way and be even better located than had been proposed in the study. It would have also cut through some rather inexpensive buildings, which the owners probably would have been glad to sell.

What the prominent Clevelander did not know was the soil findings. The highway was placed on his property because it would have required thousands of tons of material to establish a base for the highway where he suggested it should go. To his credit, once he understood the facts, he dropped his objections.

Governor O'Neill (second from right) swears in the newest member of the Ohio Pardon and Parole Commission as state senators Charles Carney (far left) and Stephen Olenick watch.

By 1956, the Highway Construction Council's days were numbered. The gubernatorial candidates that year were Republican C. William O'Neill and Democrat Michael V. DiSalle, and neither wanted a highway department that wasn't directly under his control. The council was originally conceived as the method for a Republican Senate to have some check over the highway department. Moreover, one of the council's purposes was to classify highways. That job had been completed and the money had all been authorized. So, in 1957, following O'Neill's election, the council was officially disbanded.

O'Neill subsequently appointed me to the Ohio Pardon and Parole Commission as a Democratic member. This appointment was highly unusual. Normally a governor took immediate advantage to have his party control any commission to which the appointment of a member made this possible. In this instance, a Republican governor had appointed a Democrat, leaving the commission with a Democratic majority. However, the job did not entail deciding any political questions, and I served as vice chairman.

Every month the three board members traveled to all of the state's penal institutions: the River House in Columbus; the Ohio State Reformatory at Mansfield; the Crafton Honor Camp; the Marion Correctional Institution; the Ohio Reformatory for Women at Marysville; and the London Prison Farm. At London, Columbus and Mansfield, our work usually involved spending several days there each month. We took the records of the prisoners with us, box after box, whenever we went to the prisons.

On the average, the board heard the pardon and parole cases of about 750 prisoners a month. Rarely did an inmate have to be accompanied by a guard. With their records in front of us, plus communications from judges, prosecutors and others involved in the convictions, we talked to the prisoners individually, then made our decisions.

As established by state law, every prisoner is entitled to appear before the Pardon and Parole Commission at some designated time, and it was interesting work. Some days we spent in Columbus reviewing files and made our determinations from the parole officers' reports of parolees' conduct. Prosecuting attorneys also submitted recommendations, as would investigators who worked for the commission.

In the case of prisoners incarcerated for life, after twenty years they appeared at five-year intervals before the commission. At that time, the Pardon and Parole Commission served as the board of clemency, the conscience of the governor and a carry-over from the concept of the "conscience of the king." The kings historically — some of them at least — had a religious person who served as clemency arbiters in relation to decisions involving capital punishment.

The Ohio board functioned much the same with the governor regarding capital punishment cases. Before an execution would take place, we would write our recommendations to the governor. Sometimes he commuted the sentences to prison terms; other times, he did not. Quite often the families would come to see us and appeal for clemency.

Occasionally, the board would be petitioned not to give a prisoner parole. One such case involved a wife who didn't want her husband released. "He would rape a chicken," she explained.

In cases when a prison escapee was apprehended and brought back to prison, five more years would typically be added to his term. One time, however, we had an escapee who didn't turn up for twenty years.

This man had been living in a distant city, and had become almost, if not in fact, the leading citizen of that community. So far as we could check, anyone who would name three of the most important people in that thriving community would include him as one. He had two children who were well-respected schoolteachers. After reviewing his file and current life, we decided to forget he had ever been found. After all, the purpose of incarceration is to restore prisoners as productive members of society. To that end, the prison at London, Ohio, has written above its doors the words of Governor A. Vic Donahey: "Who enters here leaves not hope behind."

One of the well-known murder cases of the late 1950s involved Sam Sheppard, the Bay Village osteopath who, after a highly publicized trial, had been convicted of murdering his wife. Sheppard was in the state penitentiary when I served on the Pardon and Parole Commission. His case did not come before the board during my service, although he would later be granted a new trial on the grounds of prejudicial pretrial publicity, and would be found not guilty.

I remember one very old fellow who had been in prison since the 1890s. He came before the board and said he didn't want a parole, explaining he wouldn't know how to live outside after having been incarcerated for more than sixty years.

We had another fellow who had been before the parole board a couple of times, and had been paroled by a previous board which later voted to rescind its decision. When I reviewed this case, I learned that some congressman residing in the inmate's community was so angry with the man's family, he kept the man from getting paroled. Without this political pressure, this man would have been paroled five or ten years earlier. The board I served on granted him parole.

The commission paroled one guy who looked to be an ambassador to the Court of St. James. He came back to prison a month later after passing bad checks for several thousand dollars at the Waldorf-Astoria Hotel in New York City. Because of the way he dressed and carried himself — looking like a great, important man — the hotel had readily cashed his checks.

The commission also dealt with an inmate whose parole was being sponsored by a Chicago company that had promised him a job as a ceramic designer at an annual salary of $35,000. He had been imprisoned for breaking into a home at night and stealing $1.50. At the time of his conviction, state law specified a long sentence for breaking into an inhabited dwelling at night. He, too, was granted parole.

While serving on the parole board, some days I would hear about one horrendous crime after another; meals after such sessions would not arouse an appetite. It is impossible to conceive the dastardliness of some performances by humans. Listening to them, one after another, a sickness clouded the mind. Then, if the commission was dealing with a mere armed robber, the air had cleared. And, occasionally, there was a case that brought a smile — such as the burglar who was apprehended because he had leaned against a newly painted garage and the mark on the garage fitted the paint on his pants.

The Ohio Penitentiary contained a few items of historical interest — most notably, the letter left behind by Confederate General John Morgan — "Morgan the Raider" — telling in detail how he had escaped from incarceration. The Columbus prison also once housed one of America's most famous writers, O. Henry, who served time there during the late nineteenth century.

Not all of the board's work involved paroles. The brother of comedian Bob Hope once came before us to discuss a charitable undertaking regarding the inmates. This is not so unusual as it may seem. In some of Bob Hope's routines, he joked that he had graduated from B.I.S. — in other words, the Boys Industrial School of Ohio. The comedian was contributing money in a philanthropic effort to aid people who had been victimized by disruptive experiences in their youth. In so doing, his organization assisted paroled prisoners.

One time when we were meeting at Marysville, the unique case of a woman came up. Because of her mental condition, she had been sent to Lima State Mental Hospital for the criminally insane. After being treated for several months, physicians determined her mind had been sufficiently restored and she was returned to Marysville prison. Officials there immediately put her into solitary confinement for violating the institution's rules before her stay in Lima. The board removed her from solitary confinement and granted her parole.

Then, as now, the parole board faced the problem of overcrowded prisons. I've been to Mansfield when prisoners were jammed in the hall, and outside three busloads of new prisoners from Cleveland had just arrived. We tried to parole prisoners who were not involved in physical terrorism or any kind of murder. Quite often, some prisoners such as pickpockets were paroled; we figured they didn't hurt anyone physically.

Roy Harmony of Troy was a member of the parole board when I served. He was always preaching to the prisoners that they should listen to their mothers. One prisoner came before the board and Roy started to preach to him about listening to his mother. I looked over the records and saw that his mother was in Moundsville prison and had a record that made her son look like a saint.

"You'd better tell him not to listen to his mother," I advised Roy.

After three and a half years of service on the Pardon and Parole Commission, I figured my sentence with the state had been served.

There would, however, be one more commission to which I would be named, an appointment that resulted from the 1962 gubernatorial campaign, when James A. Rhodes, a former Columbus mayor and state auditor, defeated Michael V. DiSalle in his re-election campaign.

A Republican, Rhodes' political activity began in the 1930s. Supporting his widowed mother while trying to work his way through Ohio State University, he appealed to the 91st General Assembly for a job and was employed as the legislative enrollment clerk for the House of Representatives. I made his early acquaintance in 1935, the first year of my state legislative experience.

Rhodes called me shortly after his election to the governorship and asked me what position interested me in state government. He told me he would give me any available job I wanted, but I told him my mind was made up not to serve in any capacity. My feeling was I should concentrate on my work for *The Vindicator* and not be so involved in state government.

Nevertheless, a few days later, he called me and said, "I have the perfect job for you," and named the Civil Rights Commission.

I replied I still didn't want to take any job with the state, whereupon he waited a few days and called me again.

"Will you talk to your publisher about the position?" he asked.

This I did, and William J. Brown told me, "By all means, I think you should take the job."

That was the beginning of twenty-two years of service on the Ohio Civil Rights Commission. Reappointed as my terms expired, I was always confirmed by a unanimous vote of the Ohio Senate.

At the time of my first appointment, February 1963, the question of race relations in Ohio, as well as in the nation, had become very serious, yet civil rights enforcement in Ohio was still relatively new.

The commission was formed in 1959, but civil rights legislation in Ohio dated to the nineteenth century. And, in the 1940s, some effective work had been done to force restaurants to serve without racial discrimination. Nonetheless, the commission was quite feeble in its operation.

In its early years, most of the cases coming before the commission involved hotels, restaurants and bars that refused to serve blacks. There was also a notable case concerning a dead body that had been kept above ground for several months by the owners of a Montgomery County cemetery who refused to permit the burial of blacks on their property. By the end of my service, issues such as these had almost disappeared from the commission's calendar — such was the new acceptance by Ohioans of equal opportunity for all.

The Ohio Civil Rights Commission is composed of five members; in practice, three from one political party and two from the other. The governor, through his appointment power, usually determines which party has a majority on the commission.

Each commissioner serves a five-year term, and as a commissioner, one serves as a free agent. Although such commissions always act as one in making any decision, the majority acts for the whole. Commissioners do not have to answer to anybody; the only way they can be removed is through misfeasance or malfeasance.

The duties of the Ohio Civil Rights Commission are to enforce the civil rights of minorities, women and handicapped persons in employment and such transactions as the borrowing of money, the rental and purchase of property and public accommodations. Ohio law on employment rights also provides protection from discrimination based on nationality and religious affiliation.

During my years as a commissioner, the area of operation was increased to include protection for women and the handicapped, and to cover fair-housing rights. Religious discrimination and such matters as employer abuse in cases of sexual harassment also widened the commission's scope. While the nature of the cases changed during my service, and fair employment agreements were reached with many companies, the number of cases remained about the same, averaging some 5,000 a year even after careful screening to keep the number down.

Civil rights laws, both state and federal enactments, are generally enforced by state civil rights commissions. Accordingly, the decisions of the Ohio Civil Rights Commission have the effect of law. A decision may be appealed to common pleas court, but if no appeal is filed in thirty days, it stands as law, and failure to comply can compel contempt-of-court action.

When the Ohio General Assembly passed a law seeking to provide access to public buildings for the handicapped, the Civil Rights Commission established rules to carry out implementation. The standards resulted from public hearings and, of course, time was allowed in meeting the new handicapped-access rules.

An examination of the main office of the Ohio Civil Rights Commission, which was then housed in the old state police headquarters in Columbus, revealed it would take some $50,000 to have the structure reach the desired standards. The incidence of large numbers of handicapped people using the building occurred only once every four years under the commission's routine of scheduling meetings with disabled persons at that interval. Construction costs to accommodate the handicapped were frequently excessive compared to the extent of use, but barrier-free buildings was the intent of state law and it had to be enforced. By 1990, indication of just how well the handicapped public-access law had been implemented was demonstrated when the Ohio secretary of state announced that all but a few voting places contained easy access for the handicapped.

While there were some interesting cases while I served on the Civil Rights Commission, a few didn't seem to amount to much. For instance, there was the case of the Columbus Sausage Company which concerned reverse discrimination against men. During a special sales promotion, the company had served a free drink, namely beer, to housewives who shopped there. The final resolution of the case was the sausage company had to give free beer to men who also shopped there.

There was a similar case involving a Dayton theater that had a special matinee for housewives with a reduced ticket price. Under the law, the theater had to give men the same price.

Another somewhat inconsequential sex-discrimination case, this time in Cleveland, regarded Playboy bunnies, which was brought by men who wanted to be bunnies. This particular claim was laughed out.

Such trivial cases excited media attention but had little meaning. The cases did, however, demonstrate the law can occasionally be asinine. Common sense has to take over; almost every law somewhere reaches a point at which it won't work.

This had previously become very apparent to me during my years in the state Senate when I was serving on the Ohio Sundry Claims Board, which was designed to award damages in instances where the state had wronged someone. Then, the ancient concept that the king can do no wrong was still followed in Ohio. An example which comes to mind is the case of a young man who legally parked his new car in front of his girlfriend's house, where it was smashed by a state truck. The Sundry Claims Board replaced his destroyed vehicle, but it always took special legislation to enact the board's decisions.

One case before the Civil Rights Commission involved Canadians being discriminated against by Toledo residents. It was resolved through a penalty ensuring that such discrimination must cease. About the same time, the problem came up concerning a southern Ohio business discriminating against the employment of Kentuckians from across the Ohio River. The law provided no penalty for such discrimination — more evidence that the law is occasionally flawed.

In another civil rights case, a woman wanted a job as a puddler in a steel mill. The company had to install full restroom facilities for her, which it did. She worked on the job only one day.

Other things happened that were rather disturbing. For instance, in Wooster, there was an elderly white woman who wanted to rent an upstairs room in her house to a white person. Suit was brought against her by several black activists from Cleveland. Interestingly, all of the blacks in the Wooster neighborhood petitioned on behalf of the householder, agreeing that it was her right to rent to the white person.

Another situation was in regard to the Columbus schools. The problem was the tendency to assign black teachers to schools where the population was largely black, and white teachers to schools that were predominantly white. The idea of the civil rights effort was to evenly distribute whites and blacks throughout the school system. The black teachers mounted a strong protest, claiming they performed better at educating black students than white teachers. They objected to the arbitrary ruling that distributed black teachers throughout the system, and argued it was actually having a reverse effect on educational accomplishment. The Civil Rights Commission insisted upon a full application of the basic principles; the schools had to be as fully integrated as possible.

The city of Cincinnati has a high percentage of black population, but in some suburban school districts in Hamilton County, there were no black teachers. Civil rights activists wanted to provide an almost equal percentage of black faculty members in all of the county's school districts. Yet, if an almost equal percentage was applied countywide, the percentage of black teachers in Cincinnati would have been reduced since the percentage corresponded with the number of blacks living in the city. This, the activists did not want. The whole idea was dropped.

That's the type of issue that faced the commission; quite often the evidence of discrimination was either very strong, very weak or nonexistent. You could usually make a clear decision one way or the other.

There were many cases involving religious groups and work rules that centered on Saturday as the Sabbath. In general, decisions in these matters were quite easy with large employers because accommodations could be made. The difficulty arose with small employers, for whom it was necessary to maintain operations with a few workers and, thus, adjustments could not be made to allow certain employees to take Saturday or even Sunday off and still retain their jobs.

A common-sense standard also had to be applied in dealing with these questions. There are many businesses, restaurants in particular, that especially need employees for Saturdays and Sundays in order to maintain trade. Hence, it is not reasonable to require them to accommodate religious days off for any great number of employees without jeopardizing operations.

Another matter came up in relation to sex discrimination in employment — there are jobs that require either a woman or a man, such as restroom operations in mental hospitals treating men or women. In such instances, the Ohio Civil Rights Commission grants authority for limited employment by sex.

A whole series of discrimination cases, some of them laughable, involved slander. Anyone who ever worked on the railroad or in a steel mill is familiar with the slanderous names sometimes given to other people in conversation such as dago, guinea, hunkie, and even some swear words. Situations developed, and someone with excessively sensitive ''skin'' would bring a case of discrimination before the Civil Rights Commission. We had to weave our way through; often the statements were made more in fun than in malice.

One of the most interesting cases centered on a home economics teacher in rural Ohio who had her students make spaghetti. She announced grandiosely to the class, ''This is a favorite dago dish,'' seemingly with no ulterior purpose. There happened to be an Italian-American in the class who became incensed and brought the case before the Civil Rights Commission.

The commission chairman was Hugo Sabato, an Italian-American schoolteacher, who observed, ''I've been a dago all my life and spaghetti is our favorite dish.''

The case ended up in the waste basket.

My appointment for what would be my last term on the commission came in an odd way. Governor Rhodes had re-appointed me but my confirmation could not take place until after the new governor, Democrat John Gilligan, had been inaugurated and the new Senate went into session.

A newspaper story that originated in Columbus reported there was some question whether Jackson would be confirmed since he had been appointed by the outgoing Republican governor and the Senate was controlled by Democrats. The front page of the morning edition of *The Vindicator* picked up the story and also reported my appointment was in jeopardy, but the newspaper's evening edition reported my appointment had been unanimously confirmed.

Gilligan preferred to appoint someone else, but when a Democratic senator got wind of it, he got up on the floor and demanded my immediate confirmation. This was, at least, an example of the Ohio Senate looking with favor on the careers of its alumni.

Under Ohio law, a commission member could be removed by the governor after he reached age seventy, unless he had his physical capacity proven by an examination every year. After I turned seventy, although I was not expecting to be in disagreement with the governor, for assurance I had a physical exam annually which was attested to by the state.

I served until 1985. By choice I retired; however, Governor Richard Celeste, a Democrat, didn't want me anyway. The director of the Ohio Civil Rights Commission wanted me to serve a few months longer to finish cases on which the commission was working. I told him I would if the governor approved. Instead, Celeste appointed a man from Cleveland.

By that time, I had retired from *The Vindicator* and didn't want to serve any longer. I was getting along in years, and the commission was becoming involved in situations I didn't particularly like — for example, wrangling over the wages that should be paid commissioners.

There had also accumulated in my memory a number of cases that were disconcerting, such as the numerous times company officials had decided not to defend themselves, finding it more cost-effective, and sometimes even safer, to simply pay out sizeable amounts of money to compensate for the alleged discrimination.

Much of civil rights work is to get people to understand each other and come to have a regard for one another. It's a tedious job, for human beings are conditioned to think first and most vigorously about their own needs, forgetting the other guy has rights, too, white or black. That is the trouble with affirmative action; by its very nature it sometimes denies rights.

In 1986, representatives from the Ohio Civil Rights Commission came to Youngstown and gave me a plaque to honor me for my service. Having served in many areas of state government, as well as pursuing a newspaper career, reflection tells me the most important service it has been my good fortune to render was in the civil rights field. It is comforting to remember that perhaps I contributed a little in bringing Ohio citizens together.

EXTRA

Civil War Diary —

Valley's Famous Son Was Loyal to Lincoln

By Clingan Jackson
The Vindicator, 1961

One hundred years ago today, when thousands of citizens were at the Civil War front, the Youngstown district and Ohio rallied to the Union ticket and placed War Democrat David Tod in the governorship at Columbus.

Instinctively, the conservative interests of Ohio had turned to the Mahoning Valley businessman who in the 1840s had twice come within an ace of winning the governor's seat.

The Union ticket was spawned at Cleveland to unite the Republicans and those among the Democrats who stood steadfastly for the Union cause, among them Stephen Douglas of Illinois, Democratic 1860 candidate, who held the hat of Abraham Lincoln at the inauguration.

"Let the Rebels of the South and their allies in the North know that we are terribly earnest in this matter," the *Mahoning Register* intoned on Oct. 3, five days before the election.

The election was Tuesday, Oct. 8, 1861, and the final returns showed 206,997 votes for Tod, the candidate of the Union Party, against 151,774 for Democrat Jewett. The margin was the highest ever given to an Ohio gubernatorial candidate to that date.

Tod had won a reputation as a War Democrat, as opposed to moderates and Copperhead sympathizers with the South in the Ohio Democracy. Southern leaders had said that the defeat of the Union Party in Ohio would be worth many battles.

Twice previously Tod had been the Democratic candidate for governor, losing to Whig Mordecai Bartley in 1844, the vote being Bartley 146,333 and Tod 145,063, and to William Bebb in 1846 when the vote was 118,869 for Bebb and 116,484 for Tod.

During the 1850s, Tod was largely active in development of his industrial and mining interests in the Youngstown area, but as the war clouds formed, he went as a delegate to the 1860 Democratic convention in Charleston, S.C.

Tod was a Douglas supporter for the presidency. He was chosen vice chairman of the convention and assumed the chair with the withdrawal of Caleb Cushing, who had been chosen chairman.

Like the leader of his party, Douglas, Tod counseled loyalty to the Union as war broke out. He took office as governor Jan. 1, 1862, and throughout his term vigorously backed President Lincoln's war effort.

There was the commissioning of many officers in the Union Army, since the governor played a much more direct role in the recruiting and staffing of troops in those days. It is believed enmities developing with these appointments were responsible for his being passed over for the party nomination in 1863.

During his term Governor Tod faced some of the most difficult problems of the war. There were Morgan's raid into Ohio and a reported boast of the Confederate chieftain that he would burn Tod's installations at Youngstown and water his horses in Lake Erie.

There also was the arrest of Clement Laird Vallandigham, who as a Copperhead Democrat stirred opposition to the war. He was arrested at Dayton over a speech delivered at Mount Vernon by General Ambrose Burnside. It was one of the notable escapades of the war.

Vallandigham finally was put behind Confederate lines at Tod's suggestion — but he made his way to Canada and while there ran for governor of Ohio. In 1864 he reappeared in Ohio to campaign against Lincoln. He had many supporters, including many in Columbiana County which he had represented in the state legislature, as well as in some Mahoning County townships.

In 1847 Tod left via canal boat for Washington and assignment by President Polk as minister to the court of Dom Pedro in Brazil. Tod's farewell to Youngstown to assume the governorship must have been impressive although doubtless sobered by the war.

Heard Lincoln's Gettysburg Speech

Governor Tod was at Gettysburg Nov. 10, 1863 when President Lincoln gave his short address which has become a classic of the English language.

Frequent trips to Washington and conferences with Lincoln and members of his cabinet were part of Tod's work as governor. Lincoln once said of him, "Governor Tod has aided me more and troubled me less than any other governor."

The story also is told that Lincoln chided him with spelling his name with only one D whereas Lincoln's wife, Mary Todd Lincoln, had two D's. Tod is said to have replied God

had used only one D and what was "good enough for God was good enough for Tod."

Leaving the governorship, Tod returned to Youngstown, and early in 1864 with the resignation of Salmon P. Chase as secretary of the treasury, there came a telegram from Lincoln, delivered by a switch engine to Brier Hill, offering Tod the treasury position.

For reasons of health, Tod turned down the appointment. Four years later, Nov. 13, 1868, he died, and some 20,000 came to his funeral.

Tod still is a name much associated with this steel valley. There is the Tod House and schools and other places named after him. His descendants likewise have contributed to the fame of the name.

Nevertheless, it is the personality of the governor which still lives here in the shadows. As a youth of 19 and opposed to the politics of his Whig father, Judge George Tod, David became a champion of Andrew Jackson.

His first political preferment was as postmaster at Warren, and there is a cane still in town which it is said belonged to "Old Hickory" and which was given to Tod. He was a friend of Lincoln and performed notable service backing the president on emancipation and the calling of the troops. Part of the reason for Ohio's great effort was this man from Youngstown.

This Sunday, Oct. 8, 1961, is the 100th anniversary of the great day when he was elected Ohio governor — a casting of the die by the Buckeyes who furnished more than their share of troops and generals and casualties in this bloodiest of American wars.

Tod was to take his place among the great of his day. His portrait still hangs in a special place in the Ohio Capitol — an imposing figure with flowing dark hair. ∎

★ ★ ★ ★ ★
The VOTER'S JOB!

Government takes too much of every citizen's income to be played with by anyone. Pressure groups must be resisted in the every action of state government and its departments, and the order of action must be determined objectively and with a view of alleviating the problems in our society. Public projects, roads, hospitals, institutions, conservation undertakings must be planned on a priority basis to meet the greatest needs of Ohio first.

But this cannot be done by public servants or political parties *alone*. Assistance by an *alert and informed citizenry* is needed to replace minority self-interests for the general welfare of all.

Clingan Jackson

Two jobs for the people of Ohio in 1958 are:

(a)—to see to it that citizens at all times know what government is doing. The avenues for the information which will enable him to be easily informed should and must be unclogged or the democratic process will become meaningless. As Adlai Stevenson put it in a recent speech: "the people need to be *told not sold*."

(b)—to assist the political parties in our two-party system to become truly civic instrumentalities, charged with the job of resolving political controversy in a *respectable and responsible* fashion, while at the same time maintain lively organized competition — *the American automatic check against unfair exploitation*.

"Businessmen know that competition is good for them — the life of trade. Too often they forget about the necessity of competition in the world of politics, which takes about 30 percent of their substance in taxes.

They grumble about taxes and, on occasion, they try to manipulate the political scene to their benefit, but they fumble much and only a few seem to realize the fine working of the mechanisms of government is the objective that is most likely to achieve lasting prosperity.

Efficiency in government depends very much on keeping up competition for public office and maintaining political parties which seek to offer candidates for competition in elections. It is discouraging to the electorate when the offering of choice is not present on ballots or the choice is too limited."

Clingan Jackson, Youngstown/Warren Business Journal, July 1991

CHAPTER 11

REFLECTIONS

arly in 1958, at a gathering of Mahoning County Democrats, I was asked to take a stand and run for governor. Having served in the Ohio House of Representatives, the Ohio Senate and as a member and chairman of a number of state commissions, it seemed to me that I was better prepared for the governorship than any of the other possibilities discussed at that time.

Knowing full well what it meant to seek the gubernatorial nomination, I set about trying to arouse the necessary support; it simply was not there. Most Ohio newspapers, particularly those in the Scripps-Howard block, took an antagonistic position partly, I thought at the time, because of *The Vindicator* takeover of *The Telegram* in 1936.

221

Through the years, mention had also been made of my handling political stories while serving in public office. This question was made most apparent when I served on the Senate Rules Committee, which met in private on some occasions. My newspaper colleagues could not understand that any information developing behind closed doors would not be used by *The Vindicator* until it became generally available to all news organizations.

I went through the motions as a candidate for governor; but lacking widespread support, my budget was kept low and I spent less money than any of the other candidates in the primary. No matter what happened, I promised my wife, I would not go broke; and I didn't.

I did well in the balloting in Mahoning and adjacent counties but poorly statewide, except for some nests of support in the Akron and Dayton districts. None of the candidates did as well as I did in their own home-county voting but in a statewide race, that had little meaning.

Having served in some capacity with all of the governors from George White in the early 1930s through Richard Celeste in the 1980s, I had a good look at all of them and did some state business with each.

White, who was from Marietta, had been national party chairman during James M. Cox's campaign for the presidency in 1920. He was governor when I first went to the Statehouse in 1935, but I came to know him more intimately after he left office. White's career began in the Klondike gold rush and he carried to the end of his life a certain gruffness acquired during his prospecting days.

White was succeeded by Martin L. Davey of Kent, who had served as congressman from the Akron district. Coming into office in the midst of the Great Depression, Davey had a sympathetic mind and effectively found ways to help suffering Ohioans with jobs and relief programs previously not regarded as any of the state's business.

Republican John W. Bricker won the governorship in 1938 over Charles Sawyer, who had beaten Davey in the Democratic primary that followed the Little Steel Strike. Bricker always impressed people as very sincere. I treasure a note from him that showed him a man of considerable structure. At a crowded gathering I had attended, he made, in jest, some unflattering remark about my being a Democrat. His letter was an unnecessary apology, but it showed him a big enough man to have respect for little people.

Frank J. Lausche, who had been mayor of Cleveland, was elected to his first term in 1944. He lost his bid for re-election in 1946 to Thomas Herbert, also from Cleveland, who had been state attorney general. A wounded veteran from World War I, Herbert served only one term. He was a family friend, and when I was a youngster he visited our home to hunt rabbits on the farm with my brother, Lamar, who was Herbert's fraternity brother in law school.

Beginning with the 1948 election, Lausche came back for three terms. His long years as governor made him into something of an Ohio institution. It was a period of general prosperity, and he presided over the state with uncommon common sense.

Lausche and his family lived in very down-to-earth means in the old state mansion on Broad Street which, in the beginning of his term, had draperies that had become ragged with age. Only minimum improvements, however, were made at the mansion, and it was staffed with trusties from the penitentiary. Dressed in a bathrobe and ancient-looking slippers, Lausche often had an early breakfast with some state worker with whom he wished to confer; scrambled eggs and orange juice was the usual fare. He never seemed to be a very partisan governor, and his voter support crossed party lines. Indeed, quite a few leading Ohio Republicans always looked with favor on Democrat Lausche, and in 1956, he was elected U.S. senator.

C. William O'Neill, a Republican, was elected to replace Lausche. O'Neill came up the political path from Washington County as a state representative, speaker of the house and state attorney general, and ended his career as chief justice of the Ohio Supreme Court. O'Neill, too, had a non-partisan twist and numbered among his close friends and supporters none other than Youngstown's George Glaros, then one of the leading Democrats in Mahoning County.

Michael V. DiSalle, who had been mayor of Toledo, was elected governor in 1958 and served a four-year term. But by 1962, Republican winds were beginning to blow and DiSalle lost some of his political clout as a result of a remark indicating he didn't care much for fairs, including the state fair. Republican James A. Rhodes, who had been mayor of Columbus and state auditor, defeated DiSalle and began the longest tenure any Ohioan has ever had in the governorship.

Rhodes served two four-year terms, sat out a term — Democrat John J. Gilligan was elected in 1970 — then came back again in 1974 for two more four-year terms. His accomplishments were mainly in the field of education. Rhodes expanded the number of state universities, including Youngstown College which evolved into Youngstown State University, and built other institutions to bring the opportunity for a college education physically near residents anywhere in the state.

Ohio was always first in Rhodes' mind and he had capable people in responsible state jobs work diligently with him. His years were good years for Ohio businesses, whose expansions he eagerly promoted.

The governor who followed Rhodes was Richard Celeste, a Democrat

July 4, 1976; the nation celebrates its 200th birthday and area residents attend a ball. From the left: Harriet Wick Schaff, vice chairman of the Mahoning-Youngstown Bicentennial Commission; Anne Hulme; Susan Jackson Ehas; Pattie Alessi, ball chairman; and the commission chairman.

who was elected to the position in 1983 after serving as lieutenant governor and with the Peace Corps. He was the last governor for whom I served somewhere in state government activities and, like many who preceded him, at one time Celeste had his eye on national office.

Many Americans would like to at least take a squint at becoming president of the United States. In my youth, I heard old-timers talk of seeing Lincoln and some even meeting him. There were also those in my family who had known Grant, Garfield, Hayes, McKinley and Taft.

My first taste of seeing someone who represented the entire nation came as a little boy when my father took me to see Vice President Thomas Marshall, who was speaking at the Youngstown YMCA. Marshall is remembered as the man who advised, "What America needs is a good five-cent cigar."

Years later, as a teenager, I sat all night by the railroad tracks below Lowellville until President Harding's funeral train went by. It was draped in black with the honor guards of the American military standing by his casket; through the large window of the railroad car, we could see their somber faces as the train took this Buckeye State president to his hometown of Marion.

From Hoover through Reagan, as a nosey reporter I had an opportunity to talk with every president. I first saw Hoover as he passed through Lowellville in 1932 and waved to a group of us assembled near the railroad tracks. Decades later at a national convention of the Republican Party, I sat immediately opposite Hoover during a press conference. He impressed me as a solid man.

The first time I saw Franklin Roosevelt was in 1936, when he was in the full flowering of his New Deal and running for re-election; in those days, it was easy to get caught up in his enthusiasm for getting America going again.

After Harry Truman became president, he reminded me of the incident at the Chicago convention when I helped him move the hotel bed to make room for a picture to be taken of his family. Truman's strut was straight out of the Missouri and Kansas border with a manhood that was the product of the rebirth of the nation in the Civil War period and the battle to make Kansas a free state. Truman always knew where he was stepping. Once I saw him come out of a side door at a hotel in Washington with Mrs. Truman. She tried to have him turn to the left to go down the hall, but he turned right.

"I told you," he said, as a reception group came from that direction to enfold him.

President Eisenhower had a soldier's stature. Clasping my hand shortly after he was nominated for president, I could tell he was still

Jimmy Carter, campaigning for the presidential nomination, arrives at Youngstown Municipal Airport. On hand to greet him is local coordinator Edward A. Cox, now an appellate court judge.

a soldier; his grasp was like that of officers commanding American regiments. The impression Ike made came not from his words but rather from his bearing.

When 1960 came, the man who would be elected president was already known to me. I first met John Kennedy at Congressman Kirwan's St. Patrick's Day party in Washington, where he asked me to send him some information about the poll I was taking. I did, and he responded with a letter.

The death of this energetic young president hit me pretty hard. He was so much alive — so much in charge — it seemed to me when I was around him, such as on various occasions when he visited Youngstown.

Lyndon Johnson was a very approachable man, but one never was quite sure he knew you were there. The tale he liked to tell the most was about George Washington's family moving to Texas, where they lived in a little hut near a mesquite tree. When George's father came home one day and saw the tree had been cut down, he asked his son who was responsible. "I cannot tell a lie, I cut down the tree," young George replied, to which his father said, "We are moving back to Virginia — Texas is no place for you."

Once, during a meeting with Johnson and Kirwan that I attended, the talk concerned what the CIO was doing politically. Johnson's will to cast events in the direction he wanted them to go was very apparent; later, as the conflict in Vietnam escalated, that would be his downfall.

I also met Richard Nixon at one of Kirwan's St. Patrick's Day affairs. He, too, was interested in polls. Years later, I was invited by Congressman David Dennison to a formal party for Nixon and his new cabinet. It was a small crowd, consisting largely of congressmen who first came to Washington with Nixon in the 1946 election, and there was an opportunity to talk with Nixon at length.

My contact with President Ford was much more limited, although I had observed him at various party affairs and had talked to him before he became president.

Like Truman, Jimmy Carter struck me as down-to-earth. His last visit to Youngstown was just before his loss to Ronald Reagan, when he conducted what he called a "town meeting."

Reagan lectured in Youngstown before he won the nomination, and I interviewed him across the table at Stambaugh Auditorium. I had met him and observed him at national conventions, but I never had a better squint at Reagan than had been my privilege following his lecture.

As I grew older, some of the younger members of the newspaper's staff used to ask me about Grover Cleveland. I never met Grover, but I usually answered them with something about his presidential campaign that I had heard from my father.

A reporter has the opportunity to meet a lot of important people, and one of the most important Hollywood figures I met was Rin Tin Tin, the photogenic canine. He walked into the office one day and came right up to my old desk beside the cuspidor and stuck his snout under my arm. I petted him until his trainer came in and had Rin Tin Tin perform tricks. Soon after, he died. *The Vindicator* published the last "interview" with Rin Tin Tin, and the story was picked up by various publications across the country.

I also had the opportunity to see Haile Selassie, ruler of Ethiopia, and General Charles DeGaulle, president of France, as they passed in the Kennedy funeral march. Most striking, however, was Black Jack, the riderless horse that followed Kennedy's bier.

It was equally impressive to see Pope John pass by me within a hand's breadth. But it did disturb me, as it would many thoughtful observers, when I saw pigeons sitting around the feet of the Moses statue in St. Peter's Basilica, directly above where the pope sat.

This scene reminded me of House Speaker Sam Rayburn when he was presiding at the 1948 Democratic Convention in Philadelphia and became aware of the doves that had been released and flew above him. Rayburn was a very human man. He told me that as a boy growing up in Texas, his mother would permit him and his brother to walk five miles to a road on Sundays so they could see someone go by.

When I was riding with Rayburn during one of his visits to Youngstown, I listed for him all the fine things about the city. Perhaps overcome by the boasting, he slapped me on the leg and laughed, "There's no place like home."

Reflection brings memory not only of good days and bad days but also of spots in life where performance has not been adequate. To be happy, however, it is necessary to insulate in the mind a pleasant ability to quickly pass over such incidents that return again.

Once while visiting Washington, D.C., my wife and I joined Congressman Kirwan; Kenneth M. Lloyd, executive secretary of the Mahoning Valley Industrial Council; Charles Cushwa Jr., then president of Commercial Shearing and Stamping Company (now Commercial Intertech); and their wives at a banquet honoring President Truman. Guests at the affair were allowed to shake the president's hand.

"I have heard of your good work," Truman said to me when I clasped his hand.

He apparently was referring to my 1948 poll, which urged citizens to watch the vote on states that bordered the Ohio River where Truman overcame Dewey. This experience and others add up to an admonition to all striving young men and women to take as truth any flattering remarks that come from politicians in high places.

At another dinner in Washington, when I was walking behind the speakers' table in a news quest, Chief Justice Earl Warren put his hands on my shoulder and said, "I never met a man before who does so many different things so well."

The chief justice had never met me; someone had informed him who I was, and his long experience in the political field had instilled the ability to find the right words to make me feel good. I never had too high an esteem for the chief justice, but after that encounter, I did.

My luckiest experience is also part of my memories. Deemed a minority member of the Ohio Senate Finance Committee, the question arose as to the total state income from the sales tax, which had been enacted in 1935. No one seemed to know the answer, including the state finance director. I was able to speak up and relate in round numbers the total sales tax revenue for each year since the law's enactment. The day before, I had written a story on the subject for the newspaper and had already done the research. Of course, I made no mention of this to the committee and, as sometimes happens, the members thought I was wiser than I am.

One of my proudest moments similarly comes to mind. During World War II, I arrived at the Columbus railroad station to find the waiting room filled and the trains running hours late. While awaiting my departure, a young lady about ten-years-old walked through the aisles and stared at everybody who was seated. Finally, she walked up to me, said she was in trouble and didn't know what to do to get to her destination. Taking her in hand, I made arrangements with the railroad to send her on her way. It always pleased me that she had looked everybody over and picked me to trust out of all of those strangers.

During the war, I was one of three Youngstown men chosen to go to Ohio State University in Columbus for civil defense training. Since I had taken some chemistry courses in college, I was assigned to specialize in chemical warfare and poison gas defense, and subsequently instructed a local group on what to do should there be an invasion. The entire civil defense system here, including in the event of an air raid, was developed by Youngstown citizens. Fearing destruction of the steel mills, which contributed much to the Allied effort, inspections were made to find out who was showing any light. Gradually, as the war went on and the U.S. was in a better position, we felt safer.

Shortly after the American declaration of war, Kirwan told me he had learned a German submarine was laying right off the Miami shore and the U.S. had nothing with which to destroy it or force it away —

so short had been American preparations for war.

Some months before Pearl Harbor, the government contracted with a Youngstown engineering firm to make special equipment for the U.S. Navy. But as of November 1941, the company was quite a few months behind schedule. I walked through the assembly line in March 1942, three months after Japan's surprise bombing, and the company was two months ahead of schedule — so much did the threat of Pearl Harbor enliven the thrust of American workmen and management to achieve what was necessary to defend the Republic.

A fact that comes to an old man who remembers the spreading bodies of Americans on the islands of the Pacific and other locations of the war is that no one should be fooled by any current promises of peace. Twice, in the first world war and in the second world war, the U.S. was caught with its "dukes" down; defense ability was at a very low ebb. Both times the great sheets of water that separate the American continent from the rest of the world served as a buffer and gave time for the development of the war might of America. The third time, given the diminishing distances on earth, there may not be time for such preparation.

As one of the world's greatest historians said, "The bloodiest wars are always preceded by the most earnest protestations of peace."

Looking to the future rather than the past has long been deemed part of wisdom. Nevertheless, it is from experience and by recording happenings and trends that prophetic minds have been able to forecast much of what is to come.

After going through the age of encountering the forests, establishing widespread farms and grazing areas, passing into and through an iron-making period with a lot of bustling as railroads and steam engines arrived, the age of steel came to Youngstown in the 1890s, marking the first century of its known history. Through two world wars, steel flowed in a fearful mass from the mills and continued to do so for a time during the long period of peace and prosperity that followed.

By the city's second hundred years, the 1990s, the age of steel had pretty much passed from this section of the land. Youngstown, perhaps more than any other Ohio city, has been victimized by the rust that has afflicted many plants in the Midwest as world economic balances changed with the remarkable industrial comebacks of Germany and Japan. Now there is a stirring to provide employment in other directions. A new age is dawning here, and looking around the Valley, many promising developments can be seen.

The area has plentiful rainfall, good flood control and an abundance of water for industrial purposes. There are dozens of small industrial enterprises cropping up, some in simple buildings with a relatively small number of workers, in spots where tree growth is recapturing the landscape. And while Youngstown's population has dropped sharply, in general the population has not walked away from this district but rather has spread into the recesses of the countryside. Homes, many of them quite majestic in size and style, have been built in the suburbs, and there is no absence of collections of small and orderly houses of a more moderate character for the population flung outward from the central city.

The biggest resource here is the people, and they represent superior strains of mankind, a situation that isn't talked about much anymore. Indeed, this district has something important to tell about the very nature of Americans and America in coming generations. This is true because of its unique experience with the people who came to settle in this section of North America during the last 200 years.

It opened first to trappers seeking furs along the rivers and streams; but with the sale of its townships by the state of Connecticut, farmers and woodcutters came in, principally from Pennsylvania, New York and some New England states. In the nineteenth century, it became a rich farming area and villages grew up at many crossroads together with some commerce.

With the opening of the canal in 1839, the middle of the nineteenth century brought the coal mines, the manufacturing of iron and then the coming of the rail transportation immediately before the Civil War; the forces of the industrial revolution had been implanted. The war itself brought a boom in iron production; and Tod's furnaces at Youngstown and Brier Hill, as well as other iron enterprises in the Mahoning Valley, raised pig iron production to a high level. In 1891, the first steel plant came.

Beginning in the 1830s, new people arrived: Scotch, English and Welsh added somewhat to the already-here mixture of Scotch-Irish, Pennsylvania-Dutch and Yankee. The Germans came in considerable numbers late in the nineteenth century and into the twentieth century; and with the steel mills arising, thousands were recruited from eastern European lands.

With World War I, there came to be colonies numbering into the thousands of Slovaks, Hungarians, Poles, Italians and Croatians. These populations were so great that Italy and other nations had consular representations in Youngstown, and immigrants read foreign-language newspapers. Near the end of the first world war, many blacks came from the South to work in the mills. Following World War II, many from Spanish-speaking countries also came here.

Mingling of cultures and peoples of different beliefs actually began with the first settlements in this section of the country. Daniel Shehy,

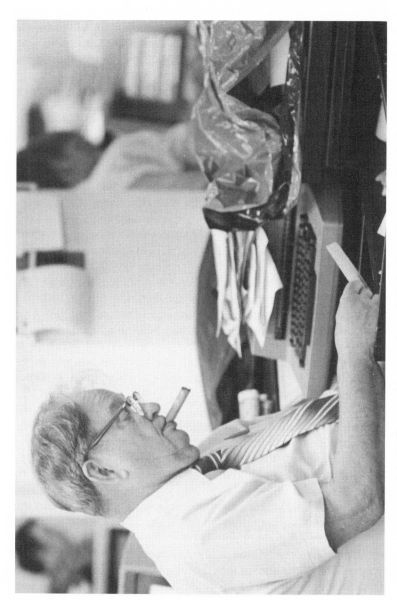

July 1983 — retirement; the political editor cleans out his desk.

who like John Young and Colonel James Hillman was a first settler of Youngstown, was a Roman Catholic while his wife was one who drew her religious inspiration from John Calvin.

As more settlers came in the nineteenth and into the twentieth century, churches of all sorts arose: Welsh, German, Italian, Irish, African, Hungarian, Polish, Croatian, Slovak, Russian, Romanian and others in the Christian tradition. Jewish temples were similarly established.

The towns were small enough, including Youngstown, that these congregations mingled. It is somewhat rare to find a Mahoning County family that doesn't have some inclusion from a foreign "tribe." What an American will look like 100 years from now is unknown, but the mix has occurred here early, and looking about one can get a predictive view.

In one of his famous stories, O. Henry tells about being "out West" at Youngstown. Then, it was a stopping place for many on their way further west. Some western Ohio counties have families whose ancestors made short hops from the Youngstown area. Stopping to talk to an aged woman in western Kansas, she told me she had heard of Youngstown and thought it was near Canfield. This woman had come by wagon across the country as a small girl from Canfield, when it was the county seat and the center of law in this region.

Over the years, some of those whose youth was spent among the trees which cluttered this maple, oak, beech and walnut wilderness that once held sway went on to great national distinction. Two of the region's congressmen became presidents of the United States, Garfield and McKinley. Ernest Moore, whose origin was in what is now Campbell, was a founder of the University of California at Los Angeles. And Julian Kennedy, whose family ties went back to a home along Dry Run Creek, became president of U.S. Steel when it was the top corporation in America. In almost every field of endeavor, including sports, this district has furnished its share of the great.

There is a reason this has happened. At the conclusion of his famous Shenandoah Valley campaign, regarded as one of the greatest feats in military history, Stonewall Jackson reportedly looked through a glass and saw Union troops marching at a distance. "With such men, this war will not be easy," he warned.

The men were regiments from the Western Reserve of Ohio, the inhabitants of the farms and other parcels sold by the Connecticut Land Company.

Still, like the U.S. Marines, the need for a robust community or city often is for a few good men — hopefully, more than just a few — as well as good land and good climate. All that is needed here is good government, and that means not too much of it.

The universally most difficult accomplishment is good government. It can't be said that government is all bad; it is, after all, one of the criminal creations the human race has never been able to escape and, yet it has some redeeming qualities.

A principal governmental problem afflicting this district comes from the overabundance of local governments, making for a patchwork instead of one efficient operation. Some of the incapacities such patchwork of governments bring have been overcome by cooperation among the separate entities and the setting up of special districts. Even so, it is insufficient compensation.

Part of the trouble is that the mother of all the inner districting — state government — hasn't done its job in modernizing local government. Some things seem to be dead wrong, such as the fact the villages of Poland and Canfield are municipalities and must be under the law, while Boardman and Austintown remain as townships since their citizens never established village government even though the townships are near the population of Warren, one of Ohio's venerable cities. Just maybe, perhaps in the next 100 years, Ohio government will implement some radical changes in the district divisions within the state. Nowhere is this more needed than in the Youngstown district, which has entity after entity competing against one another along the Mahoning River and among bedroom communities, all of which should be part of cities with municipal responsibilities.

There was something of a snugness in downtown Youngstown in the old days. The clanging of streetcars bringing in the crowds of shoppers signaled the bustling that once stirred the downtown mornings, afternoons and evenings. Then there were five or six theaters with movies showing until near midnight. One could see a couple of shows after work, stop at one of a half dozen good eating places, have a bite, go home on a streetcar and arrive before midnight. The more ribald may remember the Princess Theater, which featured dancing girls — sometimes to the extent of bringing words of condemnation from puritan mouths. It was a time when the downtown provided everything for the sacred and the profane.

The Mahoning County Courthouse, which now has only one church — the old Trinity Methodist — at its back, once looked out its front toward Christian and Presbyterian churches across Market Street and a Baptist church across Boardman Street. Wood Street was also lined with churches; some moved further out with the elimination of the Erie grade crossing. Downtown churches were needed in those days, if for no other reason than to offset brothels and gambling — the sinning that went on along Boardman and Front streets and, for that matter, reached over the hill to Wood Street, where the old First Presbyterian Church and St. Columba Cathedral still hold sway.

Less than a century ago in the old Central Square stood the original stone Man on the Monument, while the Maid on the Fountain reigned on the other side of the Diamond near the library that came to be there for a time as the march of progress began, beginning with the removal of the cannons and the tragedy some will remember when the stone Civil War soldier fell off his perch and broke. Eventually his replacement arrived, and the wags claimed it was one of Garibaldi's men, made by Italian workmen. Nevertheless, a Man on the Monument is still there, albeit in the rearranged square and not as conspicuous as he once was.

Today it takes a moonlit night and imagination in the deep silence of the waning hours when the downtown is almost uninhabited to again see and hear the noises of streetcars or the trolley buses that succeeded them in Central Square, and to remember how the pigeons once flitted about on the cannons that two American presidents helped place there as testimony to area men who went to battle in the civil strife. Although Central Square is now much changed, it has a past; and one can even smell that past if he lets his mood wander in the dead of the night. And even though Youngstown, once a thriving city with a population of 185,000, has fallen below the 100,000-population class, this should not lead to despair.

By the time the twenty-first century arrives, the Mahoning River will be framed with green and will carry purer water. The vacated farmlands about the city will be overgrown with trees, improving the landscape, and the spreading population from the city and the semi-rural households now being developed will lend a more princely atmosphere to the district. While the city now has unoccupied land as the result of the dismantling of old industrial structures and houses, this vacancy — like that of the vacated farm lands about the city — will be filled as the years pass. There will also be more trees downtown; already Youngstown has become a more scenic place than it once was.

A large part of the economic future will depend on making the central city a comfortable place for enterprises of all kinds to do business. Both the downtown and the outstretched business districts have encumbrances to development that must be overcome, but the human resource remains strong. Prosperity is associated with people who use their heads and develop good political sense. Indeed, Youngstown will become a more pleasant place than it has ever been, provided it has the leadership it deserves. And for that, much depends on the people taking seriously their responsibilities as citizens.

EXTRA

CLINGAN'S

By CLINGAN JACKSON

Youngstown/Warren Business Journal, September 1990

With all the talk about the environment, concern should also be expressed about what the Americans have recently been doing to the English language. It seems more and more like the gutter is taking it over. Words and statements keep cropping up in literature and on the airwaves that were seldom heard in ages past except, perhaps, in red-light districts.

There is no charm in such talk and anything that is needed to be said can be accounted in gentlemen terms. With all the efforts that are being made to eliminate disease and to make all women into lovely creatures by means of special diets, shouldn't attention be given to what flows from the tongues of men and women?

Congress, too, gets into the act. It isn't just bad words, it's bad ideas that get on the airwaves. Too many congressmen spend too much energy trying to get their faces and blasphemic remarks over the lines of communications so that voters will believe they are doing something in Washington rather than just having a good time.

It might be a good thing if voters would learn to have deep respect for their congressman if they simply didn't hear anything about him. It might be that he was really working diligently to do something really good for the country. Accomplishments usually come from quiet performances. Unfortunately, the crowd normally is attracted by the loudest noise; citizens seem to run in the direction of noise just as they do when they see a fire. Articulation can be a means for deeper pollution than even the chemical industry can achieve and, perhaps, a dump in your backyard.

Words can pollute the soul and most of us leave a considerable track behind us of remarks which, in afterthought, we wished we had only kept our mouths shut.

On reflection, as age sinks in, one can scarcely remember ever getting into trouble by not saying anything. That's probably the reason that animals get along with each other better than humans. Most of them don't talk very much. The ones that do, don't get along well. Ever get rid of a dog that barked too much?

Occasionally, when politicans get to talking over the airwaves from Washington or even from a county courthouse, it comes to mind that they are really barking dogs and should be gotten rid of.

The public is wrong also, for many have come to regard politicians as dogs with their purpose only to retrieve something for themselves rather than doing something for their country.

Presidents, with the aid of speech writers, come up with the highest purposes for mankind in their words. These words usually don't sink in very well, and men and television return to carping ways.

Come to think of it, what have these words just expressed been but trivia? Nevertheless, there needs to be a case of curbing the pollution of the English language and that curbing doesn't mean getting grammar or punctuation right but clearing up the ideas expressed in words to remarks befitting a civilized people talking to and about one another.

More and more, what is needed in America is an understanding that the other guy with ideas unlike yours may be equally devoted to high purpose. The trouble often in human society is that a group or tribe gets centered on its high purpose and then seeks to inflict it on others.

The pollution needs to be eliminated but it is equally urgent that the inhabitants of earth clean up their tongues and their ideas with respect for all.

EXTRA

CHRONICLES

Youngstown/Warren Business Journal, September 1991

District residents keep an eye on what's going on about this earth as well as or better than residents in other sections of the United States, and this keen attention has an impact on presidential preferences.

With this region's very mixed ethnic population of Americans who have ancestral homes and perhaps even childhood homes in different European countries, one doesn't have to look far to find local citizens who have personal feelings about the subdivisions of the Soviet Union which are now going through a period of dramatic changes, sometimes amidst a frightful balance in human relations.

As all the turmoil unfolds, national Democratic Party leaders are talking a great deal about making domestic programs the center of their efforts to defeat President Bush in the 1992 presidential election. In so doing, they seem to grant the Republican president a rather full place in international affairs, which have much engaged the nation in recent months and through most of the Bush administration.

Many political leaders believe the only issue Americans are really concerned about is the domestic program, yet this is rather far from the truth. Past elections have shown that Mahoning County voters take foreign affairs very much into consideration during presidential elections. For example, voters in this heavily Democratic region quickly swung to back President Eisenhower during the Suez crisis, which occurred shortly before the 1956 election. Indeed, in voting for president Americans make their decisions based on foreign issues affecting the nation as much as, if not more than, on purely domestic questions. The flag begins to wave and if the voter has any dreams in his life about the welfare of humanity, he is likely to want a master for the house with a wide vision and hope for all men.

By contrast, when citizens vote on congressional candidates, they are often thinking about what they can get out of Washington. Many haven't learned that whatever you get out of Capitol Hill must be considerably less than what you or some of your neighbors put into it.

Under such conditions, it is no mystery that the president and Congress often seem to be floating in different ways, even when one party has control in both the legislative and executive branches.

In fact, it is an illusion to believe there is much difference between domestic problems and international questions. The world is tied together as evidenced by oil, which led us into the Persian Gulf war.

Foreign policy has much to do with prosperity in the United States and, as years go on, developments indicate we will be more and more affected locally by what goes on abroad.

When a president is chosen next year, there will be thousands of voters living in this region who will decide their presidential votes on the basis of what Bush has done in relation to some far-off land — the home of their ancestors or the home of their childhood. Such thoughts still run deeply in many Americans, most all of whom know what faraway place was home to those in their family who first came to America.

Susan and Maryann Jackson; both walked into my heart.

CHAPTER **12**

MY THREE WIVES

ood fortune is a necessary element of most any man's success, and mine was having three farm girls for wives.

My first wife was Virginia Fenton, my high-school sweetheart. She grew up on a Poland Township dairy farm north of Lowellville and was a member of the Fenton family, which achieved some prominence in American history. Her uncle, General Chauncey Fenton, served on General John J. Pershing's staff during the first world war; he later headed the mathematics department at West Point and served as president of the West Point Association.

One day, while walking with her brother, Chester, at lunchtime in downtown Lowellville, we were inspecting the new freshman girls who had come to the high school. I pointed to one, and told Chester she was the girl I was going to marry. I didn't know that girl was his sister.

Sometime afterward, I persuaded Chester to invite me to the Fenton home for dinner; after school we walked together across the fields and reached a wire fence. It was there that Chester demonstrated his athletic ability by jumping the fence. Not to be outshone, and wanting to make an impression, I proceeded to hop the same fence, but the barbed wire caught the seat of my britches and tore a wide opening. So it was that my first meeting with my future wife included having her mother sew my pants.

Virginia and I seemed to have a natural affinity; she won my attention throughout the last two years of high school and held it through my years in college, particularly in the summer when I was home for vacation. She had long blonde hair which was usually curled, and a favorite horse that she always rode. Once when we had a spat, she rode some five miles through the rather desolate reaches of eastern Mahoning County, across the state line to where I lived in Carbon. It was a gesture of making-up. My mother invited her to have dinner with us, which she did, then later rode her horse home.

Virginia graduated from Lowellville High School in 1927, and entered Kent State University for teachers' training. By the time I graduated from college in 1929, she was employed as a teacher at Lowellville School.

From my very first meeting with her, my decision at first sight was confirmed. I was 16 years old then and she was 14, and I always thought she would become my wife. I had other girlfriends and Virginia had other boyfriends, and there were a few occasions when she may have had other notions. This was an era when having a girlfriend didn't mean you were sleeping with her, as it too often does today. We would hold hands while her father would be nearby, reading the newspaper.

A date might include a hayride or a sled ride drawn by horses. Once I got Virginia in trouble with her mother when we went for a sled ride through eastern Poland Township and into Pennsylvania, across Coffee Run, a tributary of the Mahoning River, to a stately old house. The lady who lived there served our group hot chocolate in front of the fireplace. Upon returning home, Virginia's mother reprimanded her when she learned that we had visited a "regioner," a term for people living on the Pennsylvania side of Coffee Run who in the Civil War had sympathized with the Confederacy. This happened some sixty years after the Civil War, proving sentiment dies hard.

After graduation from college, we were split up for a while — her mother, I think, had other ideas for Virginia including, I'm pretty sure, an itinerant preacher — but by 1932 we had arranged our wedding. It took place in June of that year in the living room of the Fenton home. Neighbors had provided the flowers, and we stood in front of an arch of flowers as Virginia's uncle, Reverend Barnes of New Castle, Pennsylvania, married us.

We had a wedding party dinner at the McFarland home in nearby Erskine Quarry, a residence that provided a convenient place for small gatherings. During the Great Depression, many homes were opened to the public for various functions which would bring in cash, a primary need by families trying to sustain themselves in those days.

We took off from the McFarland home for our wedding trip and headed for her brother's home in Monroe, Michigan. Ray Fenton was an engineer, who was building a rolling mill there for the Newton Steel Company.

Our first stop was Cleveland. When we arrived at the hotel and jumped from my Plymouth car, rice flew all over the garage as hotel employees whistled and applauded. They thought it was exciting to have honeymooners staying at the hotel; we were embarrassed.

From Cleveland we drove to Monroe. We had a key to her brother's home and entered the house. Night had come, and Virginia and I were just settling down when the neighbors came to see who had invaded the premises, and we had to explain who and why we were there.

Virginia's brother came home the next day, and the three of us visited Bell Island Park in Detroit; I remember little of the entertainment, being mostly fascinated with my new wife. The following day we returned home and I resumed my work at the newspaper. Virginia was on summer vacation from school.

Shortly thereafter, we rented a house at 277 Walnut Street in Lowellville for $18 a month, about one-fourth of my monthly salary. We furnished it with an old radio a friend of mine sold me for $10, some furniture that was no longer needed in our parents' homes, and a few pieces we contracted to pay for at a furniture store which had been damaged in a fire. Our "new" furniture had a smoky "flavor," and the odor lasted for many months, if not years.

It was a time when one prepared for winter very carefully. One fall day, I came home and found Virginia sitting in the kitchen with four bushels of peaches she had purchased for twenty-five cents a bushel. She canned them and we ate peaches for quite a long time.

Grapes ripened on a vine behind our house. Her brother and I put them in two-quart bottles in a routine which was supposed to make wine. All this fruit and wine, and any other vegetable that could be canned, was put in the cellar storage area to give us something to eat in the Depression winter.

This grape juice was to show up many years later when my mother lived alone in the house. Entertaining the women's association of the

Virginia Fenton Jackson

Lowellville Presbyterian Church, she thought the two-quart bottles contained grape juice and served it to the ladies, all of whom seemed to enjoy the taste. When she showed me what she had served, I sampled some and well knew it was high-grade wine. My mother had been a prohibitionist, as had the ladies, but she also had a sense of humor and commented that the grape juice made her feel pretty good.

Virginia taught school for a short time after we were married, but in those hard times, the policy of school boards generally was not to employ any married teachers unless they could show their husband was unable to work. She lost her job and never taught again.

A little more than a year later, when Virginia was visiting her parents' farm, she ran by the barn and stepped on a wheat stubble. The jag from the stubble lodged in her foot, and although it seemed to be superficial, it pained her. On the very day it occurred, I took her to the doctor, who prescribed some remedy. The following day, while she was still sleeping, I went to work early; but shortly after I arrived, I received a telephone call from her brother who had stopped by the house.

He reported Virginia was quite ill; I phoned for the doctor and hurried home. By the time I got there, arrangements had been made to transport Virginia by ambulance to North Side Hospital in Youngstown. We rode together in the ambulance, and once we arrived at the hospital, it was a bitter fight from the start — a tragic case of too-limited application of the medical knowledge needed to prevent tetanus from developing. In an effort to save Virginia, pharmaceutical supplies were flown from Philadelphia to Youngstown, but to no avail. Her death came in November 1933, and her funeral at the Lowellville Presbyterian Church attracted so many people some were unable to get near the church.

She was buried high above the village in the Poland Township Cemetery at Lowellville. The snowflakes of fall were falling; and from then on a part of me has resided there.

The shock was severe, but when tragedy strikes, one has to make up his mind that he has to go on living. I had just won election to the Lowellville Village Council, so I decided to stay in Lowellville rather than return to Carbon and my parents' home. A friend and her husband moved in with me and she kept house.

By that time, I had begun attending Democratic Party gatherings in Youngstown and Lowellville. My father had been a staunch Democrat as had his father and, about 1934, I was elected president of the Mahoning County Democratic Club. It was an active organization and, with the ferment of FDR's New Deal, a tremendous number of people were involved in politics throughout the 1930s. All you had to do was put out a sandwich or two and you could attract a crowd.

Being a councilman in Lowellville, mixing daily among people in town, I picked up every odd piece of news about any family in the area. Soon most of the town's residents would buy *The Vindicator* instead of *The Telegram*, which had been the leading newspaper in Lowellville until that time.

An incident that comes to mind is the plight of a fellow from Lowellville who had a flat tire on Gate's Hill back in 1915. He was coming down that same hill one day in 1934, and had another flat tire. When he had the first flat, he lost the keys to his car and had difficulty making arrangements to move it. As he fixed his tire in 1934, he found the key he had lost nineteen years earlier. Oddball stories such as this interested readers. Reporters from the rival newspapers were hunting for every scrap of news — anything to get another subscriber.

It was this type of activity that helped me overcome my melancholy following Virginia's death and, a few months later, the sudden death of my father. About the same time, I became a candidate for state representative, and won the Democratic nomination and the general election. From then on, I was absorbed in politics.

As a nominee for state representative, I joined party candidates in meeting with John Farrell, the Mahoning County Democratic Party chairman, for a victory dinner at the Hotel Ohio. The chairman presided as one of the waitresses, a rather comely blonde, came to serve me. He suggested, pointing to me, that there was a man for her.

"Oh, I know him. He was going to take me to the South Sea Islands," she replied.

The woman was telling the truth. She had frequently served me and other reporters at the hotel's old Purple Cow Restaurant. We took to teasing her a little as we had coffee and donuts in the morning.

I never saw this woman again until forty years later, when she walked up to me at another restaurant and reminded me how she had once served me and my colleagues at the Purple Cow.

A friend of mine was Charles Bannon, secretary of the Mahoning County Democratic Party and father of the Mahoning County Common Pleas Court judge by the same name. Eventually, he suggested that I meet a lady he knew. We arranged for a Sunday afternoon of mostly driving about.

I saw her before I was introduced. She was a brunette, and was sitting on a porch swing at her home on the South Side of Youngstown, dressed in yellow. I thought then that maybe Thelma Rex Pabst was the woman I would marry. Being regarded at this point as an eligible male, I had already been introduced to several young women.

Although she was born on a farm in Ashtabula County near Orwell, most of her early years were spent in Youngstown. Her father operated a butcher shop in a market; her mother died in the Spanish flu epidemic of 1919. Although her father remarried, Thelma never accepted her stepmother.

She entered Hall's Business College and supported herself almost from the time her father remarried. Trained as a secretary and bookkeeper, she worked several different jobs before her marriage to Russell Pabst. After their divorce, she became a secretary at Mill Creek Park and kept the books for the park commissioner.

I never knew much about her first husband. "Billy," as she was always known rather than Thelma, never talked much about him. His family was closely related to the Pabst family of brewery fame — first cousins, I believe. When she moved into my home after our marriage, there was some evidence of rather sumptuous past living. Billy brought with her a full set of original Haviland china, which she never took out of the barrel during our marriage. Since her death, it has been appraised at more than $6,000.

I did learn that Billy and her first husband owned a duplex on the city's South Side, and she never received anything from him in the way of alimony. To make ends meet during the Depression, she related she had sold an expensive diamond ring, probably a gift from her former husband.

Billy was a woman who had only a few friends, yet each of them was close. When I knew her, she lived with her girlfriend, Mary Batteiger, and her mother, whom we always called Aunt Camille.

Aunt Camille had been a close collaborator of Eugene Debs. Her husband was Pete Midney, who had been a leading Youngstown Socialist. When I knew her, Pete had been deceased for many years. She gave me a few of Debs' books that were marked with his own notes. I still have those books, and they have some historical value.

After a year of courting, Billy and I were married in July 1935. Our honeymoon was spent in Columbus — the General Assembly was in session — and my colleagues saw to it that a spotlight was focused on my new bride as she sat in the gallery. The *Columbus Dispatch* carried her picture on the front page. As part of our wedding trip, we also went to Nashville and visited The Hermitage, the home of President Andrew Jackson. Then we returned home to Lowellville and housekeeping. We were together for forty-five years and reared two daughters, both of whom we adopted as infants.

Eventually we moved from Lowellville to a home we had constructed on land I inherited from my father, part of the farm on which I was born. It was closer to my employment in Youngstown, we reasoned; I had the land plus $1,800 from my father's estate.

Thelma Rex Jackson

As the German army moved into Poland in 1939, word of the invasion came over the telegraph wire at the newspaper. That night, I went home to Lowellville and told my wife the U.S. would soon be in the war and if we were ever to have our own home, we had better build it now. I had a cellar dug, and then needed another $4,000, in addition to the $1,800 I had inherited, to build the house. Banks were not eager to loan money to me, but with the aid of some friends, I finally secured a mortgage. Interestingly, in 1942, just two years after the house was constructed, I was offered more than four times what I had invested — so much does war tend to increase the demand and price of housing. Even so, I didn't want to sell because then I would have had to buy another house and, after all, the old family homestead held a deep significance for me.

The big events in my second marriage were the arrivals of our two children. Our eldest child, Susan, came while we were still living in Lowellville. She was passed to me on a bridge in Youngstown by the Children's Services people. I carried her into the house — one of my proudest moments — and soon she walked into my heart. My wife had the same reaction.

Susan always made us proud and did very well in school. As a senior at Miami University of Ohio, she was named to the dean's list. She became a schoolteacher and has taught school in Boardman, Berea, Oklahoma, Youngstown, Connecticut and now in Twinsburg, Ohio. Her husband has served in the Army as well as in civilian jobs dealing with labor relations and personnel at various locations.

Susan lived at home while teaching at Boardman. An opportunity came to teach in Berea, and she moved there largely because her then-fiance, Allen Ehas, lived in nearby Euclid. After their marriage, Allen went to the Army and was stationed at Fort Sill outside Lawton, Oklahoma. Susan taught a split fourth-fifth grade class in Cash, Oklahoma. On a visit to Youngstown many years later, she was looking through her grandmother's scrapbooks and found a newspaper clipping about Cash Clingan, who had lived in Cash, Oklahoma. She contacted Esther Norris, a schoolteacher with whom she had worked in Cash, and asked if she had ever heard of Cash Clingan. Much to her surprise, Cash had stayed with Esther in her home while he was on a cattle drive.

In Oklahoma, Susan taught Eskimo students, Army dependents and Kiowa, Comanche and Chickasaw Indian children. She later transferred to the Lawton schools. At the completion of her husband's military service, they returned to Youngstown and lived in the Kennedy Terrace apartments when their first son was born. He was named Rex after her mother's maiden name.

Maryann, our second daughter, arrived in 1947. Like her sister, who was nine years older, she walked with a sure foot into our affections.

Maryann attended Ohio State University for a time and then was trained in computers, graduating from a computer school with perfect marks. Shortly after she married Charles Hall, he went to war as a Green Beret in Vietnam where he served two years and was shot down in a helicopter behind enemy lines. He was awarded a special medal for heroism and went on to enjoy a twenty-year military career.

Maryann and her husband have been stationed at a number of military installations across the country including Fort Dix, New Jersey, where their first son was born, and later in Germany. She has held computer-related jobs every place they have gone.

Eventually she came to work for the federal government in Washington, D.C., and continues to do so. Her husband is now a retired lieutenant colonel. Since leaving the service, he has been employed by firms supplying the federal government, particularly the Defense Department. He has top security clearance, as does Maryann.

Billy was a housekeeper extraordinaire — everything had to be clean including the furnace ductwork, which was washed regularly. She was precise also about herself and was an excellent bookkeeper. She whipped my personal finances and checkbook into precision shape for the first time.

Sometimes I had a little difficulty with her. Once, when I was chairman of the Ohio Senate Finance Committee, some state officials and a fellow senator gathered at Put-in-Bay, Ohio, to wrangle over the biennial budget. Seated at dinner with the senator from Cincinnati who headed an investment firm, Billy informed him I didn't manage my checkbook correctly. I thought that was a good recommendation for my skill as a finance committee chairman.

Billy was one of the most truthful persons I have ever known and was very forthright in her statements. A loyal wife, she perhaps had some misfortune in marrying a man who meddled in politics and tried always to make a good impression. Having a sneaking belief that most politicians were crooks, she didn't like people who referred to me as a politician. I even heard her tell several people that I was a "statesman." At times I could see in the person she was talking with some question as to whether or not she was telling the truth.

One of our greatest experiences together occurred in 1961. She had never ridden in an airplane and we had an opportunity to take a trip, sponsored by the newspaper, to eleven countries in Europe. We left the Youngstown airport and flew into stormy weather over Pennsylvania. The turbulence frightened me, but it didn't seem to bother Billy.

On the trip home, the airplane ran short of fuel and was forced to land at Gander, Newfoundland. When we finally reached Youngstown, the weather was poor and the plane circled the airport for more than an hour. Again, Billy was not bothered, but I was. This being her first experience on a plane trip, she saw nothing out of the ordinary.

In Italy we toured the towns of Milan, Venice, Genoa and Rome, where we had an audience with the pope. In Venice, I visited the old Venetian Republic Senate chamber that dated to the eighth century. I had previously studied how it operated and knew the Ohio Senate had derived many of its procedures from that governmental body.

While visiting Paris, Billy spent time shopping in the famous Lafeyette Department Store; in fact, that's where she spent all her time. Being an amateur expert on the French Revolution, my favorite part of the trip was the tour of the Palace of Versailles, its gardens and lake. Once you step outside the palace, it is interesting to see the housing of Versailles that was provided for the nobles of France, most of whom spent their time at the palace frolicking as the French economy sank under the burden of their extractions. The nobles paid no taxes, and the last efforts of the king's ministers to impose control failed before the outbreak of the revolution, which ended nobility in France.

We saw an unusual sight in France. Our hotel was first-class and had a very nice lobby. In the midst of it, seated on a plush chair, was a man who was at least twice my size. His legs were crossed and an attendant was trimming his toenails with scissors. I asked members of the hotel staff about this strange behavior and was told he was an oil-wealthy Arab sheik. I had not seen anything quite equaling that since the 1940 Democratic Party convention in Chicago, when I was taken to visit the widow of Hinky Dink, who also operated rather strangely in a first-class hotel, feeding pigeons from her plush suite.

In 1965, serious illness struck; an operation was required for my gallbladder but the surgeons found that I had been working for more than a week with a ruptured appendix and the poison had spread throughout my body. My long hospital stay included four major operations. In the darkest hours of that illness, it was Billy's countenance, coming around the door, that gave me strength and hope.

It was a slow process getting back to normal in my home relations after being discharged from the hospital; I had lost more than sixty pounds. Billy and I were to have only two years before she, too, had an affliction which plagued her the remainder of her life.

Needing help, she called me at the newspaper office one day. She had been painting the door of the garage, fell off the ladder and broke her hip. Home alone, she crawled into the house to phone me.

Billy was never able to walk again without a walker. After her accident, she was in a grocery store only once. Her practice was to list the groceries and for me to do the shopping, sometimes going to all three grocery stores in the nearby Lincoln Knolls Plaza. She was still able to make all the meals and she dominated the kitchen, not wanting any help from me. I would carry the dishes of food and we would eat many meals on trays in the living room. We hired a woman to clean a day or two each week, and she did her work in response to my wife's precise directions.

Billy suffered a stroke in July 1980. After mowing the lawn, I found her seated at the kitchen table, and she said she didn't know what had happened to her. She shook her head and I knew something was wrong. I took her to the doctor and he admitted her to North Side Hospital. An infection developed in her right leg; eventually, it had to be amputated. She never returned to good health. I came home from the hospital to get some sleep one evening, and about six o'clock the following morning I got a call to return immediately. She died just as I arrived.

Billy's death was a terrible blow. I had harbored no thoughts of ever marrying again. Soon after Billy's death, I went to visit my brother, John, in Elroy, Wisconsin. He died two months later.

After much persuading by my daughter Maryann and her husband, I went to visit them in Bad Kreuznach, Germany, in December 1980. They were located at the site of Hitler's troop headquarters, though the Fuhrer had never been there himself. Now it is the location of the helicopters and the back command for the European NATO forces. There are several blocks of American housing.

Cutting a Christmas tree in Germany was of interest during my visit. My son-in-law, grandsons and I negotiated with an elderly German on the road. He told us we could get a tree wherever we wanted. At my urging, we climbed rather high in the forest, cut down a fine specimen and dragged it to the road where the car was parked. While cutting the tree, snow littered our hats and coats. An inch or so formed around the brim of my hat, testifying to a white Christmas, unusual in this section of Germany.

To this day, it is still a matter of conjecture whether the elderly German owned the forest or was just out there collecting money for trees. Nonetheless, the tree was decorated in true German fashion. During the holiday season in Germany, fireworks begin before Christmas and don't end until January, and the decorations have their own characteristics and gimmicks.

I went to the officers' club with my daughter and her husband for a New Year's Eve party. Their two sons — Michael, then age twelve and Eric, then age nine — were supposedly staying home. It was an amusing evening. On one side of our table were airmen and on the other were anti-aircraft gunners. Much of the conversation involved various charges from both sides such as how one would knock the other out of the sky. The party lasted all night, but I departed for home about midnight.

Upon returning, I found the house empty of my grandsons. It was about an hour-and-a-half later before the boys returned and told me of their fun that evening — setting off fireworks outside the officers' club and causing quite a commotion. The boys had joined a group of army brats and were trying to annoy the officers, who included everyone from lieutenants to generals. They made me promise not to tell their parents what they had done.

Some time after Billy's death, I got in the habit of inviting the sister-in-law of my brother to dinner on Sundays after church. Her husband of some forty-seven years had died a number of years earlier. So the two of us finally decided to "hitch up" for the final stretch. Her name is Loretta Fitch.

For our wedding trip, we traveled to Ireland for twelve days. We went to Dublin and a theater there to see the famous tenor Luciano Pavarotti. They turned the spotlight on Loretta and me because we were on our honeymoon; it seems the focus of such publicity is always on people too old to get married — very seldom on the young couples.

We had a young Irish girl as a guide who lectured about everything pertaining to Ulster and the Republic of Ireland. She was from southern Ireland, and she told us about the struggle between the north and south on the Irish island, providing us a very intelligent, impartial discussion of the political issues involving the warring factions. When she finished her presentation, she stood up and waved her arms to show where she stood. She was violent in her opposition to the Protestant domination of Northern Irishmen in Ulster and didn't have any use for those Orangemen from the north. She had given us a fair account for the tour, then let us know how she felt.

Loretta, too, had been a farm girl, born in Trumbull County on a dairy farm operated by her family, the Burrows. As a girl, she assisted in the family business by driving a horse and buggy and peddling milk door-to-door on the North Side of Youngstown. She truly is an example of a woman successfully invading the business world, and she did so decades before the generations of women who followed.

In 1936, Loretta started a floral business from her home, initially without a telephone or any means of transportation. She arranged for flowers to be transported on buses from wholesale flower shops and

Loretta Fitch Jackson; her genius for horticulture made our pond blossom.

developed quite a thriving enterprise. Eventually, she was so successful that she opened a regular location at the junction of routes 616 and 422 at Coitsville with a sign, "Loretta Fitch Florist," and came to have a very substantial portion of the Youngstown area retail florist business. She was particularly successful in supplying flowers for weddings, and she can scarcely go anywhere to this day without meeting people for whom she has crafted bouquets.

In 1971, Loretta sold her shop but continued to work there for some time. Today the shop is still in operation, and although the owners have moved it to Boardman, it still bears her name.

Loretta also likes to grow vegetables as well as flowers and herbs. She dries many of the flowers she grows for winter bouquets which she gives to her many friends, and she makes arrangements year-round for the church.

Loretta and I both have great-grandchildren. Her son, George Fitch, studied engineering at Youngstown College and worked for Youngstown Sheet & Tube Company as a steelworker until his retirement. Her niece whom she reared, Mabel Storey, resides in California.

Loretta's grandchildren as well as mine live out of state, but Loretta manages to keep in touch with all of them for their birthdays and such.

Currently, four of my grandsons are in college. Michael Hall at Mason College in Washington, D.C.; Eric Hall at Virginia Polytech, near Roanoke, Virginia; Jason Ehas at the University of Cincinnati; and Curt Ehas at Bowling Green State University. My oldest grandson, Rex Ehas, is out of school, married and has presented me with my first great-grandson, William Allen Ehas.

Loretta's son has three daughters: Nancy Fitch, who has a degree from Youngstown State University and St. Elizabeth Hospital's School of Nursing and is currently working in the laboratory at a hospital in Washington, Pennsylvania; Jeanne Fitch, who owns an exotic animal shop in California that features fancy parrots, tropical fish and birds; and Susan Ansley, an accomplished florist like her grandmother who manages a florist shop and has two children, Joseph and Jessica. They reside in Irving, Texas. Mabel's children include Vicki, Joyce, Scott and Jeffrey.

Loretta has been a Republican and even now is on President Bush's advisory committee because of her many contributions. My history has been spent in the Democratic Party, but both of us have voted for some candidates from the other's party.

Our marriage seemed to be a good merger from the start; it didn't appeal to my logical mind that two people should be living and keeping up two houses when one would do. Moreover, we were both active in the same church and had many mutual friends. Some of my colleagues at *The Vindicator* learned that Loretta's business was listed by Dun & Bradstreet, which attests to her competency in financing, and I have not heard the last of that. But after all, George Washington also did well in marriage.

Loretta seemed to me to be one who would be wise enough to take me as I was during our marriage. She, I believe, has made only minor revisions in me. Albeit, if you knew Loretta, you would know that she has not been revised at all. Still, we get along handsomely.

She did put a good deal of my late wife's furnishings out on the porch and put hers in the house soon after coming here to live. And, she was thoughtful enough to arrange pictures of my first and second wives in my office, also adding the picture of her first husband, Raymond Fitch. The spirit of our marriage is to make a go of it until we go.

During the first three years of our marriage, after my brother Lamar had a stroke and was restricted in getting about, he resided with us and Loretta looked after him. Many years ago, at the age of sixteen, she had worked for Lamar and his family at Grandfather Jackson's old house when she first came to Coitsville from Trumbull County.

The three women I wed were all different. They were not the same in spirit, but all three were wonderful women.

The second Mrs. Jackson tended to keep to a minimum any philanthropic spirit for contributions that I had. As for the third Mrs. Jackson, I have to somewhat curtail her tendency to make such contributions.

Virginia was a sassy blonde, a good schoolteacher and a good horsewoman. One night she decided to have a corn roast with her girl friend, Sarah Graham. Not wanting her parents to know, they climbed out of Virginia's second-story bedroom window, got on her horse, and rode to the cornfield where they made a fire and had a wild corn roast at midnight. Virginia was in many ways an intellectual and of a very religious mind.

Billy was a brunette who had an aristocratic bearing; indeed, some would say she was stand-offish. In truth, however, she had deep consideration for other people. She brought order to my life partly, I suspect, from her training and work as a bookkeeper and secretary. Billy encouraged both of our girls to understand how to keep track of financial matters and accomplish household tasks.

Loretta has been the most outgoing of my three wives and engages everyone in friendly conversation, not only at the grocery store but also at church. This requires waiting a multitude of minutes on my part. She is able to cheerfully do things for people, even those she doesn't like. In the event of any disagreement that may arise, it is quickly resolved with absolute accommodation, and then she does what she was going to do anyway.

Billy was a household manager of absolute cleanliness and order. The house was not to contain anything that was not immediately needed and useful. Loretta has more of an accumulative nature, although equally clean. She has excellent taste in decorating — more color and contrast than Billy would have agreed to. The truth is I like the way each of them did things.

Having had three wives, I can say that the opposite sex has brought a lot of happiness and inspiration to my life. But for them, I would be less than what I am and if it not be much, it certainly is not their fault.

Two years after my marriage to Loretta, retirement came to me as a prospect for a lot of pleasure. There was always a retirement "bug" in my disposition. My devotion to work had been pinned to the proposition that life is best designed when work is merely an implementation for the leisure hours. The object, it always seems, should be to gain enough for food and shelter and leave enough time for meandering to embrace the human soul.

Leisure hours were not spent to gain in the contest for an economic place in society. Consequently, the declining years find the mind filled with pages and pages of history, poetry and infinite details about affairs that have no relation to the ability to make money.

It was to be a period of pleasant years, traveling the land that has belonged to my father and grandfather and fussing around with a yard of some acres. Enlarging the house with an enclosed porch that offered a view to the tree-lined acres and building a pond in cooperation with my third wife, who has a feel for things green, including water lilies, made it a pleasant experience in the outdoors.

Building a pond is a matter of digging and watching. Its most interesting developments come by nature. First is a period of waiting until the pond is filled with water; later, the arrival of ducks brings fish eggs to the pond and fish begin to show. Canada Geese decided to visit and became quite a chore, coming to the door of the house to be fed. A mallard duck family that took up residence in the pond for long periods also became very friendly and wandered up to the door of the garage and looked in, appealing for corn. Once a turtle was observed crossing the road. A day or so later he could be seen well across the lawn and heading toward the pond.

The fish have become items of interest for various friends who have pulled out sizeable bass and bullhead catfish. Truthfully, no fish were added to the pond to my knowledge except for a few goldfish donated by someone who was leaving town and wanted to give them a home.

"This Is Your Life" was the theme of a testimonial arranged by friends in May 1986, which culminated with a dinner at the Idora Park Ballroom, the last event ever held at Youngstown's old amusement park.

There might have been some passing person who threw other fish into the pond; but nature herself, including the known proclivity of ducks to transport fish eggs from one place to another, is the true mother.

The pond was dug on something of a deer run, and the deer quite often stop to drink, usually after dawn or late in the evening; although they are occasionally seen at the chunk of salt which serves as an attraction at the back of the lawn area. Squirrels multiplied, eating the pine cones, burying for winter-dining the walnuts and butternuts that came from the trees.

Much of this development represents the imagination of Loretta, who brought a genius for horticulture to a place that had been rather mundanely cultivated with a good stand of trees and a widespread lawn. She is a picture of the old lady in the lily pond, for often she wades into the pond, trims the lilies and pushes them about.

Everyone retired should have an opportunity to see how life develops in a new pond.

Early in the pond's experience there was a great demonstration of animal fidelity when one of a pair of mallard ducks that had made the pond their home suffered the loss of its mate to dogs. The mate continues to come to the pond every summer, but alone. Mallards mate for life.

Technology also had a lot to do with this retirement happiness; there is considerable space to mow during many months of the year. It was always dreadful to push the old-type lawn mowers, but a sufficient opulence made it possible to buy a mower to ride and move about with ease to scare the birds and clip off the dandelions.

There had to be some hangover from years of reporting news and writing about political affairs, and there was. In my final years at *The Vindicator*, it was possible to use an extended noon hour to play a little pinochle with some of my old friends in the Democratic Party. This was, of course, a means of obtaining political views. But after retirement, it became an opportunity to spend weekday afternoons joshing about old times in political affairs.

Wanting to keep "kicking" after fifty-four years as a newspaperman, I was happy to write a twice-monthly column for the *Youngstown/Warren Business Journal*, which was founded the year after my retirement. As with the book you're reading, my column is called "Clingan's Chronicles," and it was so-named by the newspaper's publisher, Andrea Wood, who has kept "kicking" me to produce this book, which should, at least, have interest to some members of my family, if not all.

In my retirement, I also had the opportunity to become more active in the church to which my allegiance has existed since birth.

Still in my possession is the record from the old cradle roll of the Coitsville Presbyterian Church. My younger years brought many periods of rather slight church activity, although there was some participation, and for a time I served as a trustee. Later years brought some eighteen years on the session of the Coitsville Presbyterian Church as well as six years as a trustee. Nevertheless, church has never been as important to me as it usually was to my wives, each of whom seemed to have a deep interest in religious activity and pulled me in the direction of the "Path Direct."

The days are now numbered until I join those who have gained my love and who have gone beyond: my wives, my parents, my brothers and hundreds of others who in their earth's passage have had high meaning for me and always will.

The final words concluding this journey of mine will have to be written by another — hopefully by someone not too scornful and perhaps, of necessity, a person who was not too familiar. The monument and mark where my gravesite is set awaits me in the Jackson Cemetery — land that was once part of Grandfather Jackson's farm — where I will lie beside my second wife who spent the years with me when our two children were growing up and came of age.

Loretta, the last bright beam of life, looks to the old Methodist Cemetery on McCartney Road where her first husband is buried. A loving wife for forty-seven years, she plans to lie next to the father of her child. This is the way we look at life in our twilight years, and it brings us much happiness as the two of us try to "keep kicking."

Our outlook much of the year is over green — with some interruption of blossoming and fruiting of the vegetation — and at other periods over white, perceiving the blast of winter's effect that leaves deciduous trees in black silhouettes. The sun rising, the sun setting and the appearance of the moon and stars come to have an appeal to the senses. It is the world that man knows, and his conjectures about the immense areas of the universe have no direct effect upon his being.

Looking out the porch windows to see squirrels and other animals, and knowing a dog rather personally, one cannot escape the conclusion that what a man knows in the great display in the universe is very comparable with what most animals understand. The squirrel looks to his comfort and looks ahead to feed for his winter supply. Much of man's effort is spent in the same way.

The squirrels bury walnuts and butternuts from the trees in the lawn to which they can return when winter's foraging becomes slim. This factor of living is met on the human level; in my case, by a lifetime of setting aside any unexpected money or property not necessary for operation in daily life, including whatever profits could be made by participation in investment clubs, four of which represented challenges in my service as their president. It always appeared to me that what I was doing was exactly what any reasonably intelligent squirrel would also do if he had the opportunity.

Confronted with the idea of the benighted state of humanity, a great scientist answered, "But who knows this anyway except men."

As years advance toward a century, consciousness arises that the period allotted to any man is short. It has to be approached by anyone committed to the real idea of a supreme being with the purpose of being able to account before the pilot. Anyone who has spanned most of the twentieth century has to recognize the tremendous awakening of humanity that occurred. And being able to live in Ohio — one of whose sons gave light and two others gave flight — is a special privilege beyond that experienced in any other century of recorded history.

There may be centuries ahead of even greater changes; but at this vantage point, the last 100 years were the best in which men could live. And yet, it is still comforting to look at the earth pretty much as men through most of history have looked at it — seeing a sun that moves up and down. That is what there is to human vision, even now when men have powerful telescopes which can see light-years away.

Still benighted we are.

SELECTED INDEX